The Science of Fermentation

ROBIN SHERRIFF

The Science of Fermentation

Explore the fascinating alchemy of fermented food and drink

CONTENTS

Foreword	6
Introduction	8
What is fermentation?	10
Microbiology	28
Fermenter's toolkit	50
Directory of ferments	64
Index	210
Bibliography	220
About the authors	221
Acknowledgments	222

FOREWORD

Imagine a world where invisible beings toil endlessly, transforming matter, shaping flavours, altering ecosystems, and, just occasionally, blowing the lids off forgotten jars and Tupperware. That world is ours. And those beings are microbes.

Fermentation is what happens when microbes throw a dinner party in your food. For thousands of years, humans have relied on fermentation – often without realizing it – to preserve food, improve flavour, make alcohol, and accidentally invent pungently delicious things like blue cheese and vinegar. Somewhere along the way, what began as survival turned into cuisine, tradition, and, more recently, part of the arsenal of award-seeking chefs and a genre of cookbooks that double as home science experiments.

Fermentation is one of the most ancient collaborations between humans and the microbial world. It predates agriculture, predates the written word – possibly even predates language itself. Our ancestors stumbled upon bubbling fruit mash or mould-covered grains and thought, "That smells... weird – let's eat it." Or at least the braver ones did.

And so began the long, joyous, unpredictable, and occasionally explosive relationship between microbes and humankind.

There is a tendency for people to think of science as something cold and precise. But fermentation is a science of warmth – of caregiving, patience, intuition, and invisible orchestration. It is the art of decay. Of time and temperature conspiring with life too small to see. Of letting go – just enough – so that something ancient and unknowable might take root and shape. And in this book, *The Science of Fermentation*, Robin Sherriff invites us inside this rich microbial choreography. With scientific clarity and infectious curiosity, he invites us to consider not just the how of fermentation, but the why – why this broad family of processes, and their spoils, from charcuterie to chocolate, from bread to booze – has shaped cuisines and cultures the world over.

This book is also a chorus of voices, as vibrant and alive as the ferments it features. Alongside the science, you'll find insights from an extraordinary cast of contributors – scientists, chefs, craftspeople, food designers – each bringing their own lens to this microbial universe. With stunning photography, step-by-step illustrations, and practical recipes, *The Science of Fermentation* is designed not just to inform, but to invite you to get your hands sticky, your jars bubbling, and your curiosity fizzing.

As a scientist and fermenter, I have spent years courting the edge where biology becomes flavour: the jump from Petri dish to pantry. Even after a decade elbow-deep in miso and kombucha, wrestling with spores and temperature swings in the world's best restaurants, I'm still awed by the quiet intelligence of fermentation. It is both delightfully unpredictable and profoundly reliable. It is the story of life rewriting itself, one cell division at a time.

So settle in, open your mind, and, perhaps, a bottle of something fizzy. You're about to enter the microscopic cosmos of science and surprises.

DR JOHNNY DRAIN

INTRODUCTION

Humans are essentially very complicated bioavailability detection machines. Life of all kinds wants to find the path of least resistance, and when it comes to food this means seeking out bioavailable nutrients – in other words, those we can successfully absorb. This is why we have taste and smell – these senses allow us to find foods that are easy to digest, and it's why these foods are often delicious to us.

Fermentation makes food particularly mouth-watering by breaking down the larger molecules we can't taste into more bioavailable ones that we can. It's what makes sauerkraut sour and kombucha tangy; it's what makes miso umami and kimchi fizz. Without it, we would be missing out on so many of the sensational flavours we take for granted every day, like chocolate, coffee, and cheese.

In the most direct terms, the dictionary definition of fermentation reads as follows: "The chemical breakdown of a substance by bacteria, yeasts, or other microorganisms, typically involving effervescence and the giving off of heat." But I find this a little cumbersome, and it doesn't really capture the spirit of simplicity that characterizes fermentation. I prefer: "Fermentation means living stuff breaking down big stuff into small stuff."

For me, fermentation is a beautiful display of systems theory – the study of complex and seemingly unconnected parts that become a cohesive whole; an interconnected symbiotic system that expands from enzymatic activity, to a multitude of cooperating and competing microbes, to unique microbiomes, to biodiversity, to soil health, to individual diet, to community, to society, and, eventually, the planet as a whole.

Fermentation enables us to bridge these seemingly disparate concepts – once you begin to see that all structures, regardless of size or type, can be broken down into smaller and smaller units by living action, you begin to see that they are all connected, from microbe to planet – from the yeast bloom on a grape to the wine we drink; from the bacteria in the air to the kimchi in our gimbap. As above, so below.

Like the many symbiotic microbes we will go on to discuss, *The Science of Fermentation* is itself the product of collaboration. It collects writings from a plethora of experts, including Dr Caroline Gilmartin, Hero Hirsh, James Read, Dr Jamie Goode, Dr Johnny Drain, Dr Josh Smalley, Dr Julia Skinner, Kenji Morimoto, Kirsten K. Shockey, Mara Jane King, Mark Dredge, Nabila Rodríguez Valerón, Olia Hercules, Payal Shah, Pratap Chahal, Rebecca Ghim, Ryan Charles Walker, and Tom Wilson.

Together, we approach fermentation from two angles. From one side, through the macroscopic human lens, we look at the practical tools, methods, and history. And from the invisible microbe's-eye view, we explore the scientific underpinnings of the various intricate microbiological processes at work.

There are many, many reasons to ferment. If you ask fermenters why they do it, you'll likely get a raft of different answers – generally very complicated ones with lots of facets. Cultural tradition, nutrition, gut health, environmental sustainability, artistic expression, and scientific intrigue are all important aspects of fermentation that get people excited.

I came to fermentation from a place of curiosity, first diving into whisky, then into saké, and from there into koji, then on to the whole wonderful universe of fermentation. So my advice for anyone looking to start is first to ferment for fun.

When you can take joy from the process and not get too bogged down in the details it will become a practice you can stick with and integrate into your life. The specifics and nerdy expertise will no doubt come later.

I hope this book inspires you to dive deep into a fermentation method, research a cultural technique, obsess over an obscure mould, and try things you otherwise wouldn't. Most of all, I hope it encourages you to put some cabbage in a jar, grow mould on some rice, and turn honey into gold. Ferment without fear and learn to love the microbes.

ROBIN SHERRIFF

WHAT IS FERMENTATION?

A timeline of fermentation	12
What are the latest advances in fermentation technology?	18
What role does fermentation play in modern cooking?	20
Why is fermented food so tasty?	22
How does fermentation enhance flavour?	24
Can fermentation bring about a sustainable future?	26

A TIMELINE OF FERMENTATION

Fermentation has a long and storied history going back many thousands of years, providing civilizations from India to Ethiopia with methods for the preservation, flavour augmentation, and even consecration of staple foods.

Traditions of fermentation are at the heart of many cultures, and for good reason. Fermenting improves flavour and bioavailability (making food more digestible), and allows people to preserve fresh produce for longer (essential for storing a harvest glut) and make alcoholic beverages. By delving into case studies of ancient civilizations, we can trace the history of how fermentation came to be so valuable to so many cultures, and why it has remained a fundamental culinary practice.

BEER
YEAST STRAINS DIVERGED FROM THOSE USED IN WINE AND BREAD MAKING IN AROUND THE 16TH CENTURY.

FISH SAUCES
WERE TRADED EXTENSIVELY THROUGHOUT THE ROMAN EMPIRE.

c. 11,000 BCE — BEER
The oldest evidence of humans brewing beer dates back 13,000 years. It was found in caves at Mount Carmel in northern Israel. The process, involving malting, mashing, and fermentation, was not dissimilar to modern beer-making, and was likely performed as part of mortuary rituals.

c. 7000 BCE — FISH
The earliest evidence for non-alcoholic fermentation comes from a 9,000-year-old fish-fermenting site discovered in Sweden. This may have been developed as a storage adaptation to preserve the catch in conditions that were too damp for drying.

c. 6000 BCE — YOGURT
One of the most ancient fermented foods, yogurt dates back to the Neolithic era. It extends the life of milk, and reduces its lactose content, which humans were then only just beginning to evolve the ability to digest. At its inception it must have been made without a starter.

A SHORT HISTORY OF FERMENTATION

The history of fermentation is a history of humanity, stretching back from our evolutionary roots, through a range of food-preservation techniques to modern-day microbiology.

With the advent of settled agricultural communities in the Neolithic period came the skilled practice of fermentation. We have archaeological evidence that humans have been actively fermenting foods for at least 13,000 years. The earliest we know of was beer, but wherever cows have gone it is likely that we have also made some form of ferment with their milk.

Consumption of fermented food, however, predates this by around 10 million years, with genetic evidence indicating that our early hominin ancestors were eating fermented (and thus slightly alcoholic) fruit around the time they descended from the trees. There is even evidence to suggest that fermentation was the first form of cooking and had a significant impact on the evolution and brain development of modern humans.

As human civilization has progressed, so has our understanding of fermentation, and the discoveries we have made can be traced throughout our history, from ancient times to the modern day.

DAHI IS A YOGURT CITED IN THE RIGVEDA, C. 1500 BCE, SOMETIMES MADE BY ADDING CHILLI STEMS TO WARM MILK.

c. 5000 BCE
CHEESE

Analysis of pottery found in Croatia showed residues of cheese and yogurt, which would have increased the portability of milk as well as allowing for earlier weaning of babies, thus reducing birth intervals and accelerating population growth.

c. 3000 BCE
VINEGAR

With alcohol as a prerequisite, vinegar naturally followed. Evidence dates from around 5,000 years ago, when the Babylonians left sun-dried dates to ferment into alcohol and then vinegar. Known as "poor man's wine", it was used for both culinary and medicinal purposes.

A history of food security

From the preservation of perishable food like fish, to the management of post-harvest gluts of cabbage, fermentation has been a critical technology for food security around the world and throughout history (up until the invention of canning and refrigeration, at least).

CULTURAL TRADITIONS OF FERMENTATION

The process of fermentation has become intrinsic to traditional foodways around the world, as it can create new flavours, reduce food waste, and preserve harvest gluts. Different cultures have found specific ways to make the most of their produce, so ferments are thus often synonymous with cultural unity and identity. From France, where cheese is of huge significance, to Japan, famous for its soy sauce, many countries have developed ferments with their own unique style and character, which have become a source of great national pride – and sometimes contention.

Chicha vessel from the Shipibo culture in the Peruvian Amazon

SACRED MEANING

HAN NOBLEWOMAN LADY DAI WAS BURIED IN 168 BCE WITH SOME DOUCHI.

c. 900–200 BCE
CHICHA (SOUTH AMERICAN)

Chicha is a beverage found all along the Andean region, although the term refers not to one drink but a multitude of ferments. It is most commonly made with corn (as *chicha de jora*), and was used ceremonially by pre-Inca Andean cultures, as evidenced by some beautiful ancient drinking vessels.

c. 500 BCE
GARUM

Garum was the favourite ferment of the classical world. This pungent fish sauce wasn't one thing: there was a simple, cheap version, similar to modern fish sauces (see p146), called *liquamen* in Latin (or *garos* in Greek), and the more refined *garum*, made with the blood and guts of larger fish.

c. 200 BCE
DOUCHI (CHINA)

The first Chinese attempt to ferment soya beans, over 2,000 years ago, resulted in dried, wrinkly little flavour nuggets known as *douchi* or *shih*. However, by 215 CE they had adapted meat and fish *jiang* (fermented paste) to create a soy version, and later decanted the liquid from the paste (see p118).

KIMCHI AND KOREAN IDENTITY

There are over 180 types of kimchi (see p84) across Korea, displaying so much variety that it is hard to define them beyond "fermented food with seasonings". Kimchi is woven into the national fabric: kimchi fridges (for proper fermentation and storage) are ubiquitous; a specially developed "space kimchi" accompanied South Korea's first astronaut; and "kimchi" is a common phrase to induce a smile for the camera.

The collective making and sharing of kimchi in autumn (*kimjang*) is a national drumbeat, heralding the changing of the seasons and unifying households in turning the vegetable harvest into kimchi for winter. In 2013, UNESCO registered *kimjang* as part of the "Intangible Cultural Heritage of Humanity".

There are challenges, however, in maintaining kimchi culture: the International Trade Centre's Trade Map reported that 98 per cent of kimchi consumed in Korea in 2014 was from China (as these imports are cheaper). Contrasting this, though, the gastrodiplomatic Global Hansik Campaign (*hansik* refers to food made with Korean ingredients and methods) has seen kimchi promoted and embraced across the world.

> **INJERA** IS SO POPULAR IN ETHIOPIA THAT TEFF EXPORTS WERE BANNED IN 2006 FOR YEARS DUE TO FEARS OF A SHORTAGE.

c. 100 BCE
INJERA

Fermented flatbreads are found across East Africa, from *lahoh*/*canjeero* in Somalia (sorghum, wheat, and spices), to *kisra* in Sudan (sorghum), and *injera* in Ethiopia (teff flour). They occupy an interesting space in breadmaking, with a sour flavour and bubbly texture, without being fully leavened.

989 CE
KVAS

The Eastern European fermented soft drink kvas (see p184), or kvass, has been made since at least the late tenth century, with written evidence dating from 989 CE. It is most commonly made with bread as a substrate, though everything from beetroot to horseradish kvas exists.

c. 1000–1100
NATTŌ

The earliest record of the alkaline soya bean ferment nattō (see p142) is in an early-eleventh-century Japanese text – though it is possible that *kinema* (a similar alkaline soya ferment) was developed earlier by the Limboo ethnic community in east Nepal.

SHOYU AND JAPANESE TRADITION

Soy sauce, though almost certainly first created in China, has been so fiercely adopted by Japan as to be inextricably linked with the country's identity. The first imported soy sauce to Europe was from Japan, and indeed the very word "soy" comes from a bastardization of the Japanese term *shoyu* (soy sauce).

Japanese soy sauce was once all fermented in huge cedar barrels (*kioke*) for months, as the soya bean brine co-mingled with koji microbes (see p110), saturating the wood, which helps to give rise to the hundreds of aroma compounds that formulate the complexity of *shoyu*. This traditional method is under threat, however, from a newer process that breaks down soya beans in stainless-steel vats using acid instead of koji. This can be completed in days at a much lower cost, and now accounts for 99 per cent of Japanese production.

A fightback is taking place, though. On the island of Shōdoshima, fifth-generation maker Yasuo Yamamoto, of brewery Yamaroku Shoyu, is one of 20 soy sauce producers still using *kioke*. In 2011, he found there was only one manufacturer left in Japan, so he started the Kioke Craftsmen Revival Project to teach others how to make them, helping preserve the heritage of traditional Japanese ferments.

> **WARU** (SEA HIBISCUS) LEAVES WERE ORIGINALLY USED TO INOCULATE SOYA BEANS FOR TEMPEH.

c. 1200–1400
LACTO-FERMENTATION

The precise origins of lacto-fermentation are hard to trace, but kimchi is first mentioned in a thirteenth-century Korean poem, and sauerkraut in fifteenth-century Germany. The technique may have been brought to Europe by a mid-thirteenth-century Mongol invasion.

1815
TEMPEH

The first mention of the word *tempeh*, referring to the solidly bound, cake-like soy ferment (see p140), is found in a Javanese manuscript from around 1815, though it may have been invented some time before this, as the text depicts events from the early 1600s.

1857
MICROBIAL FERMENTATION

Louis Pasteur presented his critical discovery that fermentation is carried out by microbes in 1857. He subsequently learned that these microbes are present in the air and on food, and went on to invent pasteurization (low-temperature microorganism elimination) in 1864.

STERILIZATION OF MILK, NINETEENTH CENTURY

FRANCE: UNITED AND DIVIDED BY CHEESE

Charles de Gaulle once said, "One cannot simply bring together a nation that produces 265 kinds of cheese." The French dairy federation CNIEL reckons there are actually over 1,200 types, and yet there is a unity to cheese – 40 per cent of French citizens eat it every day, and many French cheeses are localized to specific regions and protected, with 46 assigned *Appellation d'origine contrôlée* (AOC) status to certify their provenance and quality. However, these legal protections contend with strong pressures from industrial dairy manufacturers. In 2018, after decades of argument, large producers were to be allowed to use the label "Made in Normandy" for Camembert made with pasteurized milk (rather than traditional raw milk). The decision was met with such outrage that it was reversed in 2020.

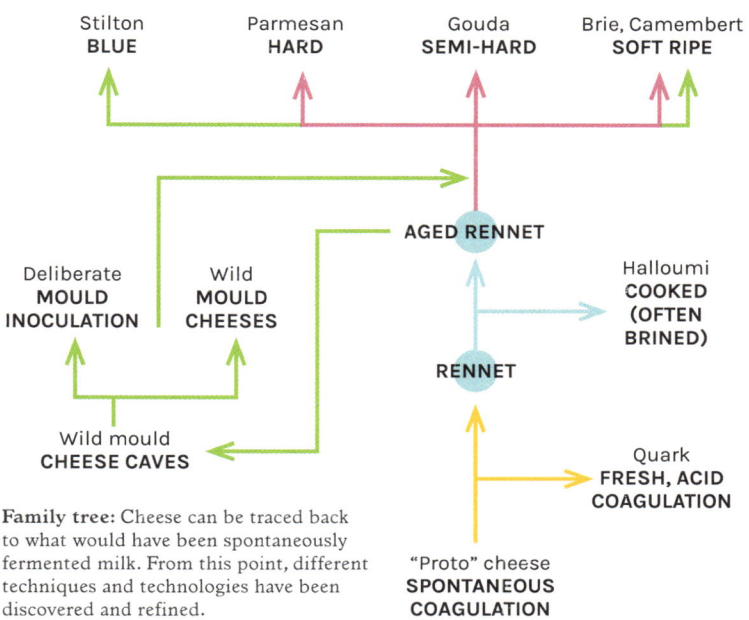

Family tree: Cheese can be traced back to what would have been spontaneously fermented milk. From this point, different techniques and technologies have been discovered and refined.

1881
KEFIR

Known to have been made by nomadic tribes in a small area around the Caucasus Mountains for millennia, kefir (see p94) was "discovered" in 1881 by German naturalist Edward Kern. He realized it could be a health tonic, kickstarting large-scale manufacture in Russia.

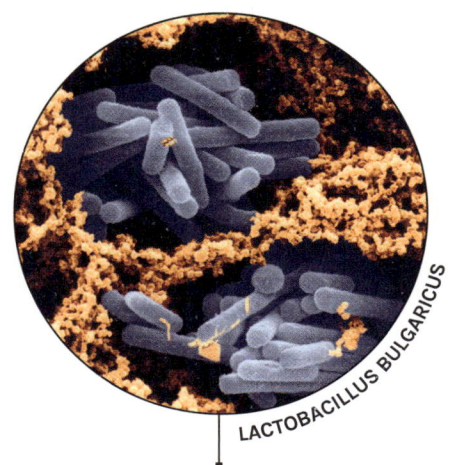

1905–1907
PROBIOTICS

In 1905, Bulgarian microbiologist Stamen Grigorov discovered the bacterial strain that turns milk to yogurt. In 1907, immunologist Élie Metchnikoff, noting that yogurt-eating Bulgarian peasants lived long lives, argued yogurt prevented "intestinal putrefaction", and so probiotics were born.

1978–2025
MODERN MICROBIOLOGY

The discovery that microbes could be genetically altered to synthesize specific compounds led to the cheap manufacture of insulin in 1978. This technology, known as precision fermentation, has more recently been deployed to create animal-free milk and egg proteins.

WHAT ARE THE LATEST ADVANCES IN FERMENTATION TECHNOLOGY?

Modern advancements in fermentation technology have had a transformative impact on sustainability, food security, and culinary innovation, paving the way for a more resilient and delicious food future.

Fermentation has evolved far beyond its traditional roots. This ancient art is being transformed into a scientific powerhouse, redefining how we grow and produce what we eat. In addition to traditional fermentation (the age-old method of using microbes to transform food), modern fermentation can be categorized into two main types.

BIOMASS FERMENTATION
Rather than transforming an existing food – like cabbage *into* kimchi – biomass fermentation creates a completely new edible mass from scratch, so that the microbes themselves are the food source. Quorn, made from the fungus *Fusarium venenatum*, is one example you may have heard of.

Biomass fermentation often involves growing fungi that can be processed into protein-rich, animal-free meat alternatives. This "mycoprotein" can end up as mince, sausages, and burgers, but companies are now using fungal biomass to grow whole-cut fillets – a rib-eye steak made of microbes, not meat.

The process involves rapidly multiplying cells in carefully controlled conditions: it can be much quicker than traditional fermentation but requires more complex processing. It can also make use of food waste – not from a compost heap, but industrial side-streams that are produced in large quantities. Imagine the spent grain from making beer or the potato peelings from the world's French fries being fermented to make mycoprotein for burger patties.

Microbes as food

Biomass fermentation harnesses fungi, multiplying them rapidly under controlled conditions. This can create sustainable, protein-rich foods made entirely by microbes.

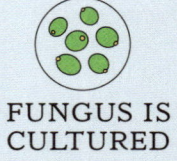

FUNGUS IS CULTURED

The starter fungus *Fusarium venenatum* is cultured under sterile lab conditions.

FUNGUS IS GROWN

Fungal cells multiply rapidly within fermentation vessels, increasing their biomass.

BIOMASS IS HARVESTED

The mycoprotein is harvested, then processed to bind, flavour, and texturize it.

FINAL PRODUCT

Protein mass is shaped into finished foods such as burgers, mince, and whole-cut fillets.

PRECISION FERMENTATION

In this process, scientists tweak the inner machinery of microbes so that they produce specific molecules like proteins, fats, or enzymes. It is a game-changer. For example, a yeast cell can be modified to produce compounds like casein proteins – the building blocks of cheese. A piece of DNA that says "make this compound" is inserted into a microbe, which then ferments sugars just like in traditional fermentation. The result is that instead of producing alcohol or lactic acid, for instance, it produces the compound its new DNA instructs it to make.

These microbial factories can even be tuned to produce specific flavour or texture compounds, allowing chefs to tailor tastes in ways once deemed impossible. Think vanilla with amplified floral notes, or yogurt with unprecedented creaminess. Precision fermentation has also propelled the development of alternative proteins, including meatless dairy, egg proteins, and even seafood analogues, as well as heralding a path towards future-proofing the ingredients of products like coffee and chocolate, the growth of which is endangered by climate change.

Compared to traditional fermentation, precision fermentation can be highly efficient and customizable – in principle you could modify the genetics of a microbe to produce anything, be it a medicine or a food. However, it is incredibly costly, requiring a lot of high-level research and

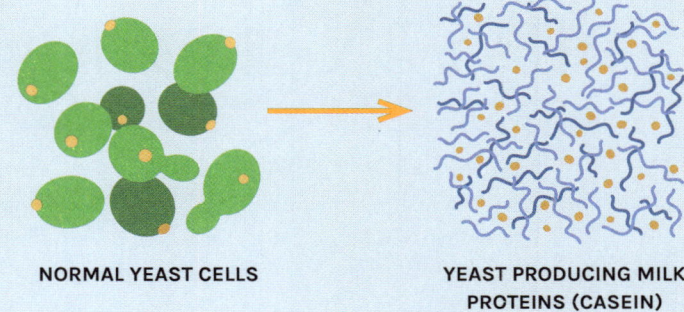

NORMAL YEAST CELLS → **YEAST PRODUCING MILK PROTEINS (CASEIN)**

Making cheese without cows: Normally casein, the key protein in dairy products, is produced by mammals, but with modified yeast, we can now produce casein without animals, using fermentation instead.

intensive control. Public perception is also an issue. Some people simply might not want to eat foods made by genetically modified microbes.

FUTURE TRENDS AND INNOVATIONS

Biomass and precision fermentation are two modern approaches that are helping us produce eco-friendly proteins, reduce food waste, and create sustainable alternatives to traditional livestock farming. But the fermentation horizon is dazzling with other possibilities. Small bioreactors may soon become kitchen staples, allowing home cooks to culture their own ingredients, from miso pastes to cheese alternatives, while specially assembled microbial consortia – communities of different fermenting organisms – could personalize fermentation processes based on household preferences, bringing terroir indoors.

Beyond food, microbes are already used to make medicines, like insulin, but may be tailored to produce custom nutrients in response to an individual's microbiome. Fermentation is even leaping from the kitchen to the cosmos, with space agencies around the world investigating how fermentation microbes behave in space – raising the possibility of off-planet food production.

Eco warriors

Fermentation isn't just about food – it's also a solution to global challenges. Microbes are cleaning waste water, generating biofuels, and even repairing soil health by transforming nitrogen levels. These microbial applications hint at a future where microbes shape both our diets and our ecosystems.

WHAT ROLE DOES FERMENTATION PLAY IN MODERN COOKING?

Fermentation is not bound by tradition. It is also a frontier of modern innovation, a means of unlocking flavours, textures, and nutritional properties that cannot be achieved through conventional cooking. As such, in the ever-evolving world of contemporary gastronomy, it is one of the most potent and exciting tools at our disposal.

CLOUDY SHIO KOJI — CAN BE FREEZE CLARIFIED, REMOVING RICE SOLIDS AND RENDERING IT TRANSLUCENT.

GINGER BEER — WASTE PULP CAN BE CAPTURED, FERMENTED AGAIN, JUICED, AND FILTERED.

Whether applied in the meticulous craft of a centuries-old cheesemaker, in the cutting-edge labs of a food-tech start-up, or in the kitchens of elite restaurants, fermentation remains one of the most essential forces shaping the way we eat.

At its core, fermentation is a process of controlled decay – one that turns humble ingredients into complex, storied foods. But beyond its sensory impact, it is a key tool for food sustainability, forming the backbone of the expanding field of alternative proteins and post-animal gastronomy, where fermentation is used to create plant-based cheeses, mycoproteins, and hybrid meat substitutes that rival traditional products in texture and taste (see p18 and p26).

It is also a driver of culinary excellence. Fermentation can be both a technique and a philosophy – transforming waste into wonder, local into global, humble into exquisite – and in recent decades it has begun to reshape how chefs understand flavour, time, and microbial collaboration. The greatest chefs, brewers, bakers, and food scientists continue to explore the potential of fermentation, pushing its boundaries to create new, deeply expressive gastronomic experiences in the world's most ambitious kitchens.

A modern toolkit of gastronomic techniques enables us to augment ferments and capture waste to produce interesting, unexpected, nuanced flavours.

Gastronomic techniques

Many traditional fermentation techniques have been adapted to bring out nuanced qualities and flavours in a restaurant setting. Through the use of modern culinary methods or niche equipment, some amazing results can be achieved, and while these techniques may seem unattainable, much of the equipment and many of the skills required are within reach for the ambitious home cook.

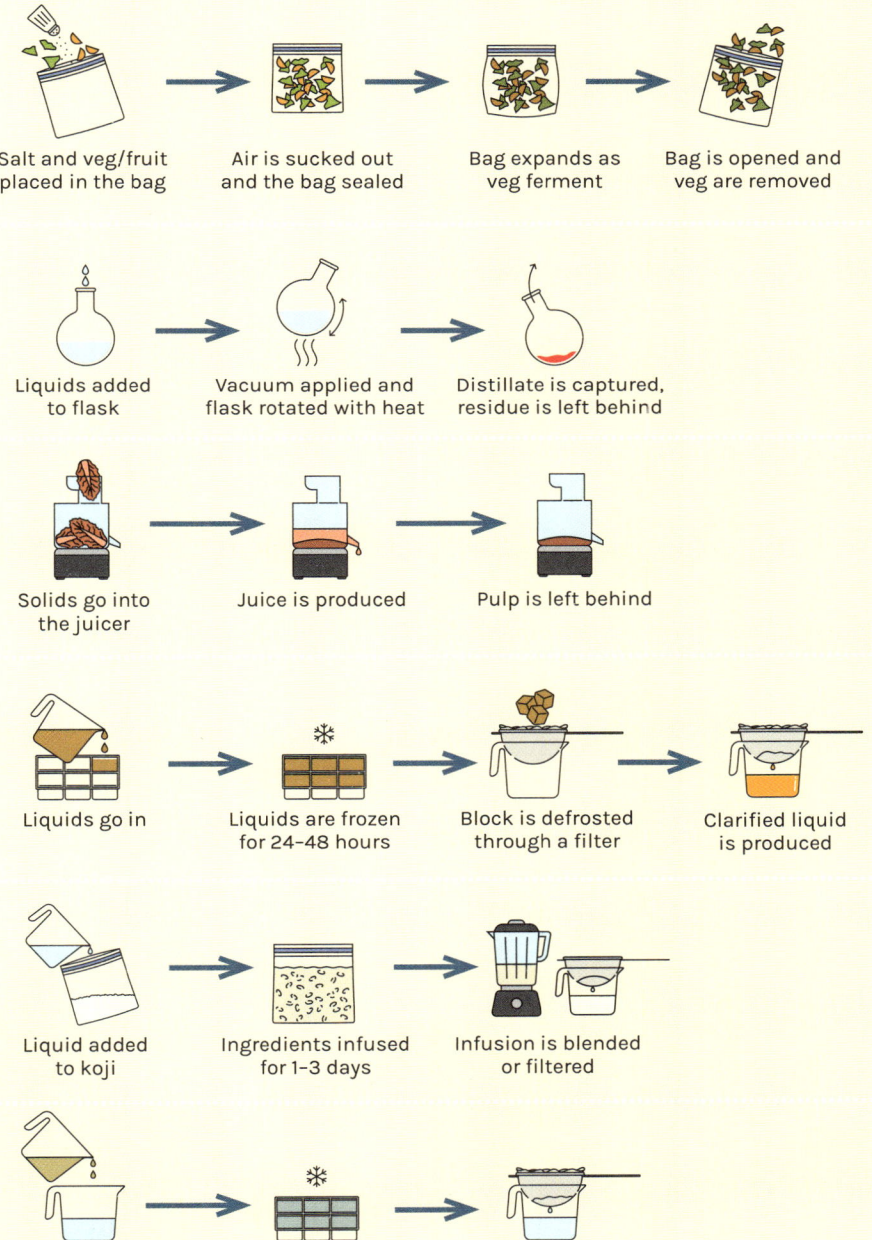

Vacuum-sealed lacto-fermentation A vacuum sealer removes air from a bag before sealing it shut. Vac-sealing vegetables with salt removes oxygen, creating ideal anaerobic conditions for lactic acid bacteria. Used in restaurants for precise, fast ferments. Takes 3–7 days.

Vacuum distillation A rotary evaporator distils liquids at low temperatures using vacuum pressure. It extracts delicate aromatics from liquids without cooking them. Takes 1–4 hours. Used in bars and R&D kitchens for capturing pure flavours or making non-alcoholic distillates.

Juicing Used to remove fibre and solids from ferments, helping to concentrate flavours and produce a thinner liquid than blending. Great for making flavour-packed bases for sauces, vinaigrettes, or drinks. Common with lacto-ferments (see p68) or shio kojis (see p116).

Freeze clarification This separates clear liquid from solids by freezing, then slowly thawing through a cloth or filter. Perfect for kombucha (see p196), shoyu (see p119), or lacto juices for brightness and clarity. Takes 24–48 hours. Used in restaurants and bars to make seasonings and cocktails.

Koji infusion Koji is a rice or grain inoculated with a specific mould that breaks down starches and proteins (see p110). Infusing it into alcohol or syrup adds umami and sweetness. Takes 1–3 days. Used in cocktails, sauces, and stocks to give buttery, miso-like, or fruity notes.

Fat washing Fat (e.g. coconut oil or browned butter) is mixed into alcohol. The mixture is then frozen and strained. The flavour of the fat stays, but the grease doesn't. Takes 6–48 hours (depending on fat/liquid used). Used in bars to add savoury depth to cocktails, kombucha (see p196), and shrubs (see p208).

WHY IS FERMENTED FOOD SO TASTY?

Key to flavoursome ferments is umami. First identified in Japan, umami has now been recognized as a distinct taste for over a century, and while certain foods are natural sources, the fermentation process can unlock and intensify its rich, savoury flavour.

For many years, scientists recognized only four basic tastes: sweet, sour, salty, and bitter. However, in the early twentieth century, Professor Kikunae Ikeda of Tokyo Imperial University identified a distinct savoury quality while studying kombu dashi, a traditional Japanese broth. He described it as "the peculiar taste we feel as *umai*", meaning "delicious", and named it umami.

Ikeda recognized glutamate as the key compound responsible for umami and developed monosodium glutamate (MSG) as a seasoning to enhance umami flavours in foods. Subsequent research revealed that umami perception is enhanced by the presence of ribonucleotides – the building blocks of ribonucleic acid (RNA), which is essential for most biological functions – specifically inosine monophosphate (IMP) and guanosine monophosphate (GMP).

By 2002, researchers had pinpointed three specific umami receptors – T1R1 + T1R3, mGluR4, and mGluR1 – further confirming umami's unique role in taste perception at a molecular level. These discoveries provided concrete scientific evidence that umami is distinct from the other basic tastes and plays an essential role in human flavour perception. For example, it leaves a mild yet lingering aftertaste that stays on the palate, enhancing the overall eating experience. It also stimulates salivation, heightening flavour perception and aiding digestion. Perhaps most notably, umami creates a rich, coating sensation that spreads across the tongue, delivering a full-bodied taste.

THE MOLECULES BEHIND UMAMI

Umami is primarily driven by glutamate. This amino acid occurs naturally in some foods and in fermented products, delivering a savoury taste. However, glutamate alone does not tell the whole story.

NATURAL UMAMI SOURCES INCLUDE AGED CHEESES, FISH, MEATS, SEAWEED, TOMATOES, AND MUSHROOMS.

MISO   PARMESAN   RIPE TOMATOES   SHIITAKE MUSHROOMS   KOMBU SEAWEED   BONITO

Synergistic taste

The nucleotide molecules IMP (inosine monophosphate) and GMP (guanosine monophosphate) can work together with the amino acid glutamate as a complex. This complex then interacts more efficiently with taste receptors, exponentially increasing the experience of umami.

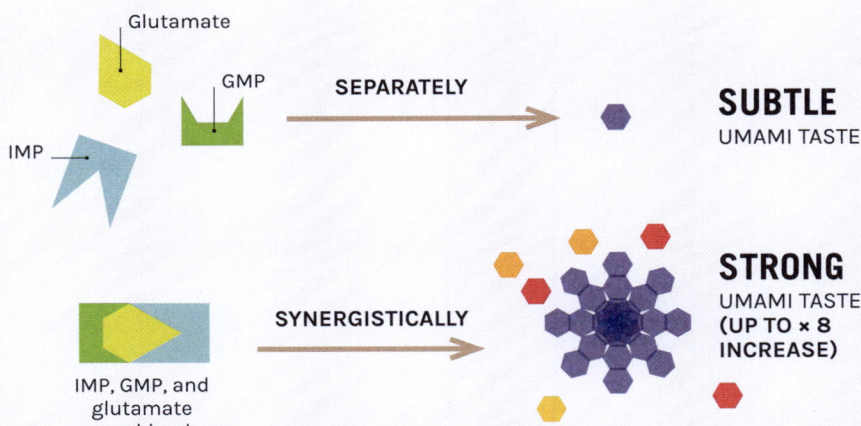

The two other important molecules, IMP and GMP, work alongside glutamate to elevate the umami experience. On their own, IMP and GMP have little impact, but when combined with glutamate they create a synergistic effect that intensifies the flavour. Research shows that this interaction can make umami perception up to eight times stronger in humans compared to glutamate alone. Understanding how these molecules interact has been crucial in advancing food science and culinary practices. The strategic pairing of glutamate with IMP or GMP is now widely used in broths, fermented sauces, and cured foods to build a more robust umami taste.

The taste of goodness

In addition to its role in enhancing flavour, umami significantly contributes to both health and sustainability. By stimulating salivation, it aids digestion and nutrient absorption – a benefit particularly valuable for the elderly. Umami-rich ingredients (alongside kokumi; see overleaf) are also pivotal in supporting the green transition, making plant-based diets more satisfying and appealing and thereby reducing reliance on animal-derived ingredients. Today, umami stands at the crossroads of flavour innovation and sustainable eating, shaping how we craft and enjoy food in an increasingly environmentally conscious world.

HOW FERMENTATION ENHANCES UMAMI

Natural sources of umami include fish such as bonito or sardines, meats like beef and chicken, as well as plant-based sources such as seaweed, mushrooms, and tomatoes. Fermentation, however, is a powerful tool for enhancing umami, transforming raw ingredients into deeply flavourful foods like miso (see p126), soy sauce (see p118), and fish sauce (see p146). During fermentation, microorganisms such as bacteria, yeast, and fungi break down proteins into free amino acids, particularly glutamate, which is responsible for umami's savoury taste. In addition, the breakdown of nucleotides releases IMP and GMP, which work synergistically with glutamate to further intensify flavour.

Traditional fermented foods owe their complex umami richness to this natural process. In miso and soy sauce production, fungi such as *Aspergillus oryzae* produce enzymes that break down soya beans and grains, unlocking glutamate and other umami-enhancing compounds over time. Similarly, in fish sauce fermentation, naturally occurring bacteria break down the fish proteins into amino acids, yielding a rich, concentrated umami profile.

This process of "umamification" can release and amplify the flavour potential of many foods. Once met with scepticism, umami is now firmly recognized as a fundamental taste, influencing not only culinary practices, but also scientific exploration.

HOW DOES FERMENTATION ENHANCE FLAVOUR?

Sweet, salty, sour, bitter, and umami define taste, but kokumi substances add koku – a rich, lingering sensation that enhances flavours and creates memorable culinary experiences. And fermented foods are a great place to find it.

KOKUMI ENRICHES A DISPARATE ARRAY OF FOODS, FROM WINE AND SOURDOUGH BREAD, TO CHEESE AND MISO.

In 1990, Japanese researchers uncovered something interesting: adding a garlic-water extract to soup created a taste experience that could not be explained by the usual sweet, salty, sour, bitter, or umami profiles. They called it kokumi, a word rooted in the Japanese term *koku*, meaning "richness", often used to describe food with incredible depth, combining texture, aroma, and taste.

However, kokumi is not a taste or aroma in the traditional sense. It is more a sensory enhancement – a thick, rich mouthfeel that amplifies the flavours around it. The science? Unlike the basic tastes, which involve specific molecules activating taste receptors, kokumi molecules interact with calcium-sensing receptors (CaSR), which typically sense calcium ions. This interaction boosts the perception of sweetness, umami, saltiness, and also fat sensation.

FLAVOUR ENHANCEMENT

Kokumi comes from small molecules called peptides, with glutathione being the first identified as a key

Kokumi or koku?

In Japan, the term kokumi is not widely known. Instead, when talking about complexity and depth in food, the Japanese use the word *koku*. It captures that full, satisfying sensation you experience when everything – taste, flavour, and texture – comes together perfectly. So, how do koku and kokumi relate? Think of koku as the overall feeling of richness in a dish, while kokumi refers to the specific molecules that help create it.

contributor. Glutathione is a tripeptide – a short chain of three amino acids: glutamate, cysteine, and glycine – and its discovery marked the beginning of a deeper understanding of kokumi's unique ability to enhance flavour.

Scientists have since identified a family of gamma-glutamyl peptides as crucial kokumi agents. Composed of two or three amino acids and always starting with glutamate, these peptides are responsible for kokumi's signature richness and continuity. Among them, glutamyl-valyl-glycine (cEVG) stands out as one of the most potent kokumi compounds. Others, such as glutamyl-valine (EV), glutamyl-leucine (EL), and glutamyl-phenylalanine (EF), also contribute to the thick, lingering sensation that amplifies other flavours.

SOURCES OF KOKUMI PEPTIDES

Fermented foods are a good place to find kokumi peptides, as these compounds develop naturally during the fermentation process. Soy sauce and miso, for instance, are rich in kokumi, contributing to their deep, complex flavour profiles. Fermented shrimp, sourdough, and brewed beverages such as beer, wine, and saké also provide significant amounts of kokumi peptides. Regional delicacies like fish sauces are notable sources, while long-aged cheeses such as Gouda and Parmesan are particularly rich in these flavour-enhancing compounds.

Kokumi peptides are not limited to fermented foods, however; they can also be found in raw ingredients that are staples in many cuisines. Vegetables like garlic, onions, and mushrooms naturally contain kokumi compounds. Fruits such as durian and avocado, along with edible beans and cocoa beans, are also sources of these peptides.

SUSTAINABLE FLAVOURS

Kokumi peptides are amazing, as they can cut back the need for salt, fat, and sugar in foods without losing flavour. Even better, during fermentation, a process called gamma-glutamylation reduces bitterness naturally. Peptides like EF and EV not only tone down harsh flavours, but also add that rich, full kokumi sensation. Kokumi research also highlights its importance in sustainability. Kokumi peptides are naturally produced through the fermentation of food by-products such as wheat bran and brewer's spent grain, which can be used to elevate plant-based dishes with richer, more balanced flavours. By making these products more enjoyable, kokumi peptides could help more people embrace plant-based eating.

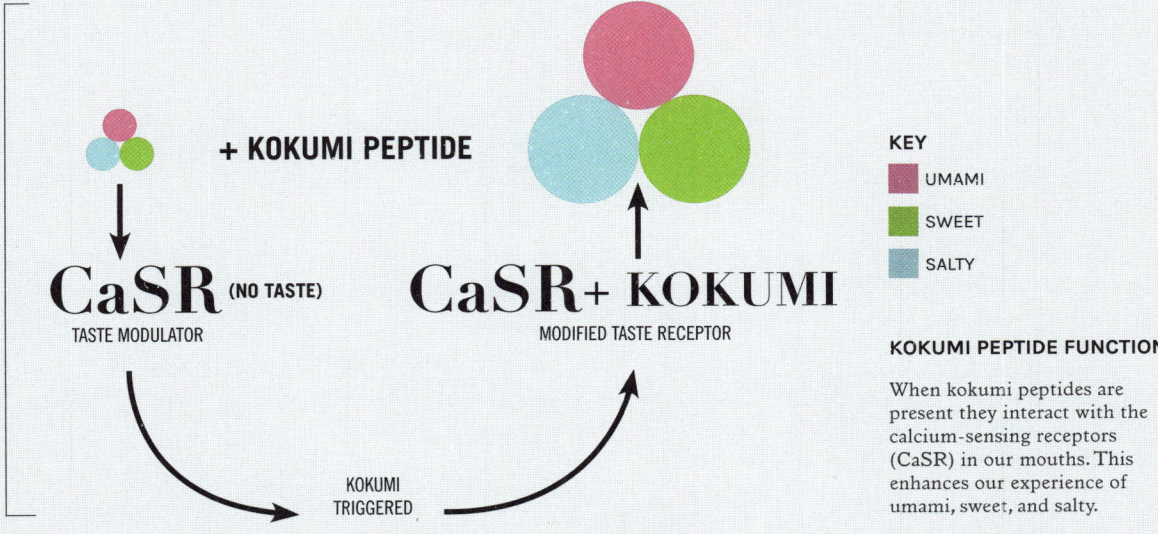

KOKUMI PEPTIDE FUNCTION

When kokumi peptides are present they interact with the calcium-sensing receptors (CaSR) in our mouths. This enhances our experience of umami, sweet, and salty.

CAN FERMENTATION BRING ABOUT A SUSTAINABLE FUTURE?

Some of the most significant innovations in food production developed out of necessity, to preserve produce and tackle food insecurity. But the consequences of industrialization have been dire, for our health and our environment. In the fight to make our global resources sustainable, fermentation can have a huge impact.

The industrialization of food was intended to increase efficiency, improve resistance to disease, and lower costs. And to some degree, it has succeeded – fewer people experience famine, and food is more abundant in the Western world than ever before. But it has come at a cost. The over-processing of food, excessive use of synthetic fertilizers, and reliance on chemical pesticides have led to an explosion of diet-related diseases and contributed to massive soil depletion, water contamination, and biodiversity loss. The issue is not just the quantity of food we produce but the quality and the impact of how we produce it. So, how do we begin to rethink food production to mitigate these issues? And how does fermentation fit into the picture?

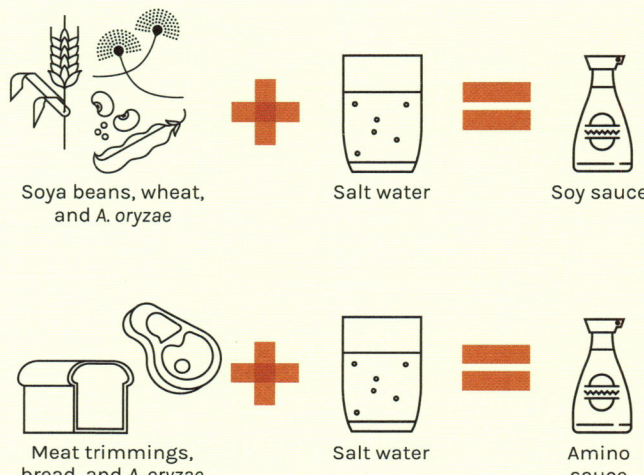

Soya beans, wheat, and *A. oryzae* + Salt water = Soy sauce

Meat trimmings, bread, and *A. oryzae* + Salt water = Amino sauce

FROM SURPLUS TO SUSTENANCE

Fermentation allows us to take ingredients with little to no perceived value and, through the transformative power of microbes and enzymes, create foods that are not just preserved but enhanced in both flavour and nutrition. The key shift in thinking is to stop seeing food waste as "waste" at all. Take spent bread and meat trimmings – two common restaurant byproducts. In conventional kitchens, they would be discarded, but if we look at them scientifically, we see something different. Spent bread is starch. Meat trimmings are proteins and fats. And this is where fermentation offers a solution.

Consider soy sauce (see p118): traditionally, it is made by fermenting soya beans (rich in protein and fat) and cracked wheat (rich in starch) with *Aspergillus oryzae* and salt water for about a year. What if we took meat trimmings in place of soya beans and spent bread instead of wheat? The result? A fermented umami sauce that is indistinguishable from traditional

---

An ancient solution to a modern problem

None of this is new. Fermentation has always been a means of maximizing food efficiency. The ancient Romans and Greeks used fermentation to produce garum (see p146), a fish sauce that transformed scraps into an essential seasoning. Lower-quality garums were made with whatever fish remains were available, while high-end garums were crafted from single-species fish and valued as highly as perfumes.

soy sauce, made from ingredients that would have otherwise been discarded.

BEYOND FOOD

Fermentation isn't just about food, though. It is also being used to transform waste into energy, providing sustainable alternatives to fossil fuels. Through anaerobic fermentation, organic food waste can be converted into biogas, which can be used for electricity, heating, or even as fuel for transportation. This process is already being used on an industrial scale to reduce landfill waste while generating energy from organic material.

In addition, fermentation-derived bioethanol is emerging as a sustainable alternative to petroleum-based fuels. Traditionally, bioethanol is produced from corn or sugarcane, but recent innovations are focusing on using agricultural waste and inedible food byproducts to minimize reliance on virgin food sources.

Even outside of energy, fermentation is shaping sustainable materials. From biodegradable plastics to textiles, scientists are using microbial fermentation to create materials that can replace petroleum-based products, reducing plastic pollution and resource consumption.

At its core, fermentation is a low-waste, high-value process that is uniquely suited to solving modern sustainability challenges. It turns surplus into sustenance, overlooked ingredients into culinary gold, and food waste into energy. But fermentation is not just about practical applications – it is a philosophy. It forces us to rethink our relationship with food, shifting our mindset from excess and waste to efficiency and transformation. Whether it's being applied in fine dining, home kitchens, energy production, or large-scale biofuel research, fermentation offers one of the most effective, scalable, and proven solutions to some of our greatest food-system challenges.

PRECISION FERMENTATION COULD REDUCE GLOBAL GREENHOUSE GAS EMISSIONS FROM FOOD PRODUCTION BY UP TO

80%

FERMENTATION CAN CONVERT AGRICULTURAL WASTE INTO HIGH-PROTEIN FOODS.

SOLAR-POWERED BIOREACTORS ELIMINATE FOSSIL-FUEL ENERGY RELIANCE.

PRECISION-ENGINEERED YEASTS PRODUCE EDIBLE FATS.

KIMCHI WAS BORN FROM THE NEED TO PRESERVE GLUTS OF VEGETABLES DURING KOREA'S HARSH WINTERS.

MAKING CHEESE PRESERVED SURPLUS MILK BEFORE REFRIGERATION AND PREVENTED DAIRY SPOILAGE.

Korean kimchi, Japanese miso, European blue cheeses, and even beer brewing all evolved as ways to extend the usability of seasonal and perishable ingredients.

MICROBIOLOGY

Microbiology 101	30
Food-fermenting microbes	32
How do microbes evolve?	34
What are enzymes?	36
How do enzymes drive fermentation?	38
How do niche microbes influence fermentation?	40
Why is gut health important?	42
How do fermented foods affect our gut health?	44
What are functional foods?	46
How can I include functional foods in my diet?	48

MICROBIOLOGY 101

Understanding a little microbiology will help you understand microbes, and that will help you understand fermentation. Put simply, microbiology is the study of living organisms, such as bacteria, yeasts, and moulds, that are too small to be seen individually with the naked eye.

Microbes predate humans by billions of years. We didn't know they existed until the late 1600s, when the first microscopes were invented, but we now realize they are the most abundant life forms on Earth, occupying every niche. They cover our bodies inside and out, forming the gut microbiota (see p42); they enable plants to grow by associating with their roots and fixing nitrogen; they break down organic matter; they even change the colour of water.

Microbes, and specifically bacteria, have gained a bad reputation as the agents of disease. Yet of the estimated trillion microbial species, only about 0.0000001 per cent are known to cause disease in humans. Most are either helpful or harmless.

Microbes may be small, but they are not simple. Many consist of just a single cell but contain everything they need to generate the universal energy molecule, ATP (adenosine triphosphate), for their growth and reproduction.

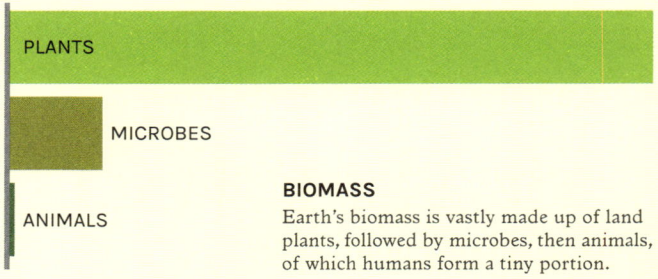

BIOMASS
Earth's biomass is vastly made up of land plants, followed by microbes, then animals, of which humans form a tiny portion.

There are five major types: bacteria, archaea, fungi, protozoa, and algae. They can also be described as either prokaryotic or eukaryotic. Prokaryotes evolved first; their machinery for growth and development mills about in the cell cytoplasm (gel-like liquid). Bacteria and archaea fall within this group. Eukaryotes, including yeasts, moulds, protozoa, and algae, are more related to humans, with DNA in a cell nucleus, separate organelles (specialized structures), mitochondria where energy is made, and Golgi apparatus (a type of organelle) and endoplasmic reticulum, where proteins are created and processed.

EXTREMOPHILES ARE ARCHAEA AND BACTERIA THAT OCCUPY EXTREME HABITATS, OBTAINING ENERGY FROM IRON, SULFUR, OR EVEN METHANE.

Timeline of life

Humans have only existed for a tiny proportion of the Earth's history. Microbes, however, have dominated for the vast majority of the planet's existence.

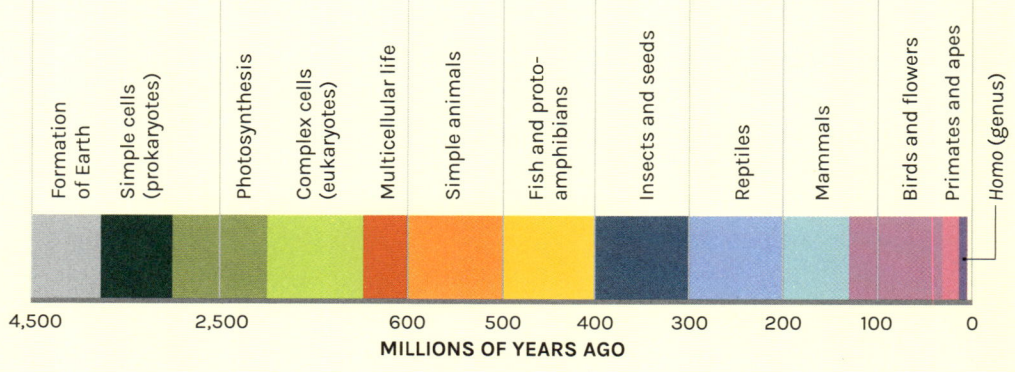

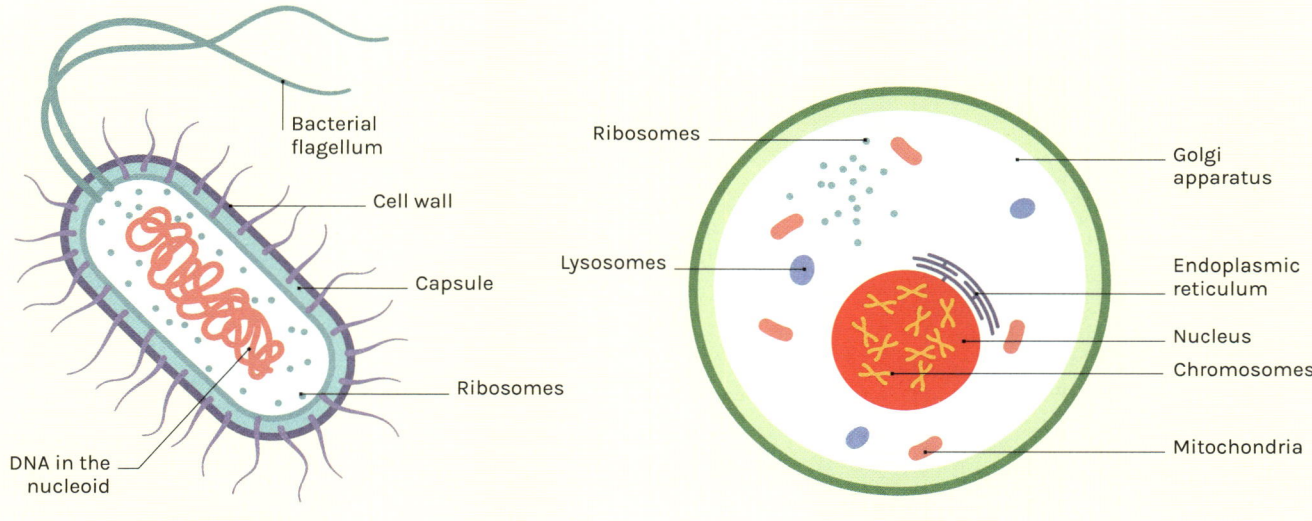

PROKARYOTIC CELL

EUKARYOTIC CELL

ENERGY SOURCES

Microbes can also be subdivided according to what they use for energy. Most are heterotrophs, which means they get their nutrition from existing organic (carbon-containing) matter; they can't make their own food. Yeasts, moulds, and most bacteria fit into this category. Others are autotrophs; they can produce their own food by photosynthesis or chemosynthesis, and live on virtually nothing but a few molecules.

This is just the tip of the iceberg in terms of classification: microbes can also be subdivided according to whether they are aerobes (oxygen requiring) or not, or according to morphology, reproductive mechanisms, or growth characteristics. We'll look at some of the major characteristics of the food-fermenting microbes later: bacteria on p68 and p190, moulds on p104, and yeasts on p150.

All our fermenting microbes are heterotrophic and also absorptive feeders; they release enzymes into their local environment, which break down organic matter such as carbohydrates into simple molecules that they can then absorb via their cell membranes. As moulds can create hyphal structures with thread-like filaments penetrating over a huge surface area, they can grow very quickly, as you will see if you use *Rhizopus oryzae* to make tempeh (see p140), for example: a thick mat will appear in around 36 hours.

While bacteria and yeasts are single-celled organisms, that doesn't mean they always live alone. On a suitable substrate, they can reproduce and form colonies; a single microbe can subdivide many times to produce one colony – "spots" that can be visible on a flat surface. Interestingly, in food fermentation situations, microbes aren't static enough to make colonies in this way.

Microbes are amazingly adaptable. Sometimes, to be able to occupy a niche, they benefit from building symbiotic relationships with other microbes: in food fermentation terms, we see this collaboration in the form of biofilms (p192), which form cellulose mats in kombucha (see p196) and vinegar mothers (see p204), or milk or water kefir grains (see p94).

What about viruses?

Viruses are tricky. They are microscopic, but they aren't really "alive" in the same way as the micro-organisms we're discussing here. They contain genetic material but can't reproduce independently without being inside a cell. They can, however, infect all other forms of life. Those that infect bacteria are called bacteriophages, and can cause trouble in the dairy industry by wiping out bacterial cultures.

FOOD-FERMENTING MICROBES

The main microbes involved in food fermentation are bacteria, yeasts, and moulds. Each brings their own unique microbial characteristics, life cycle, and methods of reproducing to the fermentation process, resulting in vastly different products.

BACTERIA

Several types of bacteria are involved in food fermentation, including lactic acid bacteria (LAB), found in lacto-fermented vegetables (see p68), yogurt (see p90), and kefir (see p94); acetic acid bacteria (AAB), found in kombucha (see p196), vinegar (see p204), and water kefir (see p94); and *Bacillus subtilis*, found in nattō (see p142). Some have an outer cell wall; some don't. Some have flagella that help them to swim; some don't. Some require oxygen to survive, others thrive without it, but they are all prokaryotes (see p30), with (relatively) simple cellular machinery for carrying out their metabolic functions, all in the cell cytoplasm. Bacteria reproduce through binary fission (see right), where a cell splits in two, with each inheriting a copy of the original cell's DNA. After a lag phase where they get used to their environment, they go through an exponential growth phase; one cell becomes two, then four, eight, 16, 32, 64, and so on, so they can grow to massive numbers: you need very few microbes to start a fermentation. This "doubling time" can be as little as 20 minutes or as long as several hours, depending on a particular microbe's optimal conditions. As well as the main clump of nucleoid DNA, they may contain plasmids; small circular molecules of DNA that carry genes that can add a selective advantage -- for antibiotic resistance, for example. These are transferred during binary fission and can also transfer to other bacteria via "horizontal gene transfer". As heterotrophs they break down organic substrates into simple molecules that can be absorbed. As they lack mitochondria, ATP (adenosine triphosphate; the main energy source of cells) is made through chemical pathways that occur in the cytoplasm. The end products of metabolism, like acetic and lactic acid, are excreted by channels in the cell membrane, to avoid them causing toxicity to the cell.

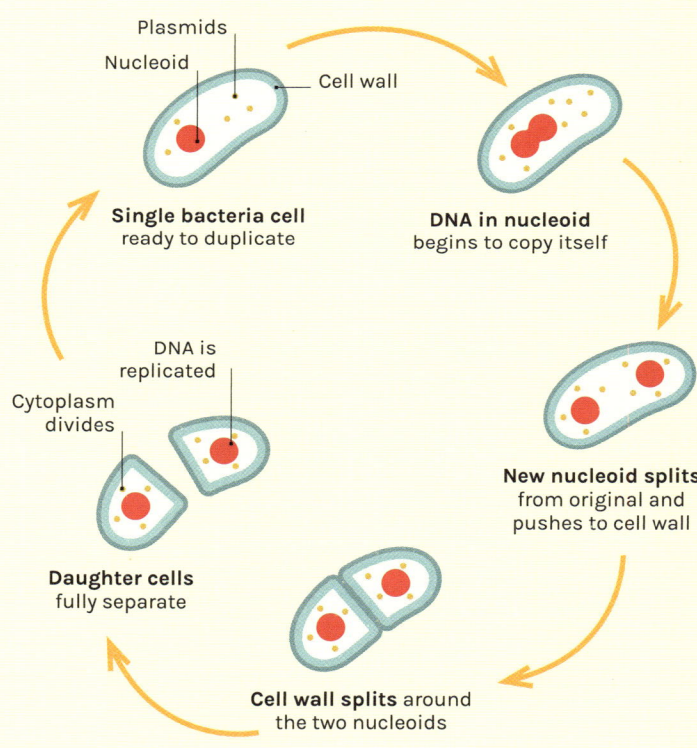

Bacterial binary fission

Bacteria reproduce rapidly by a process called binary fission. This is when one cell divides into two identical daughter cells.

- **Single bacteria cell** ready to duplicate (Plasmids, Nucleoid, Cell wall)
- **DNA in nucleoid** begins to copy itself
- **New nucleoid splits** from original and pushes to cell wall
- **Cell wall splits** around the two nucleoids
- **Daughter cells** fully separate (Cytoplasm divides, DNA is replicated)

RESISTANT SPORES ENABLE BACTERIA TO ENDURE LONG PERIODS OF DORMANCY IN HARSH CONDITIONS.

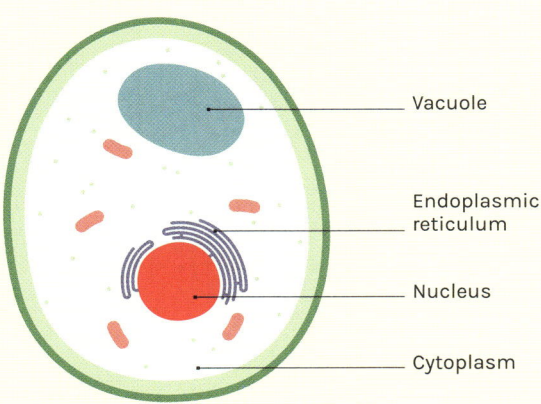

YEAST CELL
- Vacuole
- Endoplasmic reticulum
- Nucleus
- Cytoplasm

YEASTS

Species of *Saccharomyces* (brewer's and baker's yeast), *S. kluyveromyces* and *S. brettanomyces*, are commonly found in kombucha (see p196), kefir (see p94), and wine- and beer-making (see p162 and p168). As eukaryotes, they contain more complex cellular machinery and cell walls, but this isn't noticeable in the way we use them: like bacteria, they grow exponentially, via a slightly different process called budding (see p150). A small outgrowth forms on the cell, into which is passed a duplicated copy of the original cell's DNA. The bud then separates from the parent cell, forming a new, genetically identical one. More rarely yeasts can undergo a type of sexual reproduction that involves two haploid cells (each with only one copy of DNA) fusing together to make one diploid cell with the full complement of DNA. They can grow in colonies, or separately in liquid substrates, or in long chains, and are sometimes visible as dark-brown clumps in kombucha. Like bacteria, some species can form spores when stressed, although it's a more complicated process, and designed for reproductive purposes, not just for survival.

MOULDS

Although yeasts and moulds are both eukaryotic fungi, on the surface they appear much less alike than yeasts and bacteria. Moulds are often known as filamentous fungi, as they can grow and penetrate their substrate by producing hyphae, long filamentous structures spread throughout a substrate and forming a mycelium or mat. These become multicellular, with the hyphae being split into separate sections by walls called septa, with each new section having a new DNA-containing nucleus.

Filamentous moulds have various methods of reproduction, both sexual and asexual, depending upon the species (see p104). For example, *Rhizopus oryzae* forms asexual structures called sporangiospores along the surface of a hypha, on a minuscule stalk called a sporangiophore. They can also undergo sexual reproduction when opposing mating types of hyphae meet each other and produce a new structure called a zygospore. It's clear from these names that filamentous moulds are spore formers – not so much for preservation but to reproduce and spread. The spores are dispersed by air currents, water, and insects.

> **DRIED YEAST**
> ISN'T DRIED SPORES; IT'S DEHYDRATED LIVE CELLS, WHICH CAN BE ACTIVATED WITH WATER.

> **MYCELIUM**
> CAN PENETRATE AND SPREAD TO METRES OF GROWTH FROM THE INITIAL INOCULATION SITE.

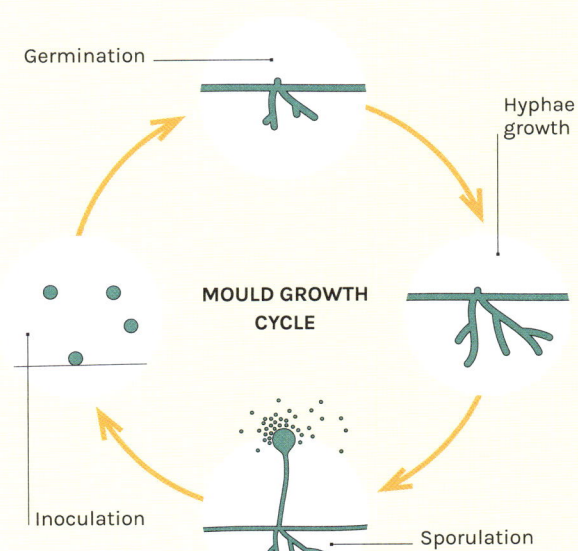

MOULD GROWTH CYCLE
- Germination
- Hyphae growth
- Sporulation
- Inoculation

HOW DO MICROBES EVOLVE?

Charles Darwin is often paraphrased as saying, "It is not the strongest of the species that survives, nor the most intelligent. It is the one that is most adaptable to change." And this is certainly a feature of our microbial friends.

Microbes have several features that make them extremely adaptable and evolution ready. They have huge populations; a colony could easily contain a billion, and each replication event gives the chance for mutations to occur. They reproduce rapidly, giving more opportunities for inheriting changed DNA. And the plasmids in their cytoplasms, which can transfer between bacteria of the same and different species, can also spread genetic alterations.

Microbial evolution isn't always linear; similar traits can arise without shared common ancestors. When microbes are unchallenged, there's little need for evolution, but they are readily able to adapt if necessary. For example, in response to the challenge of antibiotics, microbial resistance genes have arisen, creating serious issues in medicine.

This adaptability offers the potential for positive change, too. *Ideonella sakaiensis* produces an enzyme that can break down PET plastics, and recent research suggests some gut microbes could detoxify unhelpful food additives. Food fermentation microbes have all evolved specialisms that we have learned to exploit.

Single nucleotide polymorphisms (SNPs)

These are single base changes in DNA that result in genetic variation, and one of the major drivers of natural selection across all forms of life. If these tiny changes affect traits that influence reproduction or survival, they can become more or less prevalent over time. Evolution is also brought about by other types of genetic change, including insertions, deletions, and chromosomal rearrangements.

LACTIC ACID BACTERIA (LAB)

This diverse group is heavily intertwined with human existence: they are natural colonizers of our skin and mucosal surfaces, may be pathogenic, are essential components of soil, and are now invaluable to us in fermentation (see p68). *Lactobacillus*, *Leuconostoc*, *Pediococcus*, *Lactococcus*, and *Streptococcus* are all believed to have a common ancestor. As facultative aerobes, they can happily survive with or without oxygen (already a huge selective advantage), which suggests that they existed some 3.5 billion years ago, before oxygen was present. LAB that are involved in food fermentation exhibit moderate to high salt tolerance. They ferment sugars to lactic acid, making an acidic environment that helps inhibit the growth of other microbes, allowing LAB to triumph – an example of competitive exclusion (see p58), one of the tenets of safe food fermentation.

FILAMENTOUS FUNGI

Eukaryotes evolved around 2 billion years ago, after an event in which one cell type engulfed another, which started to provide energy and eventually became mitochondria. Filamentous moulds have been around for 750 million years. When we examine the development of two major food fermentation moulds, *Aspergillus oryzae* and *Rhizopus oryzae*, we see that although the results appear similar, whether fermenting rice to make koji (see p110), or soya beans to make tempeh (see p140), they diverged long ago. *Aspergillus* and yeasts developed from an event that split from *Rhizopus* about 100 million years ago, so despite the confusing similarity in their names, *Aspergillus oryzae* is a closer relative to yeast than *Rhizopus oryzae* (see above). Their ability to penetrate

The phylogenetic tree of microbial evolution

All life shares a last universal common ancestor (LUCA), which probably existed about 3.8 billion years ago. A phylogenetic tree maps how species evolved from that ancestral being, branching into bacteria, archaea, and eukaryotes across evolutionary time.

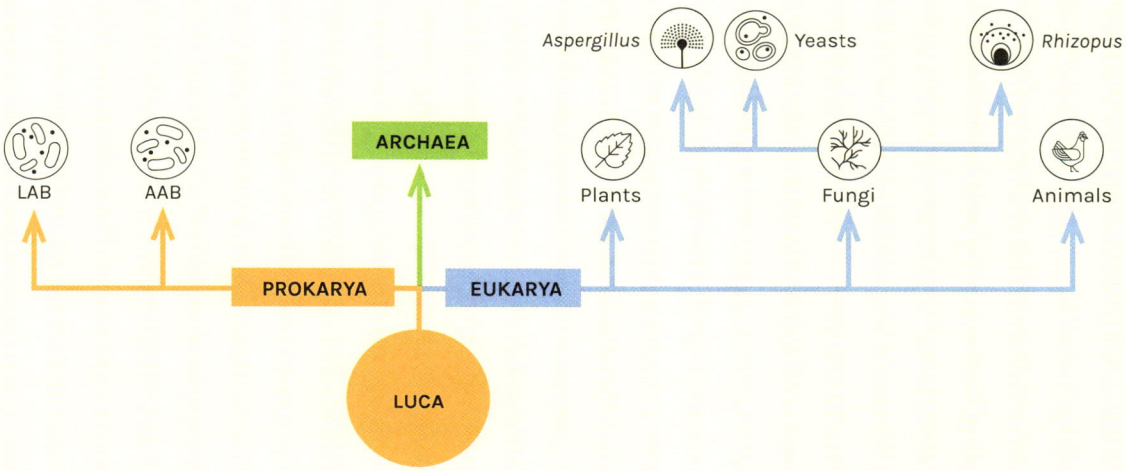

surfaces that others cannot is a useful survival strategy; we harness them for their production of enzymes and their ability to break down antinutrients.

YEASTS

Yeasts are descendants of filamentous fungi and probably lost their hyphae around 400 million years ago to occupy alternate niches, such as liquid environments; however, under the right conditions, many yeasts can switch to filamentous growth.

Yeasts as we know them today developed about 130 million years ago, after fruiting bodies appeared. When fruits ripen, there's fierce competition for the resulting sugar from microbial communities, and yeasts have become specialized at exploiting this through the rapid conversion of sugars to ethanol (see p150). As alcohol is toxic to many species, it gives yeasts a selective advantage. They can also catabolize ethanol, breaking down what they have made to produce more energy. Alcohol production by yeast has been harnessed since Neolithic times, as well as its ability to produce large quantities of CO_2, which is useful in most breadmaking (see p156).

ACETIC ACID BACTERIA (AAB)

Aerobic bacteria evolved sometime after cyanobacteria started to photosynthesize, about 3 billion years ago. Acetic acid fermentation likely evolved after alcoholic fermentation, as it depends on the presence of ethanol. Since ethanol-producing yeasts evolved early in fruit-rich environments, AAB emerged later to metabolize this new substrate. The selective advantage held by AAB lies in tolerance to both alcohol and acid, and the production of protective cellulose (see p192). We harness this now in vinegar production (see p204).

FRUIT BLOOM IS A WAXY COATING OFTEN COLONIZED BY WILD YEASTS.

WHAT ARE ENZYMES?

An enzyme is a type of protein that speeds up chemical reactions. Enzymes underpin all biological processes. Without them, life itself wouldn't be possible – let alone fermentation.

Each enzyme acts like a biological key, unlocking specific molecules and breaking them down into smaller, more usable parts. This transformation increases bioavailability and digestibility.

Most people are familiar with digestive enzymes that are produced in the human body and help us digest food. Fermentation uses the same principle, except the work is outsourced to microbes. In this way, fermentation acts like an external digestive system, partially breaking down food before it's eaten. It also suggests that the gut microbiome extends beyond our bodies and into the food cultures and preparation methods we participate in.

Enzymes are present and active in all microbial activity, though the conversation around them often centres on mould-based fermentations. The three main enzymes of interest in culinary fermentation are amylase, protease, and lipase.

AMYLASE

Amylase breaks down starches into simple sugars. Starch is a compact way for plants to store energy – long chains of sugar molecules that must be unlocked before microbes (or humans) can use them.

This unlocking is central to the production of sweet ferments, alcohol, and vinegar. Sugars released by amylase can be consumed by yeasts and converted into alcohol, which can then be transformed into acetic acid by acetic acid bacteria. It's how beer becomes boozy, and kombucha and vinegar develop their signature tang.

> ENZYMES BREAK DOWN BARLEY STARCHES INTO SUGARS, WHICH ARE FERMENTED INTO ALCOHOL, THEN DISTILLED INTO WHISKY.

Enzymes convert proteins, starches, and fats in base ingredients to produce complex layers of flavour.

> **PECORINO**
> AMINO ACIDS LIKE GLUTAMATE GIVE AGED CHEESE AND FERMENTED MISO THEIR UMAMI DEPTH (SEE P22).

AMYLASE
Amylase converts complex starches into simple sugars, fuelling fermentation and enhancing sweetness.

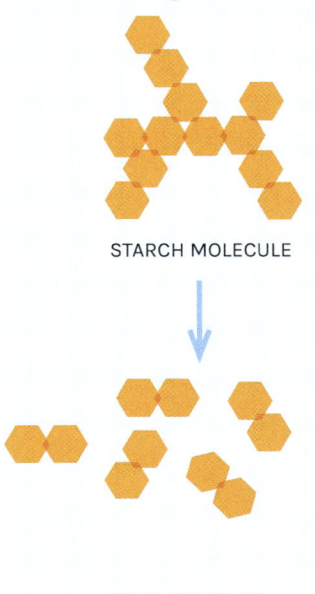

STARCH MOLECULE

↓

SIMPLE SUGARS

PROTEASE
Protease breaks down proteins into smaller peptides and amino acids, unlocking umami and savoury flavour.

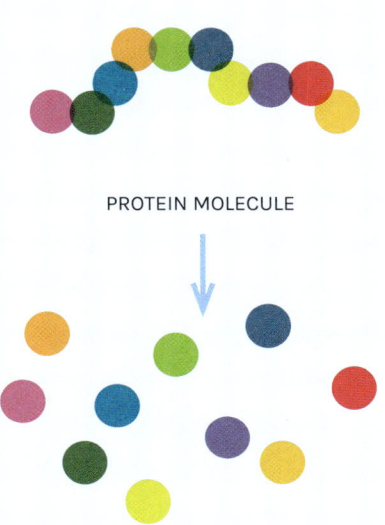

PROTEIN MOLECULE

↓

AMINO ACID MOLECULES

LIPASE
Lipase breaks fats into fatty acids and glycerol, releasing rich flavours during fermentation or ageing.

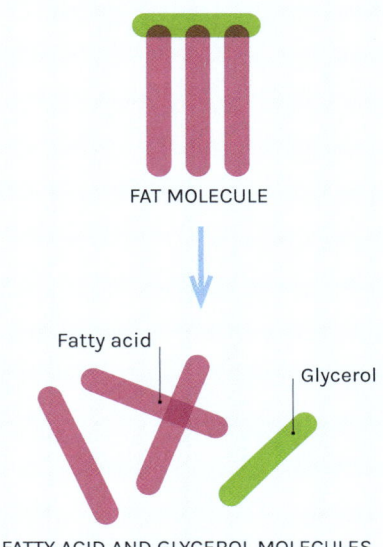

FAT MOLECULE

↓

Fatty acid

Glycerol

FATTY ACID AND GLYCEROL MOLECULES

Amylase is present in many plants and is responsible for natural sweetness: it is why bananas sweeten as they ripen, and why a roasted sweet potato can be so sugary. Malted barley is rich in amylase and forms the enzymatic foundation of saké, beer, and whisky.

PROTEASE
Protease breaks proteins down into amino acids and peptides: the molecular building blocks of life. These molecular subunits are responsible for the umami taste, signalling that valuable protein is available.

Like amylase, protease is naturally present in many foods. In aged or cured meats, it softens texture and deepens flavour. In fish, it enables the production of garum (see p146) and Southeast Asian fish sauces. By utilizing protease-producing moulds such as *Aspergillus oryzae* or *Rhizopus oligosporus*, it's possible to transform nutritionally dense but hard-to-digest ingredients such as soya into flavourful, nourishing ferments such as miso.

LIPASE
Lipase is responsible for the breakdown of fats (lipids) into their building blocks: glycerol and free fatty acids. This process, known as lipolysis, plays a crucial role in fermentation. In cooking, lipase activity can dramatically affect flavour development, particularly in cheese. In traditional Italian cheeses like pecorino or Gorgonzola, lipase contributes to sharp, piquant notes by liberating short-chain fatty acids such as butyric acid, which are highly aromatic.

These liberated fatty acids are also responsible for rancidity in fats, which is why butter can go off. When fats are broken down and oxidized, the resulting compounds can smell unpleasant or sour.

Lipase is also a key ingredient in many biological washing powders. Because fatty acids are more water-soluble than intact fats, lipase helps break down greasy or oily stains on fabrics, allowing them to be rinsed away more easily during washing. This highlights the enzyme's versatility.

HOW DO ENZYMES DRIVE FERMENTATION?

Enzymes are catalysts – biologically produced molecules that speed up chemical reactions without being used up themselves. They do this by enabling dramatic transformations that would otherwise be too slow to proceed under normal conditions.

Like microbes, certain enzymes favour certain pH and temperature environments. For example, proteases in fish sauce (see p146) work best in acidic to neutral conditions, while serine proteases thrive in alkaline ferments like nattō (see p142). Heat increases enzyme activity up to a point, after which they denature, and lose structure and functionality. This is why fermenters often balance warmth to encourage enzymatic action, but avoid overheating.

Each enzyme is highly specific – a lock-and-key mechanism where only particular substrates (reactant molecules) will fit into an enzyme's active site. A more accurate model, known as "induced fit", shows that enzymes naturally shift their shape slightly to better accommodate the molecule they're working on. This helps stabilize the reaction and makes it run more smoothly.

This is why, even within the three broad categories of enzyme discussed on p36 (protease, amylase, and lipase), there are countless specific types, all of which operate in very specific ways, leading to nuanced outcomes.

In the amylase family, alpha-amylase cuts starch chains at random points, quickly thinning out thick mashes and producing shorter sugar chains called

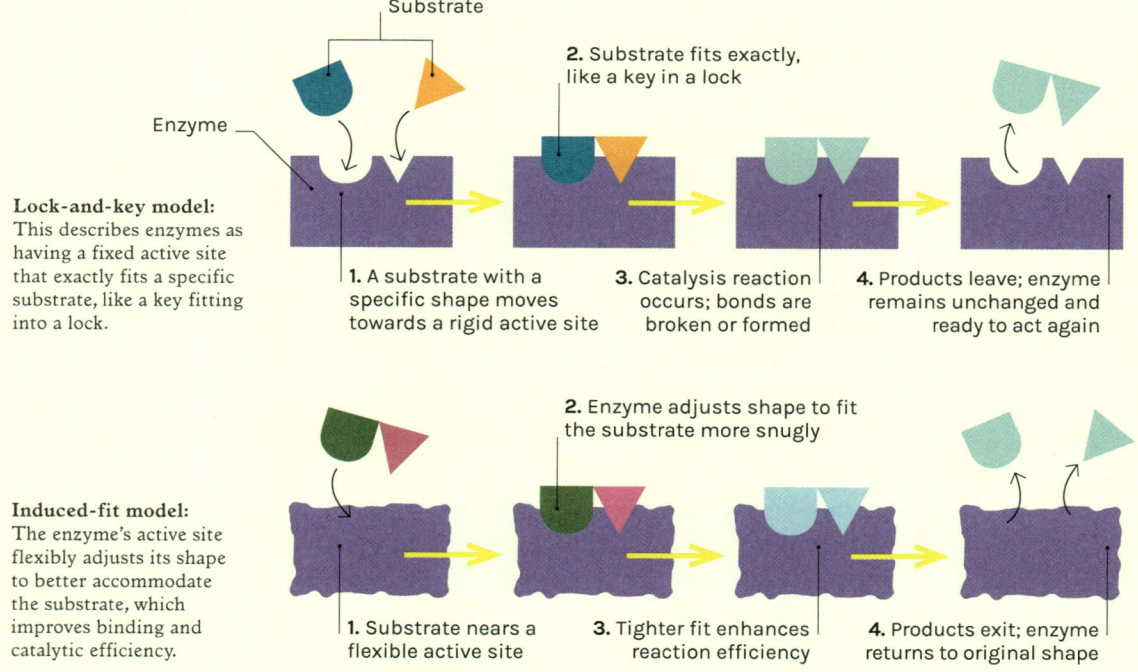

Lock-and-key model: This describes enzymes as having a fixed active site that exactly fits a specific substrate, like a key fitting into a lock.

Substrate
Enzyme

1. A substrate with a specific shape moves towards a rigid active site
2. Substrate fits exactly, like a key in a lock
3. Catalysis reaction occurs; bonds are broken or formed
4. Products leave; enzyme remains unchanged and ready to act again

Induced-fit model: The enzyme's active site flexibly adjusts its shape to better accommodate the substrate, which improves binding and catalytic efficiency.

1. Substrate nears a flexible active site
2. Enzyme adjusts shape to fit the substrate more snugly
3. Tighter fit enhances reaction efficiency
4. Products exit; enzyme returns to original shape

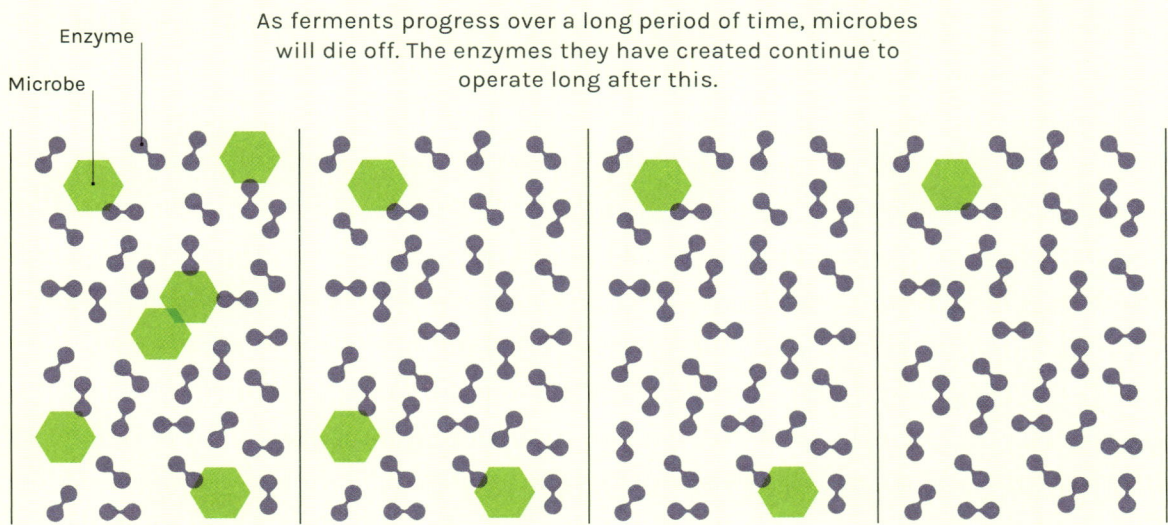

Microbe and enzyme density over time

As ferments progress over a long period of time, microbes will die off. The enzymes they have created continue to operate long after this.

dextrins. It's most active in the early stages of fermentation, especially at warmer temperatures of 65–72°C (149–162°F). Beta-amylase works more slowly and precisely, snipping maltose units from the ends of starch chains to create simple sugars that yeast can easily ferment. It prefers slightly cooler temperatures of 55–65°C (131–149°F).

Other enzymes outside these three main groups perform equally transformative roles in fermentation. Pectinases and cellulases, for instance, are present in plant-based foods to break down cell walls and soften texture, which can be unwelcome.

STAYING POWER

A surprising truth about fermentation is that microbes don't need to be alive for their impact to continue. This is because enzymes, once created, continue to function independently – long after the organism that produced them has died or been rendered inactive.

This is especially apparent in long-ageing ferments such as miso (see p126). Early in fermentation, microbes proliferate wildly and secrete a flood of enzymes. As the ferment progresses many microbes die off but their enzymes persist, quietly continuing their work.

In some cases, such as brewing and fruit juice clarification, microbes are never involved at all. Enzymes can be harvested, purified, and added directly to food or fermenting substrates to work their magic. These industrial enzymes are often derived from fermentation but used independently, precisely because they are so efficient and predictable.

In essence, enzymes are the molecular machinery of fermentation and transform, soften, and unlock flavour long after the microbial action is over.

Cooperative enzymes

In fermentation, enzymes often act in coordinated sequences, with one enzyme breaking a large molecule into intermediates that become substrates for the next. A protease might first cleave a protein into peptides, which are then further refined by more specialized proteases into individual amino acids. This cascading action allows for complex, layered transformations, with each stage unlocking new textures, nutrients, and flavour.

HOW DO NICHE MICROBES INFLUENCE FERMENTATION?

A vast array of lesser-known microbes can make unique contributions to the fermentation process, shaping flavours and textures, and influencing future possibilities in food innovation.

In many parts of the world, fermentation is associated with a few well-known microbial players: *Saccharomyces cerevisiae* (brewer's yeast), *Lactobacillus bulgaricus* (used to make yogurt), and *Aspergillus oryzae* (used to make soy sauce) spring to mind. However, beyond these, vast microbial diversity exists, which plays an equally crucial role in shaping the flavours, textures, and nutritional profiles of our favourite ferments. As our appreciation for this microbial diversity grows, so does the potential to harness some of the more niche organisms to push the boundaries of fermentation science.

UNCOMMON ESSENTIAL PLAYERS

While industrial fermentation typically relies on a handful of microbial starter-culture species, spontaneous ferments teem with a vast number of different microbes, many of which significantly contribute to their characteristics. Some commonly uncommon examples include:

- *Pichia kudriavzevii* This wild yeast strain, found in cocoa and coffee fermentations, plays a key role in flavour development, contributing to fruity and floral notes.
- *Brettanomyces* Often associated with funky barnyard flavours in sour beers and natural wines, these prized yeasts were historically perceived as a flavour taint in conventional winemaking.
- *Kluyveromyces marxianus* Able to ferment at high temperatures, this yeast is emerging as an important player in dairy- and plant-based fermentations, producing fruity esters and improving texture and mouthfeel by generating creamy polysaccharides.
- *Tetragenococcus halophilus* A lactic acid bacterium that can survive in high-salt environments, meaning it can amplify flavour in salty ferments such as soy sauce (see p118) and miso (see p126). It can also produce bioactive peptides that enhance digestibility and introduce health benefits such as antihypertensive properties.

BACTERIA   **YEASTS**   **MOULDS**

- *Cupriavidus necator* (bioplastics)
- *Xanthomonas campestris* (xanthan gum)
- *Deinococcus radiodurans* (medical use)
- *Yarrowia lipolytica* (fat production)
- *Schwanniomyces occidentalis* (fat production)
- *Rhodotorula glutinis* (fat production)
- *Fusarium venenatum* (mycoprotein)
- *Aspergillus niger* (citric acid production)
- *Trichoderma harzianum* (industrial enzyme production)

Different families of microbe – moulds, yeasts, and bacteria – have different qualities. Within these families, certain species and strains have been found and engineered to produce specific materials via fermentation.

Yeast strains known to produce little or no ethanol are selected and "brewed" just like regular yeast, under conditions designed to minimize ethanol production. The brewer also coaxes flavour and mouthfeel from the yeasts.

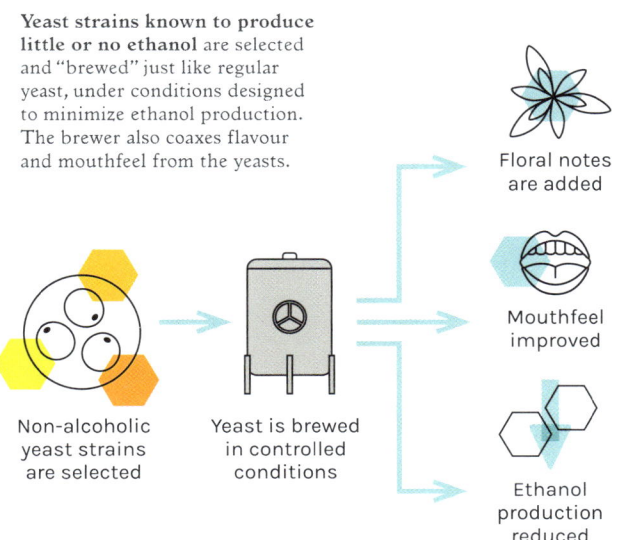

Non-alcoholic yeast strains are selected

Yeast is brewed in controlled conditions

Floral notes are added

Mouthfeel improved

Ethanol production reduced

LOW- AND NO-ALCOHOL YEASTS

As demand for alcohol-free beverages rises, non-alcoholic yeast strains are gaining attention. Unlike traditional brewing yeasts, which produce ethanol as a primary byproduct, certain yeast species can generate complex flavours without significant alcohol production. *Hanseniaspora uvarum* is one such wild yeast used in kombucha (see p196) and low-alcohol beers, known for producing high levels of fruity and floral aromas. *Torulaspora delbrueckii* is used in winemaking to enhance glycerol production, improving body and mouthfeel without excessive ethanol production, while *Saccharomycodes ludwigii* is commonly employed in crafting alcohol-free beers.

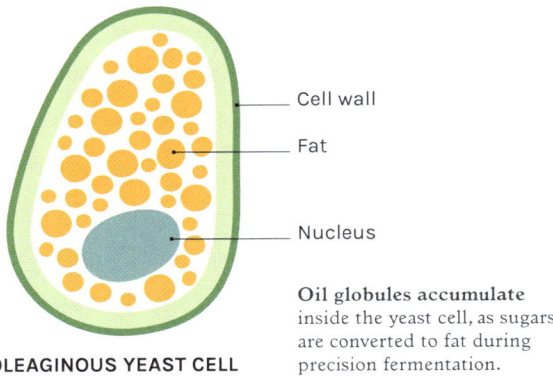

Cell wall
Fat
Nucleus

OLEAGINOUS YEAST CELL

Oil globules accumulate inside the yeast cell, as sugars are converted to fat during precision fermentation.

Blowing hot and cold

Inspired by life in the extreme parts of our planet, researchers are cultivating microbes that can withstand severe cold or heat, to design ferments that extend shelf life or thrive in unconventional settings, including space. For example, bacteria from the Antarctic are being trialled for low-temperature fermentations that preserve delicate flavours in fish.

FATTY FRIENDS

Oleaginous yeasts are a unique group of microbes capable of accumulating high amounts of fats in their cells. This makes them ideal for precision fermentation, where fat is the desired end product. These yeasts are being used to create sustainable alternatives to cocoa butter, palm oil, and animal fats, addressing ethical concerns in the food industry. Some of the most common strains include:

- *Yarrowia lipolytica* A well-researched strain, known for producing tailored lipids, including those mimicking animal fats and cocoa butter.
- *Cryptococcus curvatus* This yeast can accumulate up to 60 per cent of its biomass as lipids, making it an excellent candidate for microbial oil production.
- *Rhodosporidium toruloides* A yeast recognized for its ability to synthesize complex lipids and carotenoids, contributing to both nutritional and functional properties in fermented food.

What sets oleaginous yeasts apart is their ability to convert simple carbon sources, such as sugars, agricultural byproducts, or food-waste side streams, into the same fats found in traditional animal- and plant-based products. Their lipid profiles can be fine-tuned through metabolic engineering, allowing for customized fat compositions suitable for chocolate, alternative dairy, and even cultured meat. As scientific exploration and consumer interest in fermentation expand, embracing this kind of microbial diversity will be key to unlocking the next wave of culinary and industrial breakthroughs.

WHY IS GUT HEALTH IMPORTANT?

Gut health affects every organ in your body, and is governed by the gut microbiota, a population of about 100 trillion microbes of many hundreds of different species, which live in your large intestine.

Our dietary and lifestyle choices can significantly affect our gut microbiota, and therefore our underlying state of health. Fortunately, there are some very easy ways to maintain a healthy gut, and one of these is the regular consumption of nutritionally enhanced fermented foods, with their complement of potentially probiotic microbes.

THE GUT MICROBIOME

Our gut microbiome (or microbiota; see box below) is often described as a virtual organ, superorganism, or "second brain", because it is so important to our health. It contains bacteria, viruses, archaea, fungi, and protozoa – of which the bacterial interactions are the most well understood. It provides functions that we don't have the genetic space for in our own DNA, a bit like outsourcing components in a factory production line. Crucially, it produces metabolites that are complementary to those produced by our own cells, which are essential for digestion and myriad other functions, including breaking down fibre (which we ourselves lack the enzymes for) to make short-chain fatty acids that are essential for gut-wall health, the synthesis (or making) of vitamins, the modification of bile acids for fat and fat-soluble vitamin absorption, modulating responses to allergens, making neurotransmitters, aiding absorption, hormone production, training the immune system, and controlling inflammation and blood sugar levels.

Everyone's gut microbiome is unique, containing many hundreds of different species, but from that baseline, we've learned that the number and type of organisms can be heavily influenced by external factors, including diet, environment, antibiotic use, stress, age, and disease. As a result, some people's microbiomes function better than others.

WHAT WE KNOW TODAY

The greater the diversity of the microbes present in your gut, the more likely you are to be metabolically healthy, because a greater range of beneficial metabolites are produced. Patterns are beginning to emerge from the latest research. We are learning that the presence of certain species is beneficial – *Bifidobacterium animalis* and/or *Prevotella copri*, for example, are linked to better blood sugar control – while the presence of others, like *Ruminococcus gnavus*, seems to be detrimental, as it is associated with poor fat metabolism and increased inflammation in the body.

The term "dysbiosis" is used to describe a gut microbiota that is compromised, which is linked to the development of a range of disorders, including

Microbiota or microbiome?

These two terms are used interchangeably and can therefore be confused, but there is an important distinction. The microbiota refers to the community of different types of living microbes in your gut, while the microbiome is a much broader concept, and includes these microbes, all the genetic material they contain, elements of the environment they occupy, metabolites they produce and how they interact.

systemic inflammation, type 2 diabetes, obesity, cancer, and psychiatric issues, so maintaining good gut health is crucial. Fortunately, as you explore this book, you will discover that the consumption of fermented foods is one of the major ways that your gut health can be enhanced, which in turn can help to improve a whole range of metabolic markers, such as insulin sensitivity, inflammation levels, and glucose tolerance. The more we learn about the importance of the gut–brain connection, the more the findings also suggest that eating for gut health can change the way we feel, bringing to life the maxim "you are what you eat".

Functions of the gut microbiota

- ✓ Regulating the immune system
- ✓ Making vitamins
- ✓ Aiding food digestion
- ✓ Influencing hormone production
- ✓ Producing neurotransmitters
- ✓ Producing and metabolizing short-chain fatty acids
- ✓ Controlling inflammation
- ✓ Modulating the response to allergens
- ✓ Maintaining the gut lining
- ✓ Controlling blood sugar levels
- ✓ Protecting from infection
- ✓ Modifying bile acids involved in the absorption of lipids and fat-soluble vitamins
- ✓ Breaking down dietary fibre

How a healthy gut works

Epithelial cells form a protective barrier, keeping food and microbes in the gastrointestinal tract and preventing leakage into the surrounding membranes, which triggers inflammation.

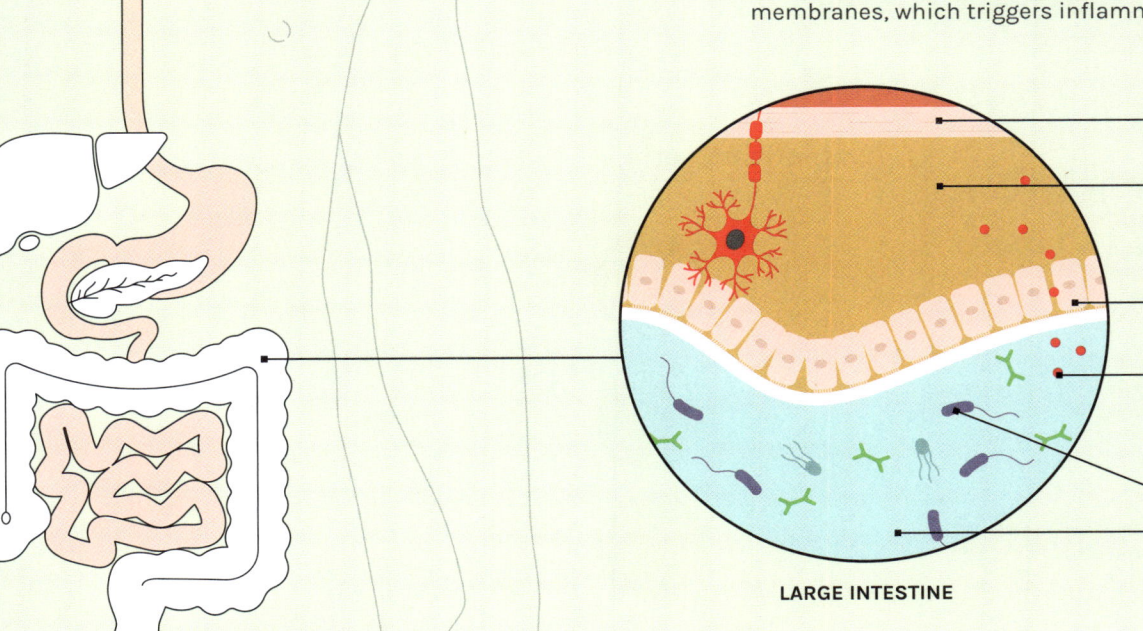

- The gut–brain connection influences mood, digestion, and general health
- The gut is also linked to skin health
- Muscle layer
- Lamina propria (connective tissue)
- Epithelial cells (like colonocytes) protect the gut lining
- Microbes, toxins, and antigens can invade surrounding areas through a leaky gut
- Gut bacteria
- Gut lumen within the gastrointestinal tract

LARGE INTESTINE

HOW DO FERMENTED FOODS AFFECT OUR GUT HEALTH?

Humans have been consuming fermented foods for over 10,000 years, but in recent decades their health benefits have been intensively investigated. In almost every case, the nutrient composition of food increases after fermentation.

Over 100 years ago, Nobel Prize-winning scientist Élie Metchnikoff first realized the link between fermented foods and gut health when studying longevity in Bulgarian peasants, who drank fermented milk (containing *Lactobacillus bulgaricus*, which is found in almost every commercial live yogurt). It has taken massive leaps in DNA technology, however, to enable us to study the microbes and processes involved in this complex relationship. And although we are only about 25 years into this journey, we have learned a lot in a very short period of time.

KEY GUT-FRIENDLY MICROBIAL PLAYERS

There is a huge – and growing – list of microbes involved in fermentation that could benefit gut health by competing with pathogens, modulating the gut microbiota, and offering immunity, anti-obesity, anti-diabetic, and anti-cancer effects. These benefits, however, are strain-specific, as opposed to species-specific – in other words, not all members of a species will necessarily be effective. Those that have been studied and proven to be beneficial are termed "probiotic" (see below and p46).

FERMENTATION AND BIOAVAILABILITY

As their populations grow during the fermentation process, microbes bring enrichment through the production of bioactive molecules – those that affect living organisms. These include organic acids, antioxidants, vitamins, minerals, and enzymes, which can nourish our own gut microbes. Fermentation also decreases the presence of anti-nutrients such as phytates (which can bind to minerals, reducing their absorption), making bioactives easier for our bodies to absorb.

Probiotic bacteria

Lactic acid bacteria (LAB)
Lactobacillus bulgaricus, L. kefiri, and *L. kefiranofaciens* from milk kefir (see p94), *Weissella* species from kimchi (see p84)

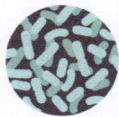
Acetic acid bacteria (AAB)
Komagataeibacter xylinus from kombucha (see p196)

Thermophilic LAB
Streptococcus thermophilus from yogurt (see p90)

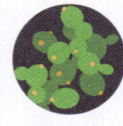
Yeast
Saccharomyces boulardii from kombucha (see p196) and kefir (see p94)

LAB
Bifidobacterium species, from kefir (see p94)

Bacteria
Bacillus subtilis from nattō (see p142)

Fermentation of dietary fibre

Probiotic microbes ferment dietary fibre in the colon, breaking it down into short-chain fatty acids like acetate, propionate, and butyrate – fuel for gut cells and key to gut-brain health.

LONG-CHAIN FIBRE MOLECULES

Indigestible but water-soluble dietary fibre, such as inulin, beta-glucans, and fructooligosaccharides.

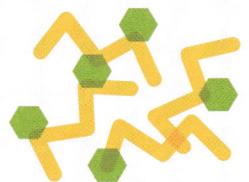

MICROBES SPLIT CHAINS

Probiotic microbes snip apart the long polysaccharide chains into smaller units.

DIGESTIBLE FATTY ACIDS

Bioavailable short-chain fatty acids are ready to be digested.

SHORT-CHAIN FATTY ACIDS

Microbial fermentation processes don't just occur in our fermented foods. One of the primary jobs that we humans outsource to our gut microbes is the manufacture of short-chain fatty acids (SCFAs), which are a useful byproduct of the fermentation in our guts of dietary fibre (see above) that we can't ourselves break down.

The three most important SCFAs are acetate, propionate, and butyrate. The latter is arguably the most important, as it provides food for your colonocytes (a type of epithelial cell that lines your gut; see p43), and also has potential anti-cancer, anti-inflammation, and glucose-regulating activity. Propionate plays an important role in gluconeogenesis (the process of making glucose from non-carbohydrates) and satiety signalling, while acetate is an essential compound for the growth of other gut microbes, and is used in cholesterol metabolism. Eating fermented foods containing prebiotic fibres and/or probiotic microbes (see p46) can positively influence the gut microbiota, so that more SCFAs can be produced.

THE GLOBAL PICTURE

When we look at world longevity statistics, the three countries at the top of the table are Hong Kong, Japan, and South Korea – all known for being big consumers of fermented soya products and kimchi-type pickles. It would be easy to draw the conclusion that this is evidence of a direct link between eating fermented foods and gut health. If only it were that simple.

When we dig deeper, we can see that other nations where fermented foods don't form a large part of the diet, like Italy, Spain, and Switzerland, aren't far behind. Wealth, high-quality healthcare, low stress, a traditional diet, and low consumption of ultra-processed foods (UPFs) all seem to help. The Hadza tribe in Tanzania are said to have the best microbiota in the world due to the huge variety of foraged foods they eat, including copious amounts of honey, and yet they consume virtually no fermented foods.

The conclusions we *can* draw are that increasing consumption of fermented foods, decreasing the reliance on UPFs, and eating a diet containing fresh vegetables and pulses could benefit any population.

Dietary fibre

Dietary fibre is only found in plant foods and refers to complex carbohydrates that our bodies can't digest. There are various types, some of which provide a source of carbohydrate for gut microbes; others (like cellulose) are bulking agents to aid digestive transit. Resistant starch, for example, resists digestion in the small intestine; this provides food for beneficial gut microbiota, and reduces the starch that is broken down into glucose, helping to regulate blood sugar levels. Sourdough bread (see p156) is a good source.

WHAT ARE FUNCTIONAL FOODS?

While there isn't a universal definition of functional foods, they are usually viewed as those that provide health benefits beyond basic nutrition, including disease prevention and treatment. Fermented foods, with their enhanced nutritional status, fit right into this category.

Fermented foods are rich in probiotics. According to the official definition of that term (see opposite), we can only say they are "potentially" probiotic, but that's OK – we don't need officially defined microbes to know that fermented foods are good for us, as there is plenty of evidence. The presence in vegetable and soya ferments of prebiotic fibres that can feed our gut microbes adds another layer of functionality, and let's not forget the presence of short-chain peptides (chains of 2–25 amino acids) in milk kefir and glucuronic and other organic acids in kombucha, all of which facilitate numerous biological processes.

The five Ks

Many of the most common fermented foods happen to have names beginning with K – kimchi, kefir, kombucha, kraut, kvas – which leads to the excellent saying, "One of the Ks every day."

KOMBUCHA IS RICH IN GLUCURONIC ACID, WHICH HAS DETOXIFYING PROPERTIES.

MILK KEFIR CONTAINS A LOWER PROPORTION OF LACTOSE THAN MILK.

KIMCHI HAS BEEN FOUND TO CONTAIN OVER 5,000 STRAINS OF MICROBE.

KIMCHI (SEE P84)

KEFIR (SEE P94)

KOMBUCHA (SEE P196)

HEALTH BENEFITS

The benefits of probiotics are numerous, often offering an enhancement to the existing functions of your own gut microbiota, like the competitive exclusion of pathogens (see p58), production of SCFAs (see p45), regulation of intestinal transit, gut-barrier reinforcement, neutralization of toxins and carcinogens, and enzyme and vitamin production – to list but a few. They are also able to influence the growth or suppression of microbes in your microbiota. Some of the mechanisms are still a bit of a mystery, but they are likely to involve bacterial cross-talk using chemical messengers.

The addition of fermented foods and/or fibre to the diet can have marked beneficial effects on the gut microbiota, and consequently markers of inflammation and metabolic disease – especially in those with previously poor gut health.

Additionally, a recent study that explored the effects of a diet enriched with either fermented foods or fibre concluded that while both had benefits, there were specific effects for each. The high-fibre diet improved some metabolic markers, whereas the diet high in fermented food increased microbiota diversity and also decreased signs of inflammation. Hopefully, a combination of the two would magnify these effects.

SAUERKRAUT IS AN EXAMPLE OF A SYNBIOTIC FOOD, AS IT CONTAINS BOTH PROBIOTICS AND PREBIOTICS.

KRAUT (SEE P74)   KVAS (SEE P184)

Definitions and differences

Here are some definitions for the new vocabulary that's emerging in this field, from the International Scientific Association for Probiotics and Prebiotics (ISAPP).

PROBIOTICS
Live microorganisms, including strains of LAB, *Bacillus subtilis*, and yeast *Saccharomyces boulardii*, that, when eaten in adequate amounts, confer a health benefit. To earn this label officially requires isolating and testing the microbe to prove it, so those that are untested in functional foods are described as "potentially probiotic". This doesn't mean they aren't beneficial or probiotic, it just means it hasn't been officially proven yet.

PREBIOTICS
Carbohydrates (fibre in plants, such as those found in fruits and vegetables like bananas and cabbage) that our bodies can't break down as we don't have the enzymes. These carbohydrates arrive in the colon to nourish our gut microbes.

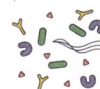

POSTBIOTICS
A preparation of inanimate microorganisms and/or their components that confers a health benefit when eaten. Probiotic microbes don't necessarily need to be alive to exert positive effects on our bodies. Sometimes their metabolites, or even the presence of their protein coats, are enough.

SYNBIOTICS
A mixture comprising live microorganisms and substrate(s) selectively utilized by our gut microbes, which confers a health benefit. This is basically something with both probiotic and prebiotic properties – sauerkraut, for example, which contains live microbes along with plant fibres that we can't digest.

HOW CAN I INCLUDE FUNCTIONAL FOODS IN MY DIET?

It's true to say that the typical Western diet is not aimed at creating optimal gut health. Fortunately, functional foods contain microbes that can help, as well as the right sort of nourishment for your microbiota. They are also easy to bring in to your diet, even if you don't make your own fermented foods.

Just as in all aspects of diet, variety is key when it comes to incorporating fermented foods. A daily shot of milk kefir (see p94), either on its own or with a mixture of nuts, berries, and seeds, is a fairly good start to the day. Kimchi (see p84) goes brilliantly with both eggs and cheese, so load up your toasties, and, like sauerkraut (see p74) can add a splash of acidity to most dishes. Miso (see p126) works well in dressings and marinades, and lacto-fermented vegetables can be eaten like a salad, dressed with olive oil to brighten the flavours (though don't include oil in initial fermentation; see p57). It's also easy to add a spoonful of mayonnaise or kefir to convert sauerkraut into coleslaw.

Sourcing functional foods

You can easily incorporate functional foods into your diet by focusing on ferments and certain plants.

JERUSALEM ARTICHOKES HAVE HIGH LEVELS OF INULIN – A KEY PREBIOTIC FIBRE.

KOMBUCHA OFTEN CONTAINS A LARGE NUMBER OF SPENT YEAST CELLS, FITTING THE DEFINITION OF POSTBIOTIC.

PROBIOTIC
Kefir (see p94), sauerkraut (see p74), kimchi (see p84), all other lacto-fermented vegetables, yogurt (see p90), and kvas (see p184) are all rich in potential probiotics.

PREBIOTIC
Plant fibres are rich in micro-accessible carbohydrates (MAC). A particular favourite of gut microbes is inulin, the best sources of which are Jerusalem artichokes, garlic, onions, leeks, apples, and bananas.

POSTBIOTIC
Kombucha (see p196) ticks this box. Miso and other koji ferments do also, as they contain microbially produced enzymes, as well as tempeh (see p140), which is always cooked before consumption.

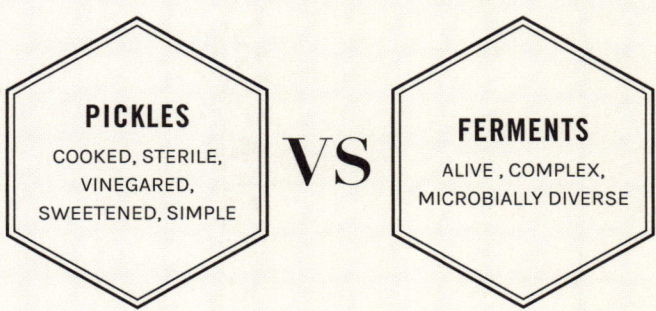

Eating a varied diet with as many different types of fruit and vegetables as you can muster – 30 a week is a recommended target – will provide your microbes with a variety of prebiotic fibres.

PICKLE OR FERMENT?

"Pickle" is a confusing term that seems to be applied to both pickles and ferments indiscriminately. Really, any type of acidic preserved food that you can find in a jar can be called a pickle, from an onion or gherkin in sweet vinegar to an Indian lime chutney – but they are not necessarily fermented. To confuse things further, pickling can also mean preserving in brine, vinegar, or salt. In summary, all vegetable ferments are pickles, but not all pickles are ferments!

Non-fermented pickles are usually less beneficial to gut health, as they lack the additional bioactive compounds that are produced from the fermentation process and more often than not contain large amounts of sugar. It's not all bad news, though, as the acetic acid component of pickles has been shown to have positive effects on blood glucose levels (although this could be outweighed by the amount of added sugar).

Can "dead" ferments still be of value? Yes, it seems that so-called "postbiotics" (see p47) can still have some positive effects, though this is a very new field of research and it's not likely that the microbes that make beer, for example, will produce health effects to outweigh the negatives of the alcohol itself.

Types of food fermentation

Many foods and drinks consumed daily are the products of different microbes. These are a few common examples and the microbes responsible.

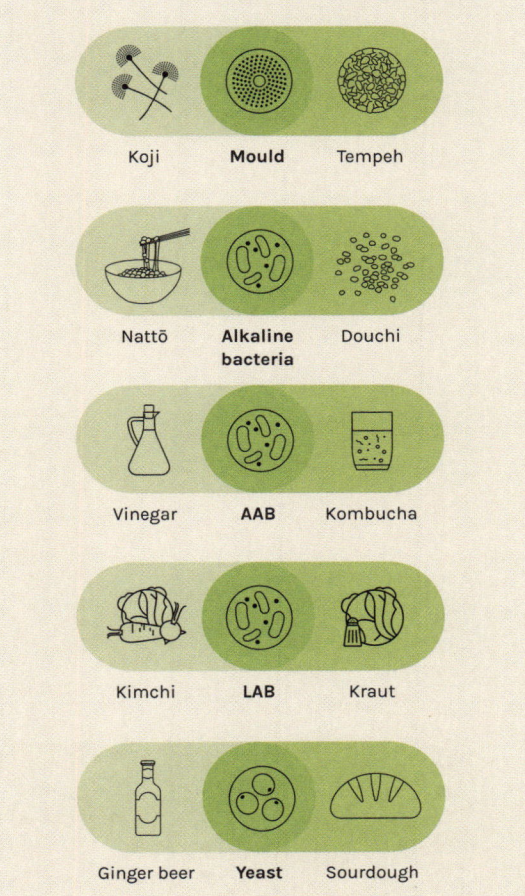

Fighting disease

In any nation rife with metabolic disease, increased consumption of fermented foods is likely to improve the health of the people. A study from Stamford University showed that a 10-week diet high in fermented foods enhanced gut-microbe diversity and lowered molecular signs of inflammation.

FERMENTER'S TOOLKIT

Basic equipment	**52**
Useful extras	**54**
Should I be worried about pathogens?	**56**
Fermenting safely	**58**
Key principles	**60**
Troubleshooting common issues	**62**

BASIC EQUIPMENT

Even if you invest in nothing else, you can attempt the majority of the ferments in this book using just basic kitchen staples. Most containers and kit you might have at home can be used for fermentation – with some caveats.

USE ROUND BOTTLES
SQUARE GLASS BOTTLES CAN EXPLODE MORE EASILY UNDER PRESSURE.

GLASS
SHOULD ALWAYS BE FREE FROM CRACKS. SCREW TOPS WILL FIZZ RATHER THAN POP WHEN OPENED SLOWLY.

REPURPOSED PLASTIC TUBS
The large plastic containers that your supermarket ice cream comes in are ideal. Stackable, food-safe, and great for everything from salting veg to maturing miso. Any plastic container should be made of food-grade plastic.

MIXING BOWLS
Get the biggest bowl available. You'll always wish it was bigger when massaging salt into 3kg of cabbage!

KNIFE
Your go-to for prep. A standard 20cm cook's knife works for almost everything.

AVOID CLIP-TOP LIDS
WHICH CAN POP OR EXPLODE WHEN OPENED IF CO_2 IS PRESENT.

BOTTLES
Essential for bottling carbonated drinks such as kombucha or tepache. Look for those rated for pressure, or repurpose ones that have been used for carbonated beverages before. Avoid using clip-top bottles; choose screw tops instead.

GLASS JARS
Used for everything from brining veg to catching wild ferments. Go for ones that seal well but won't be a pain to open. Avoid using clip-top jars; choose screw tops instead.

TEA TOWELS
Any inexpensive cotton tea towels will do. Use to cover aerobic ferments, to strain liquids without the need for muslin cloth, or to clean up.

FERMENTER'S TOOLKIT 53

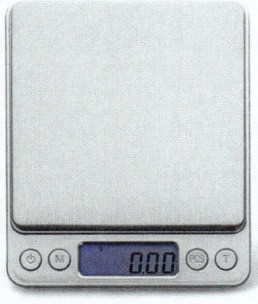

DIGITAL KITCHEN SCALES
Accuracy is everything – especially with salt percentages (see p61). Get one that measures to at least 1g.

TRAYS
Useful for drying, pressing, or salting ingredients. Steel gastronorms (the deep trays often found in hotel buffets) are workhorses and stack well. Any metal should be high-quality stainless steel to avoid corrosion.

SIEVE
A plastic sieve is best, as it's softer than metal and won't break kefir grains apart when straining.

Some crocks have a water moat around the top, which acts as an air seal.

FERMENTATION BOXES
Purpose-built for lacto-fermentation, these are airtight with an internal seal to weigh down ferments. Well worth having if you make lacto-ferments regularly.

CHOPPING BOARD
Nothing fancy, just a board that is solid, heavy, and easy to clean. End-grain wood is ideal. Wood needs to be maintained with regular use and cleaning.

CROCKS
Usually glass or ceramic, these are the traditional containers for kraut and kimchi. The water-seal type is especially good at keeping air out but needs regular topping up. Any ceramics should be made with food-safe glaze or of unglazed pottery that doesn't leach.

NOTEBOOK
Every fermenter needs a logbook. Record weights, ambient temperatures, and hunches you want to test later.

MASKING TAPE AND MARKER
For dating and labelling jars. Blue decorator's masking tape doesn't disintegrate when wet, comes off without leaving gunk, and is easy to spot if it drops into food.

KETTLE
Quickly brings water to temperature for soaking, steeping, or sanitizing. Also useful for sugar dissolving and miso washing.

USEFUL EXTRAS

Once you've got the hang of fermenting and want to advance to the next level, these additions to your kit will make more projects possible, as well as easier, more precise, and better organized.

Bamboo steamers usually have several layers

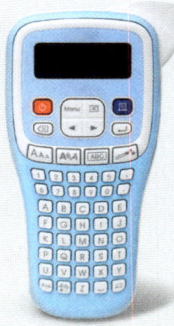

MULTIFUNCTION COOKER
Useful for quickly pressure-cooking beans, or holding a constant temperature for yogurt or amazake. (Rice cookers and yogurt makers can serve much the same function.)

STEAMER AND LINERS
Essential when steaming rice for koji. These help maintain structure and stop clumping. Silicone liners are reusable and easy to clean.

PICKLE PACKER
Used to press veg tightly into jars. Speeds up brine release and helps prevent air pockets.

LABEL MAKER
Tidier than tape, and handy for long-maturing ferments. Especially useful if you're working with larger batches in multiple containers.

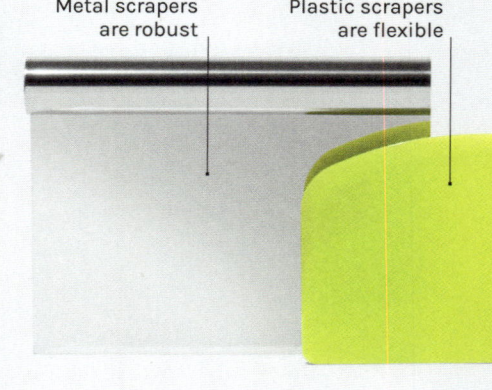

Metal scrapers are robust

Plastic scrapers are flexible

TOP WEIGHTS
For keeping vegetables submerged during lacto-fermentation. Glass and glazed ceramic are the easiest to clean; stone versions are also available. You don't need top weights if fermenting in a sealed aerobic environment.

PH STRIPS
A basic method of pH monitoring, useful for checking when lacto- or acetic ferments hit safe levels. Not precise, but better than guessing.

DOUGH SCRAPER
Not just for dough. Perfect for tidying up after chopping vegetables, moving salted cabbage into a crock, or cleaning your board mid-session. A basic one can be made of plastic, or choose metal for something stronger.

How to make your own incubator

A basic, low-tech incubator can be put together easily using an insulated box, cooler, or plastic tub.

- Place a hot-water bottle wrapped in towels in the box.
- Place the ferment in the box, then seal.

A 40 × 40 × 60cm box (approx. 100 litres) holds a fairly stable 30°C (86°F) for 10-12 hours before the bottle needs to be refilled. A more controlled environment can be achieved by swapping the hot-water bottle for a heat mat paired with a temperature controller.

FOOD THERMOMETER
Ideal for checking koji, liquid temperatures, and general environmental monitoring. A digital version with a decent probe is best – they are fast and accurate.

Airlocks are particularly useful for home-brewing

FERMENTATION AIRLOCKS AND BUBBLERS
These release gas while keeping oxygen (and flies) out. Great for alcoholic or lacto-ferments that risk pressure build-up or mould.

GLASS DEMIJOHNS OR CARBOYS
For larger liquid ferments like mead, vinegar, or wine. Clear glass helps you track fermentation visually, and they fit airlocks as standard.

Advanced equipment

Below is a useful list of more specialist equipment you can invest in for diving into more complex fermentation projects.

INCUBATOR
Useful for koji, yogurt, tempeh, and nattō. If you don't have one, you can use a microwave, an oven at its lowest temperature, or make your own (see left).

MICROSCALE
For weighing things such as bacterial starters, enzymes, or koji spores. Look for one that goes to 0.01g.

DEHYDRATOR
Typically with six or ten trays. For drying koji to preserve or making powdered lacto-ferment salts.

IMMERSION CIRCULATOR
A tool to precisely control the temperature of a water bath. Great for fermenting koji, yogurt, amazake, or even warm-stage garums.

VACUUM SEALER
For anaerobic fermentation, compressing fruit or veg pre-ferment, or sealing bags for freezing. Look for one with a manual seal function to avoid liquid spillage.

PERFORATED TRAYS (½ GASTRONORM)
Used for koji. The perforations allow air to circulate freely. Also useful for slow draining or pressing.

TEMPERATURE AND HUMIDITY CONTROLS
Connect to a fridge, heat mat, or humidifier to regulate koji rooms, long ferments, or curing chambers. Simple plug-and-play units, so they are very accessible.

HEAT MAT
Reptile heat mats or propagation heat mats are usually inexpensive and effective. Tuck under a tray or in a box to keep things gently warm.

HYDROMETER/REFRACTOMETER
Monitors sugar levels in alcoholic ferments to work out ABV. A hydrometer is more affordable; a refractometer needs a smaller sample and works faster.

RACKING CANE AND AUTO-SIPHON
For cleanly separating liquid from sediment in vinegar, beer, or mead. Avoids oxygen exposure and mess.

SILICONE SHEETS
Non-stick surface for drying miso, koji, or fruit leathers.

SHOULD I BE WORRIED ABOUT PATHOGENS?

Contamination of fermented foods with pathogenic (harmful) microbes is extremely rare. If you're following the rules for safe fermentation, and using your senses to guide you, the risks are minimal, but it's still useful to know what could happen if you don't.

The vast majority of about a trillion microbial species on Earth (including bacteria, viruses, yeast, and moulds) are either beneficial to us or of no consequence, but a tiny proportion can be agents of disease in humans. Some could even be present in or on the products you're planning to ferment. However, through naturally occurring microbial processes, with a little added human intervention, we can eliminate almost all of the risks of pathogenic contamination, and with more practical considerations like kitchen and personal hygiene, you can reduce the risks to the absolute minimum.

POTENTIAL SOURCES OF PATHOGENS

A healthy soil ecosystem can contain up to a billion microbes per gram but will also be a natural reservoir for potential pathogens such as *Listeria monocytogenes* (the agent of listeriosis), *Bacillus cereus* (whose toxins can cause a nasty stomach upset), or *Clostridium* species, including *C. botulinum* (the cause of foodborne botulism). Other pathogens, including Shiga toxin-producing *Escherichia coli* (STEC) and *Salmonella*, can be introduced via animal faeces. A vast array of mould spores is also present; any of these could find their way onto soil-grown vegetables.

SALT IS ESSENTIAL IN SAUERKRAUT TO PREVENT PATHOGENS. IGNORE ANY RECIPES THAT ARE SALT-FREE.

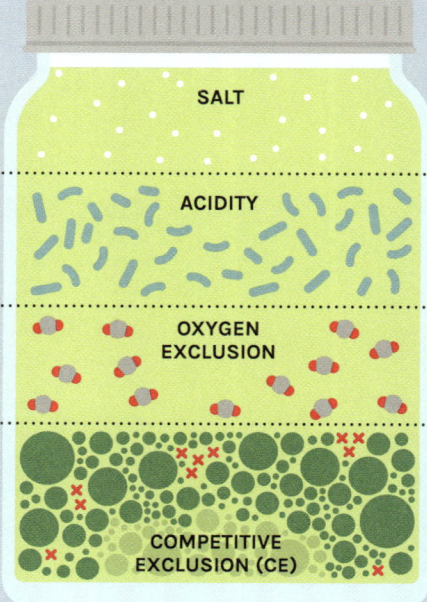

Fermentation naturally controls pathogens. During fermentation we can influence several parameters to promote the growth of helpful microbes, which will naturally suppress the pathogens.

SALT — In vegetable lacto-fermentation, salt (2% minimum) is added as the first line of defence. Luckily, lactic acid bacteria (LAB) are more salt-tolerant than most pathogens, and will begin to quickly multiply, gaining a head start.

ACIDITY — LAB in vegetable ferments and kefir produce lactic acid, lowering the pH of the ferment and suppressing acid-sensitive pathogens.

OXYGEN EXCLUSION — LAB also produce CO_2, which is heavier than oxygen and so displaces it in the headspace of a fermentation jar. In the absence of oxygen, moulds struggle to grow.

COMPETITIVE EXCLUSION (CE) — As populations of beneficial microbes increase, pathogens are crowded out through competitive exclusion (CE); they can't compete for resources to feed themselves. LAB also produce bacteriocins: antimicrobial peptides directed against pathogens.

Unpasteurized milk can be contaminated with *E. coli, Klebsiella* species, or *Campylobacter* species via mammary glands or faeces, while processing equipment and contaminated irrigation water can also occasionally be sources of human pathogens, including *E. coli* (STEC).

First discovered in 1982, *E. coli* (STEC) are thoroughly unpleasant bacteria that can cause serious gastroenteritis, though fortunately cases are rare. They can contaminate soils and grow inside plant tissues so are hard to simply wash off. Resistant to acid, salt, and microbial inhibition, they can even survive the fermentation process, though they don't thrive. As terrifying as this may seem, if you're prepared to eat raw vegetables, there is no greater risk in eating fermented ones, especially your own; all reported incidents of this pathogen in fermented food have been from large-scale commercial production.

MYTHS AND MISCONCEPTIONS

Perhaps you have heard that you can get botulism from fermented foods, or you have worried about mould growth when fermenting? Rest assured, such scare stories are often misleading. Myths about the dangers of fermentation may have arisen from some confusion with the canning process, where non-fermented foods are preserved in cans or jars by heating at high temperatures and vacuum sealing. When this is done incorrectly, there is indeed a risk of spores of *C. botulinum* germinating and making toxins, but that risk does not derive from fermentation.

After all, fermentation is an ancient art, and one that involves an extremely well understood set of processes, with many more levels of protection against pathogens. The aforementioned *E. coli* (STEC) is the one microbe that seems to be able to avoid all the defences offered by fermentation, and that is fortunately very rare.

Safety guidelines for fermentation

Using your common sense goes a long way when fermenting, but below are some specific guidelines you should always follow:

RECIPES
ALWAYS FOLLOW THE METHOD AND GUIDELINES FOR WHATEVER YOU'RE FERMENTING.

HYGIENE
ALWAYS FOLLOW BASIC HYGIENE PRACTICES FOR KITCHEN/PERSONAL CLEANLINESS.

INGREDIENTS
SHOULD BE GOOD-QUALITY, CLEAN, AND FRESH. USE CULTURES FROM KNOWN SOURCES.

SENSES
USE SIGHT, TASTE, SMELL, TEXTURE, AND EVEN HOW THE FERMENT SOUNDS TO GUIDE YOU.

AVOID OIL
NEVER ADD OIL DURING FERMENTATION – ONLY WHEN INSTRUCTED IN VERY SPECIFIC METHODS.

Accidental fermentation

Most cases of unsafe fermentation occur accidentally – for example, flavouring oil with raw garlic, which is often a vehicle for *C. botulinum* spores. In a salt-free, room-temperature, acid-free, low-oxygen environment, the spores can germinate and make botulism toxin. Lacto-ferments, meanwhile, can be contaminated by using containers with lead in them. The lead can leach into the ferment and react with the lactic acid, leading to toxic lead levels.

FERMENTING SAFELY

While fermentation is inherently a safe practice and has been carried out for thousands of years, there are a few techniques that can be employed and good housekeeping rules to follow that can ensure you ferment confidently.

If your kitchen is kept clean, then you are ready to start fermenting. For the most part, the microbes do the work of creating a safe environment within your ferment. That being said, it is still important to know why and how to cultivate the right conditions.

COMPETITIVE MICROBES

Competitive exclusion (CE, see p56) is a fundamental concept to understand when learning about safe fermentation. All microbes are constantly struggling for space and resources, and although many species are symbiotic or benign to one another, most are at war.

Microbes employ many different strategies to try to dominate the micro-environments in our ferments. One of the simplest methods they use is growth. If one or a select few microbes dominate a system, they will control the resources and space – forcing everything else out. Many mould species produce powerful antimicrobial compounds to kill off competition; lactic acid bacteria (LAB) and acetic acid bacteria (AAB) create acidic conditions that most microbial life can't tolerate; yeasts synthesize alcohol to the same end.

Most of the microbes we want are specialized for specific conditions, such as *Lactobacillus* and halotolerant yeasts, which survive in high-salt or anaerobic environments.

ENCOURAGING THE RIGHT MICROBES

Knowing which conditions favour our desired microbes helps us to encourage the ones we want and exclude the ones we don't. These are some simple ways to create environments that give the microbes you want the competitive edge:

- **Including at least 2 per cent salt** in lacto-ferments to inhibit pathogens and encourage LAB.
- **Excluding oxygen** using sealed containers (like screw-top jars, see p52) or an airlock to make your ferment anaerobic.
- **Creating an acid environment** by dosing your ferment with a little lemon juice or vinegar to lower the pH.
- **Inoculating with a starter culture** to dose the ferment with an overwhelming microbial load that we favour.
- **Using "magic spray"**, a simple, protective solution of alcohol, acid, and salt (see opposite).

The microbial out-competition process

In a LAB ferment, first salt is added. This inhibits pathogen growth and promotes LAB proliferation. The LAB then produce lactic acid, which kills any remaining pathogens and prevents them from repopulating.

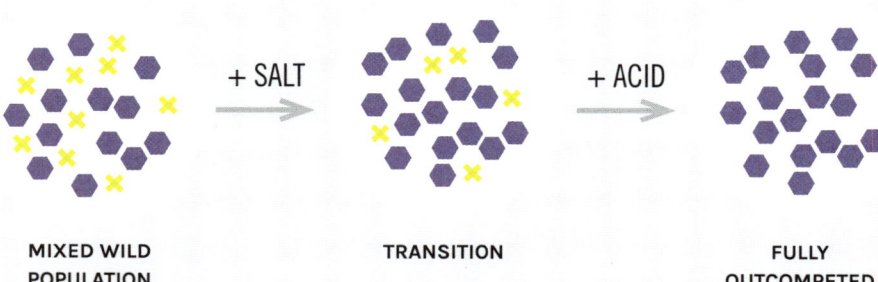

MIXED WILD POPULATION → + SALT → TRANSITION → + ACID → FULLY OUTCOMPETED

MAGIC SPRAY

This simple safeguarding solution can be used liberally on ferments, either to create the perfect starting conditions, or as a balm if anything starts to go awry in a ferment. It won't hurt any of the microbes that we want in our ferments. You can use it to coat the inside of jars and containers before filling, spray the top of ferments as a protective layer, or spray the top of ferments after removing kahm yeast (see p62) or mould.

Sanitizing vs sterilizing

Sanitized equipment reduces the level of microbes and excludes potential contaminants – cleaning with hot, soapy water is more than enough. By contrast, sterilization is the destruction of microbial life, generally using high heat or chemicals – not required in most home contexts outside of brewing.

MAKE YOUR OWN MAGIC SPRAY

EQUIPMENT
- scales
- jug
- spray bottle

INGREDIENTS
- 200ml vodka
- 200ml distilled white vinegar
- 200g salt

1. **Combine the ingredients** with 400ml of boiling water in a jug and mix until the salt has dissolved.
2. **Decant into the spray bottle** and store at room temperature. Shake before use to dissolve any precipitated salt.
3. **Replace your magic spray** every few months.

40% WATER

20% SALT

20% VODKA

20% VINEGAR

MAGIC SPRAY

VODKA – PROVIDES ALCOHOL TO EMULATE THE ALCOHOL PRODUCED BY YEASTS.

VINEGAR – PROVIDES ACID TO EMULATE THE ACID PRODUCED BY LACTIC ACID BACTERIA OR ACETIC ACID BACTERIA.

The magic formula of salt, alcohol, and acid inhibits pathogens and favour the yeasts and bacteria in many ferments. To scale up this recipe, use a ratio of roughly 1:1:1:2 vinegar, vodka, salt, and water.

KEY PRINCIPLES

These pages serve as a quick guide to using this book. Leave a bookmark here and refer back to double-check terms or when trying to modify a recipe or method.

The general rules of fermentation are simple: keep things clean, follow the methods, trust your senses, and walk before you can run. As your knowledge and confidence increases, you will be able to tease out more nuance from ferments by altering various elements – tweaking the salt percentage, changing an ingredient, or augmenting fermentation time.

A KEY TO MICROBE ICONS

The ferments in the book have been categorized according to their primary microbial agents, and the icons below are used to identify the main ones at play in each recipe. It is worth noting, however, that in almost all natural fermentation there will be far more than just one type of microbe at work. In most cases, ferments will be a complex of many microbe categories cooperating and competing, with one type eventually dominating the system.

 Bacteria Single-celled organisms that reproduce quickly and perform chemical processes in various environments (see p32).

 Moulds Multicellular fungi that grow in filaments and produce spores for reproduction and survival (see p104).

 Yeasts Microscopic fungi that consume sugars and release gases, alcohols, or other byproducts (see p150).

 Enzymes Biological catalysts that speed up specific chemical reactions without being consumed themselves (see p36).

Glossary of key fermentation terms

AAB Acetic acid bacteria; produce acetic acid.
Aerobic Requires oxygen to function.
Anaerobic Functions without oxygen.
Autolysis The self-digestion of cells by their own enzymes.
Backslop To inoculate with a previous ferment.
Brine Saltwater used to preserve or ferment.
Culture A population of selected microbes.
Fermentable A substance microbes can break down.
Inoculation Adding microbes to a substrate.
Kahm yeast A harmless surface yeast; white and wrinkly.
LAB Lactic acid bacteria; produce lactic acid.
Pasteurization Heat treatment to kill pathogens.
Pathogen Microorganism that causes disease.
pH Scale measuring acidity (<7) or alkalinity (>7).
Sanitization Reducing harmful microbes to safe levels.
SCOBY Symbiotic culture of bacteria and yeast.
Spoilage Undesired microbial activity causing off flavours.
Starter Pre-made culture to start fermentation.
Sterilization Completely killing all microorganisms.
Substrate The material microbes grow or feed on.
Wild fermentation The process of fermenting using ambient/environmental microbes.

FILL LEVELS

Fill jars to 80 per cent to allow for expansion during lacto-fermentation. Fill bottles to 90 per cent when sealing to carbonate beverages.

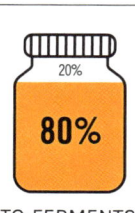 

LACTO-FERMENTS — CARBONIZATION

TEMPERATURE
UNLESS OTHERWISE SPECIFIED, ALL FERMENTS IN THIS BOOK HAPPEN AT ROOM TEMPERATURE: 18–23°C (64–73°F).

FERMENTERS' PERCENTAGES

Although fermentation has been carried out for millennia without the use of scales and numbers, now that we have these tools, we should use them. The technique below ensures that ferments will remain consistent within the methods you are using, making scaling up or down simple and developing and adapting recipes easy.

When working with percentages, it is best to use mass – in other words, weighing everything in grams, even liquids – although sometimes with larger volumes it is easier to just use a measuring jug, knowing that 1ml is roughly equal to 1g, depending on liquid density.

HOW TO CALCULATE SALT PERCENTAGE

This method is based on bakers' percentages, where the percentage is calculated as a proportion of the total weight of the other ingredients, not the total weight of the final mixture.

QUICK FORMULA
SALT (G) = (TOTAL WEIGHT OF OTHER INGREDIENTS IN G) × (SALT % ÷ 100)

 Weigh all your ingredients, except the salt.

 Add together the weights of all your base ingredients.

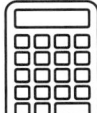

EXAMPLE

Ingredient X = 1000g	
Ingredient Y = 200g	
Ingredient Z = 100g	
Base total = 1300g	

 Let's say you're using a salt percentage of 6% (or 0.06 in decimal figures). You can now calculate the salt weight by multiplying the base total weight by this percentage: **1300g × 0.06 = 78g salt.**

Weigh out 78g salt and add it to the rest of your ingredients.

RATIOS AND HOW TO FERMENT ANYTHING

By using ratios you can easily adapt a recipe to suit the amount of ingredients you have, or the size of container you are using.

WORKING OUT SALT FOR A RECIPE

Chillies = 100g
Cabbage = 500g
Spring onion = 50g
Base total = 650g
Salt target = 2%
650g × 0.02 = 13g salt

HOW TO WORK OUT A RATIO

RECIPE

Chillies = 100g
Cabbage = 500g
Spring onion = 50g
Salt = 13%
Total mass = 663g

Then divide each ingredient by the total mass:

Chillies: 100 ÷ 663 = 0.15
Cabbage: 500 ÷ 663 = 0.75
Spring onion: 50 ÷ 663 = 0.08
Salt: 13 ÷ 663 = 0.02

USING THE RATIO

Multiply each ingredient by the new target mass to calculate the new recipe. For example, for 1000g of this recipe:

Chillies: 0.15 × 1000g = 150g
Cabbage: 0.75 × 1000g = 750g
Spring onion: 0.08 × 1000g = 80g
Salt: 0.02 × 1000g = 20g

TROUBLESHOOTING COMMON ISSUES

Sometimes, even with best practice, things can go wrong in fermentation. Thankfully, the most common problems are salvageable, and even if the ferment can't be saved and needs to go in the compost bin, every attempt is a learning opportunity.

	ISSUE	CAUSE	SOLUTION
	**CLOUDY OR SEDIMENT BUILD-UP** Cloudy brine and visible sediment build-up at the bottom of the fermentation vessel.	Dead yeast and natural fermentation byproducts.	This is normal. Can be strained out or left as is.
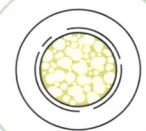	**KAHM YEAST** Silvery surface film that can look like white mould. Completely harmless, but can lead to off flavours and soft lacto-ferments.	Wild yeasts form on the oxygen-rich surface of a ferment.	Skim off, apply "magic spray" (see p59), and continue. If it recurs, reduce oxygen exposure by using an airlock or sealed container (remember to burp). Soft lacto-ferments can still be used in condiments.
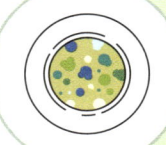	**WHITE/GREEN/BLUE MOULD GROWTH** White/green/blue growth on ferment. Can appear fuzzy or smooth.	Surface mould due to oxygen exposure, chance exposure, or poor sanitization.	Compost affected area plus 1cm beneath. Apply "magic spray" (see p59). Resalt surface if making miso; submerge substrate if brine lacto-fermenting.
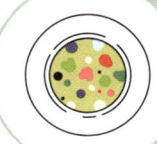	**RED/BLACK/PINK/UNKNOWN/ DEEP MOULD GROWTH** Red/black/pink/unknown growth on ferment. Can appear fuzzy or smooth.	Mould growth due to oxygen exposure, chance exposure, or poor sanitization.	Red/black/pink/unknown mould growth, or any mould growth deeper than 1cm: compost.
	**ROTTEN SMELL** Putrid, sulfurous, or rotten odour.	Salt miscalculation (too low) or microbial contamination.	Compost the batch. Ensure proper sanitization and double-check salt concentration.
	**TOO SALTY** Unpleasantly salty taste.	Salt miscalculation (too high).	Use as a seasoning in small amounts, dehydrate and powder into a flavoured salt, or dilute with other ingredients when using (soups and stews are great for this).

ISSUE	CAUSE	SOLUTION
 **TOO SOFT (NO KAHM)** Loss of texture or mushy consistency.	High temperature >18°C (64°F) expediting pectin breakdown.	Ferment at lower temperatures – 15–18°C (59–64°F) – to retain crunch.
 **NO BUBBLING OR ACTIVITY AFTER 48 HOURS** No signs of fermentation after a few days.	Temperature too cold, too much salt, or low initial microbial load.	Ensure the environment is warm enough. Check salt concentration for lacto-ferments; dose with more starter for yeast ferments. Compost if there is no activity after 3 more days.
 **TOO SOUR** Over-acidic flavour.	Too long, or too high temperature >18°C (64°F) speeding microbial activity.	Ferment at lower temperatures or for a shorter period.
 **SMELLS LIKE NAIL POLISH REMOVER** Strong, solvent-like aroma.	Yeast stress due to inconsistent temperature or oxygen levels.	Maintain stable fermentation conditions and mix to aerate. Compost if the smell remains overwhelming.
 **JAR OVERFLOWING OR BURSTING** Brine leakage or jar rupture.	Pressure build-up from trapped CO_2 released during fermentation.	Use an airlock or burp jars daily and leave adequate headroom. Store on a tray.
 **FERMENT TURNED SLIMY** Ferment has an undesired, mucilaginous texture.	*Lactobacillus*, *Leuconostoc*, or *B. subtilis* thriving in warm temperatures.	Ensure the environment is cool enough – <18°C (64°F) – and double-check salt concentration. If the ferment is palatable, use in sauces, chutneys, and salsas. If not, compost it.
 **NON-ALCOHOLIC FERMENT SMELLS ALCOHOLIC** Strong wine- or beer-like smell from brine.	Yeast overgrowth or low salt allowing yeast to dominate.	Maintain stable fermentation conditions – 15–18°C (59–64°F) – and mix to aerate. Double-check salt concentration. Compost if the smell remains overwhelming.
 **LID IS BULGING OR BOTTLE IS HARD TO OPEN** Pressure build-up inside a sealed container.	Too long, or high temperature >18°C (64°F). Potentially high sugar concentration on bottling.	**GO OUTSIDE!** Open very carefully to release pressure slowly.

DIRECTORY OF FERMENTS

Lactic acid bacteria	**66**
Moulds and more	**102**
Yeasts	**148**
Acetic acid bacteria	**188**

LACTIC ACID BACTERIA

Lacto-fermentation	**68**
Lactic acid bacteria	**70**
How to lacto-ferment anything	**72**
Sauerkraut	**74**
Dill pickles	**76**
Umeboshi	**78**
Hot sauce	**80**
Kimchi	**84**
Yogurt	**90**
Kefir	**94**
Cheese	**98**

LACTO-FERMENTATION

Around the world, we have lacto-fermentation to thank for many of our most loved and iconic foods. This natural preservation method is responsible for soured milk products, sourdough breads, preserved meats, miso, soy sauce, infinite varieties of soured vegetables, coffee, and chocolate.

Present in the soil, and on fruits and vegetables, lactic acid bacteria (LAB) have been at work on this planet long before humans. Their exact evolutionary timeline is complex, and their associations with plants and animals date back millions of years. These microorganisms are crucial to the breakdown of complex carbohydrates, proteins, and other substances. In doing so they create acid, which inhibits spoilage, so they are particularly useful in food preservation.

Fermentation has always been a part of the human experience: as hunters and gatherers we would have benefited from these microbial transformations, with ripe, spontaneously-fermented fruit forming part of our diet. But around 8,000 to 10,000 years ago, intentional use of LAB to make yogurt and cheese emerged. Beyond the superpower of creating acid, LAB also make foods more digestible and bioavailable, as well as producing metabolites that our bodies need, like vitamins, short-chain fatty acids, and bioactive compounds.

THE LIFE CYCLE OF SUGAR

Photosynthesis creates the glucose that feeds fermentation. Sugar, made by plants through water, carbon dioxide, and sunlight, is the driver of everything on our planet. In lacto-fermentation, the LAB feed on this sugar to create acid and, in some cases, carbon dioxide. It is this acid and the subsequent lowering of the pH that preserves the fermentation substrate. For example, milk is soured into yogurt, cheeses, and other more stable products, while fruits and vegetables are acidified so that other microbes cannot spoil them.

> LACTO-FERMENTATION HAS A LOW CARBON FOOTPRINT COMPARED WITH INDUSTRIAL PRESERVATION METHODS.

Fresh fruit and vegetables, milk, and soya can all be preserved and enhanced by lacto-fermentation.

How photosynthesis enables fermentation

Plants are capable of utilizing sunlight and carbon dioxide to produce sugars which are consumed by microbes like LAB to create ferments.

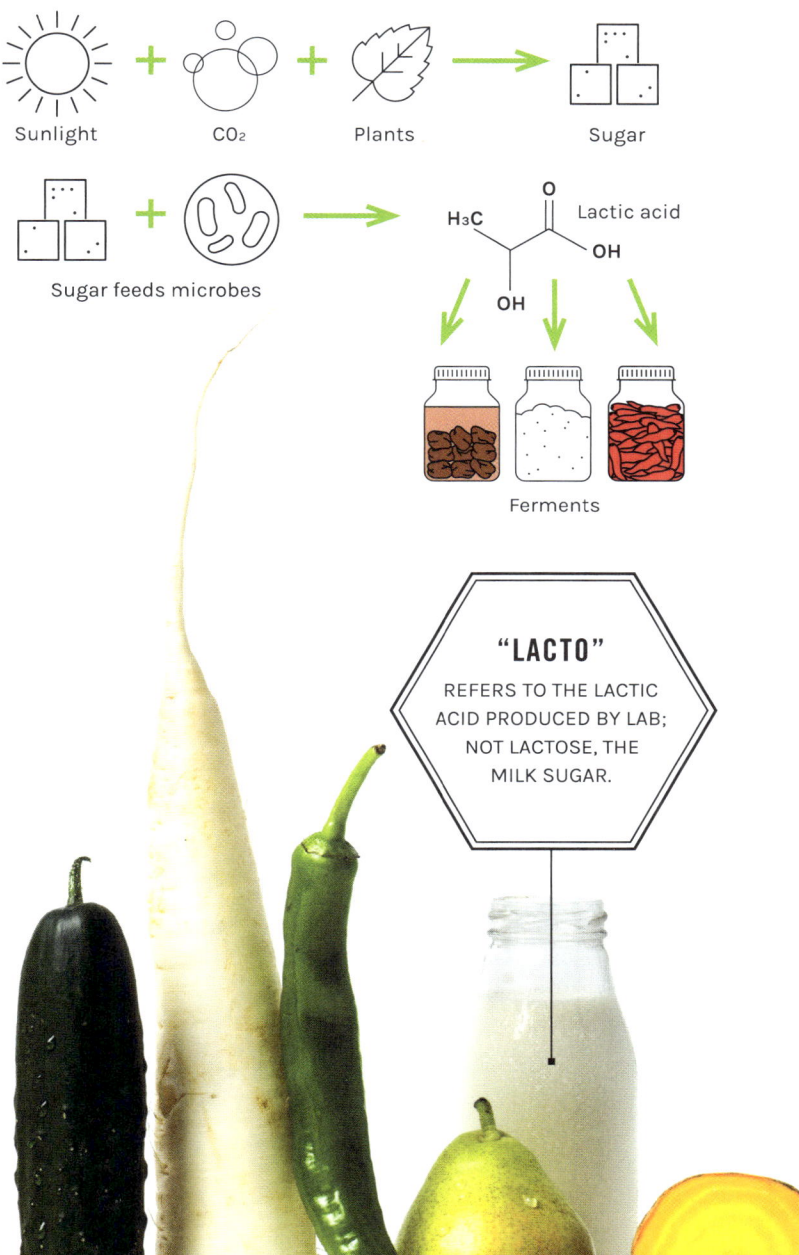

"LACTO" REFERS TO THE LACTIC ACID PRODUCED BY LAB; NOT LACTOSE, THE MILK SUGAR.

THE ORIGINAL PRESERVATIVE

Salt is also used in the lacto-fermentation of meat and fish to draw out moisture, hindering microbes of decay. In vegetables, salt helps control fermentation, as well as keeping them crisp in pickles.

Lacto-fermentation is still the easiest, low-energy way to stabilize, keep, and enhance the safety of fresh vegetables. For example, in some parts of the world, fresh vegetables may not be safe to eat raw, as they can be tainted with *E. coli* or other bacteria, often from water supplies. Yet when they are fermented they can be eaten safely, as pathogens cannot survive the acid developed during fermentation.

This kind of fermentation also amplifies food's nutritional benefits. Microbes not only acidify the vegetables, but also break down carbohydrates that our bodies cannot digest, increase vitamins, and make the nutrients more bioavailable. They also create digestive enzymes, making food easier for us to digest. Many lactic acid ferments also include probiotics and parabiotics (inactivated probiotic bacteria that become prebiotics for our gut microbes). There is a growing body of research to suggest that these microbes, dead and alive, interact with our microbiota, and are good for our well-being.

Natural helper

Lactic acid can work wonders on soil, too, improving aeration and moisture retention, and neutralizing alkalinity. Indeed, one study found that sauerkraut juice could be used for soil remediation: the juice contains *Lactobacillus plantarum* and is reported to degrade glyphosate (a common pesticide). When tested on crops, this method was found to reduce soil glyphosate levels by 80–90 per cent within six or seven months.

LACTIC ACID BACTERIA

Lactic acid bacteria function in every aspect of life on Earth. They ferment and decompose. They can detoxify pesticides and provide antibiotics. They give us life and make space for what comes next.

Lactic acid bacteria (LAB) are gram-positive (meaning they have a thick cell wall to protect themselves), non-spore-forming microorganisms that require little or no oxygen to survive. They are so widespread that it is challenging to find a location where they are not present, engaging in dynamic interactions with their hosts. They inhabit plant surfaces and soils, and are present inside humans and animals, in oceans and glaciers, throughout numerous diverse ecosystems, and in our food.

There are two different groups of LAB: homofermentative and heterofermentative strains. Heterofermentative strains can ferment sugars to create carbon dioxide, ethanol, and acetic acid. They contribute to the flavour of foods like sauerkraut (see p74), kimchi (see p84), and other vegetable products.

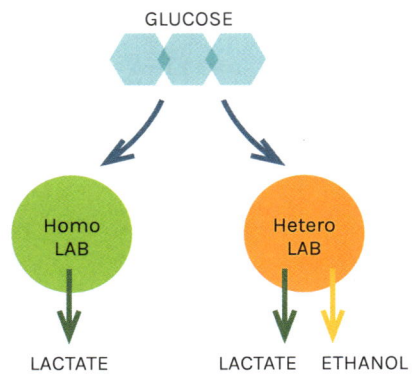

HOMOFERMENTATIVE VS HETEROFERMENTATIVE

Homofermentative and heterofermentative LAB produce different metabolites. The former produce only lactic acid, whereas the latter can produce lactic acid (lactate) and alcohol (ethanol).

Stages of fermentation

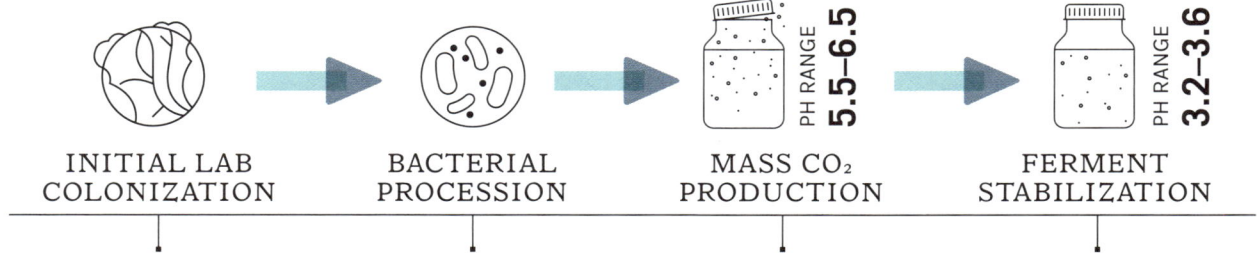

INITIAL LAB COLONIZATION

In vegetable fermentation, the heterofermentative strains start the process. In general, *Klebsiella* and *Enterobacter* are first to start metabolizing the sugars because they can handle the still-neutral conditions of fresh vegetables and brine.

BACTERIAL PROCESSION

They are followed by *Leuconostoc mesenteroides*, which thrives in a wide pH range. At this point there will be so much carbon dioxide produced that if you're making sauerkraut it will almost be bubbling out of the jar.

MASS CO$_2$ PRODUCTION — PH RANGE 5.5–6.5

If you are using a jar with a tightened lid, you will need to burp it constantly by this stage, and if you have a crock with a water seal, you'll hear a satisfying *bloop, bloop* sound as the carbon dioxide bubbles leave. *L. mesenteroides* thrives at this point, causing the pH level to drop lower than the bacteria's ideal range of 5.5–6.5.

FERMENT STABILIZATION — PH RANGE 3.2–3.6

Lactobacillus brevis* and *L. plantarum and possibly one of the *Pediococcus* genus will be active next – of these, only *L. brevis* is heterofermentative. The ferment slows down but is still becoming more acidic. The homofermentative *L. plantarum* is responsible for much of the fermentation but none of the bubbles.

Homofermentative strains consume glucose and only produce lactic acid; they like warmer temperatures and are used to produce meats, yogurt (see p90), kefir (see p94), cheese (see p98), brined olives, and miso (see p126).

LAB AND ALCOHOLIC FERMENTATION

In wine fermentation (see p162), there is a secondary stage where heterofermenter species *Oenococcus* and *Leuconostoc*, and homofermenters *Lactobacillus* and *Pediococcus*, feed off the sugars left after the initial yeast-based alcohol fermentation. Each of these plays a role in shaping the flavours, which can be both positive and negative. One of the most significant processes is malolactic fermentation, during which malic acid is converted into gentler lactic acid by *Oenococcus oeni*. This process shifts the pH, which is beneficial for grapes, which can be quite acidic.

LAB give many fermented foods their signature tang. Kimchi, sauerkraut, hot sauce, and yogurt all get their acidity from different species.

Beneficial microbes

LAB are essential to the human microbiome, living inside all of us, and are primarily located in the gut, the female genital tract, and our mouths. They have a beneficial role, producing lactic acid and other necessary metabolites (small molecules that influence digestion, immunity, and well-being). A balanced population offers numerous benefits. The lactic acid produced by these bacteria helps maintain a healthy, acidic environment that promotes digestion, inhibits pathogen growth, prevents inflammatory diseases, and modulates our immune system.

SUGARS

ANY AVAILABLE SUGARS IN PLANTS WILL BE FERMENTED INTO LACTIC ACID BY LACTIC ACID BACTERIA.

HOW TO LACTO-FERMENT ANYTHING

While it would be impossible to cover the nuances of lacto-fermenting every ingredient, these are some general principles that you can follow to get started with most fruits and vegetables.

By assessing the density and sugar levels of your ingredients, you can categorize them into distinct groups, each with their associated fermentation technique. Whichever ingredient you choose, the core lacto-fermentation principle remains the same: weigh the ingredients, add 2 per cent salt by weight, and exclude oxygen. This formula will work in almost all circumstances, though it won't necessarily get the best out of the ingredient used. The aim is to create an environment that benefits your desired microbes – in this case lactic acid bacteria (LAB) – and keeps out unwanted bacteria, yeasts, and pathogens.

Start out using these methods outlined in the guide, opposite, then, when you gain confidence, you can begin to tweak the fermentation time, salt percentage, and method, taking notes along the way. You will uncover further nuances the more you ferment. Finding a process that suits each ingredient and your specific set-up, rather than following a strict recipe, is what will make your ferment really sing.

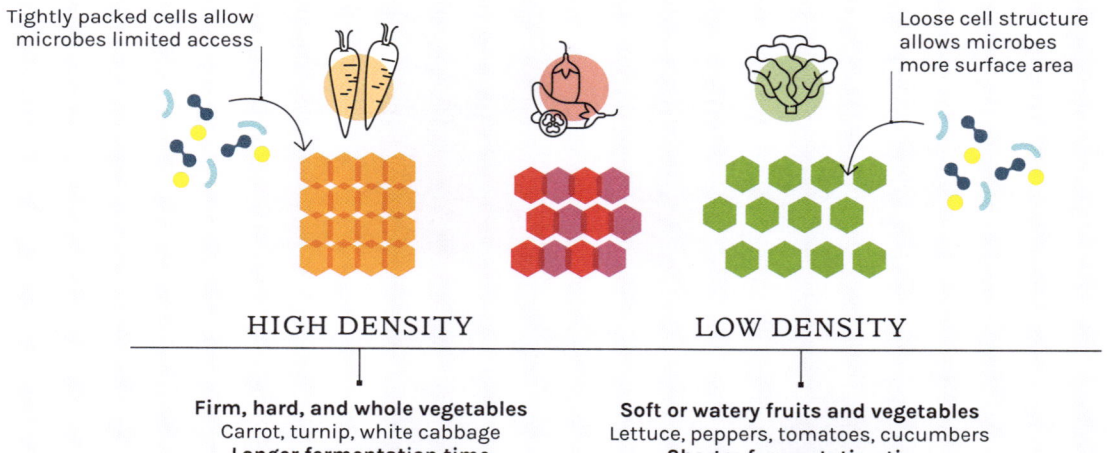

Tightly packed cells allow microbes limited access

Loose cell structure allows microbes more surface area

HIGH DENSITY
Firm, hard, and whole vegetables
Carrot, turnip, white cabbage
Longer fermentation time

LOW DENSITY
Soft or watery fruits and vegetables
Lettuce, peppers, tomatoes, cucumbers
Shorter fermentation time

GROUPING BY DENSITY

Fruits and vegetables vary in density – and the more tightly packed their cell structure is, the harder it is for the microbes to penetrate during fermentation. The tougher, drier, or denser the ingredient, the more difficult it is for the bacteria to access the sugars inside, slowing the fermentation. The reverse is also true; soft and watery ingredients are more accessible to the bacteria, hastening fermentation. Particularly tough vegetables won't give up any moisture for some time after salting, making the dry brining method less viable.

A guide to lacto-fermenting by ingredient

When fermenting multiple ingredients, tailor your method to the ingredient that makes up the largest proportion of the recipe.

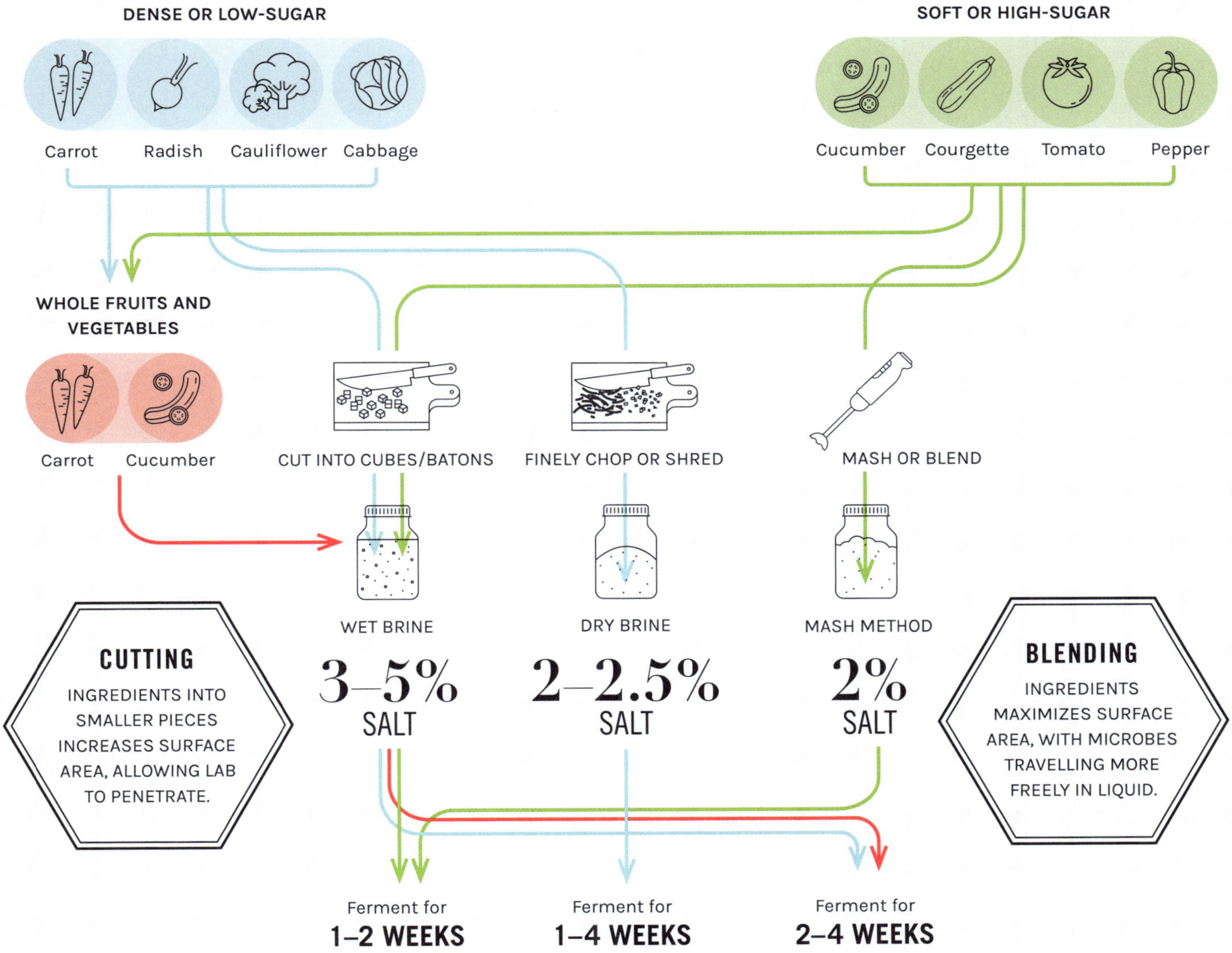

DENSE OR LOW-SUGAR
- Carrot
- Radish
- Cauliflower
- Cabbage

SOFT OR HIGH-SUGAR
- Cucumber
- Courgette
- Tomato
- Pepper

WHOLE FRUITS AND VEGETABLES
- Carrot
- Cucumber

CUT INTO CUBES/BATONS → WET BRINE — **3–5% SALT** — Ferment for **1–2 WEEKS**

FINELY CHOP OR SHRED → DRY BRINE — **2–2.5% SALT** — Ferment for **1–4 WEEKS**

MASH OR BLEND → MASH METHOD — **2% SALT** — Ferment for **2–4 WEEKS**

CUTTING INGREDIENTS INTO SMALLER PIECES INCREASES SURFACE AREA, ALLOWING LAB TO PENETRATE.

BLENDING INGREDIENTS MAXIMIZES SURFACE AREA, WITH MICROBES TRAVELLING MORE FREELY IN LIQUID.

GROUPING BY SUGAR LEVEL

The amount of sugar available will significantly change the microbial community that establishes itself in the ferment. Higher sugar content provides far more easily available material for the microbes to consume, accelerating the process. Higher sugar will also encourage yeast growth, making alcohol production and off flavours a consideration.

Low-sugar vegetables
White cabbage, beans, asparagus
Longer fermentation time

High-sugar fruits and vegetables
Beets, carrots, peppers, apples, pears, berries
Shorter fermentation time

SAUERKRAUT

This is often the first ferment that beginners will try, and a favourite of many seasoned fermenters. With just salt and time, a simple, ancient technique turns cabbage into a tangy, crunchy, versatile delight.

Sauerkraut (from the German for sour cabbage) is often associated with German and Eastern European cuisines, where it has hundreds of years of culinary history. However, its origins are likely earlier, with records of fermented cabbage in China stretching back thousands of years.

Made via lacto-fermentation, there are many strains of lactic acid bacteria (LAB) involved in the process. The early colonizers (*Leuconostoc mesenteroides*) create lactic acid, acetic acid, and alcohol, along with other by-products such as carbon dioxide, as they eat up sugars present in the raw cabbage leaves. The later-stage LAB almost exclusively produce lactic acid. Beyond acidifying the cabbage during their metabolism, these microbes create unique flavour compounds, transforming fresh cabbage into a complex, savoury treat.

CHOOSING INGREDIENTS

Experiment by adding herbs, fruits, spices, and other vegetables to the method opposite for different flavour profiles – curry powder, chillies, cauliflower, cranberries, cumin, cardamom, or Sichuan peppercorns all work well.

As long as most of the mix is made up of firm cabbage (red or white), fermentation will progress as per the method opposite. Less dense cabbages like sweetheart or Savoy will ferment more quickly, in two weeks or so, to create a less complex (but equally delicious) younger kraut.

Stages of fermentation

● **EARLY STAGE**
(0–3 DAYS/PH 5.5)
L. mesenteroides

L. mesenteroides quickly produces an abundance of lactic acid, lowering the pH and creating a pathogen-free environment. CO_2 forms as tiny bubbles, raising the pressure in the jar if sealed.

Flavour Bright, slightly acidic, with most of the sweetness of the fresh cabbage still present.

PECTINASE
ENZYMES BREAK DOWN PECTIN IN PLANT CELLS DURING FERMENTATION.

CRUNCHY
KRAUT COMES FROM COOLER TEMPERATURES (15–18°C) WHEN PECTINASE IS LESS EFFICIENT.

0–3 DAYS

DIRECTORY OF FERMENTS • Lactic acid bacteria 75

MAKE YOUR OWN

This method will make basic, tasty, consistent, white cabbage sauerkraut.

EQUIPMENT large bowl • 500ml jar • plate
INGREDIENTS 400g white cabbage • 8g salt

 LAB L. mesenteroides, L. brevis, P. pentosaceus, L. plantarum | **2–4 WEEKS**

1. **Choose a fresh, firm head of cabbage** for best results, with no soft spots or mould. Wash, remove the outer leaves, and then shred 400g.

2. **Add the salt and shredded cabbage** to a bowl and massage thoroughly for around 10 minutes until plenty of brine has accumulated as the crushed cabbage leaves release water.

3. **Pack the cabbage and brine** into a clean jar, pressing it to submerge it in its own brine.

4. **Seal the jar and store** at room temperature, away from direct sunlight, and place on a plate to catch any brine that leaks out as the CO_2 builds up.

5. **Burp the jar every few days** by opening the lid briefly to release any gas build-up.

6. **After 14–30 days, start tasting.** Once the sauerkraut has reached your desired level of acidity, transfer to the fridge to slow the fermentation. It will keep well for 6–12 months.

Troubleshooting

- If kahm yeast (see p62) or white surface moulds develop, scrape off, then spray the surface with vinegar or "magic spray" (see p59).

- If the moulds are green, pink, black, or penetrate beyond the surface, or the kraut smells rotten, discard.

- If white "veins" form at the bottom, or the top layer turns grey in the fridge, don't worry, the kraut is fine.

- Slimy kraut can happen due to an early overgrowth of L. mesenteroides. Subsequent bacteria populations will usually wrestle back control, so try waiting it out, but if it's still slimy after a week, discard and start again.

● **MID-STAGE (3–14 DAYS/4.5 PH)**
Lactobacillus brevis and *Pediococcus*

As the acidity increases, *L. mesenteroides* die back and *L. brevis* and *Pediococcus* dominate, producing lactic acid and developing flavour. A slight fizz from the CO_2 build-up will be visible.

Flavour More acidic, with a slight sulfur aroma from the production of dimethyl sulfide and hydrogen sulfide.

● **LATE STAGE (14–30+ DAYS/3.4 PH)**
Lactobacillus plantarum

As the sauerkraut ages, the *L. plantarum* population steadily rises. These homofermentative bacteria exclusively produce lactic acid. After 30 days the ferment will have a pH of 3.2–3.6 and a lactic acid content of around 2.5 per cent. The sauerkraut will have darkened in colour.

Flavour Tangy, sour, with complex fruity flavours from esters, and umami from glutamic acid.

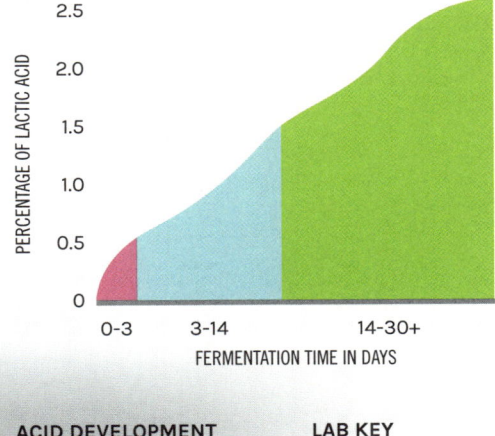

ACID DEVELOPMENT
At 18°C (32°F) lactic acid rises until it reaches 2.5 per cent.

LAB KEY
● Early stage
● Mid-stage
● Late stage

3–30+ DAYS

DILL PICKLES

As long as we have been growing cucumbers, we have been fermenting cucumbers. The practice of sea-water brining was recorded in Mesopotamia nearly 4,000 years ago, but it is likely that any cultures with cucumbers and salt have done the same.

Many of us have only been made familiar with dill pickles through thin slices on burgers or perhaps cornichon jars in the grocery store. Most likely these are preserved by hot vinegar pickling, rather than lacto-fermentation. This technique certainly has its place, but the process renders the pickles microbially inert and loses out on the complex flavours real fermentation can create.

True dill pickles, like those found in a traditional New York deli, are brine ferments. This means they are submerged in salty water, which creates an anaerobic environment that promotes the growth of lactic acid bacteria (LAB). These are ambient bacteria so they are found everywhere – in the air, and on our hands, the vegetable, and the jar – but the bulk of the microbial load comes from the vegetable itself. As the LAB metabolize the sugars in the cucumbers, they release carbon dioxide and increase the acidity of the ferment with lactic acid, creating a safe and delicious environment.

Adding tannins for crunch

Tannins are molecules found in ingredients like fig, oak, vine, or tea leaves. You can add these ingredients to your pickles to keep the cucumbers crunchy. Tannin molecules bind to proteins in the cucumber cell walls, forming a strengthened matrix, and slow down pectinase enzymes which would otherwise break down the cucumber cell walls.

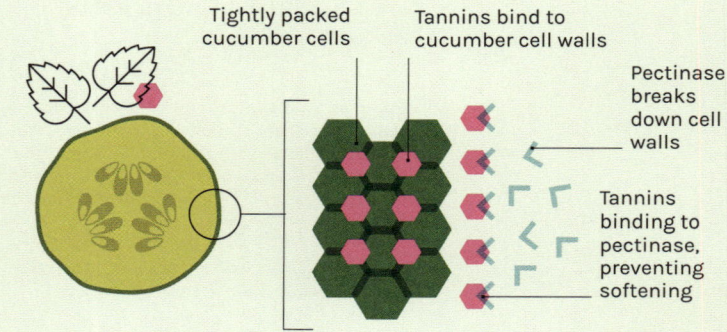

RAW PICKLING CUCUMBER

Flesh is crisp due to intact, water-filled cells

Stages of fermentation

Over the course of 5–10 days, the LAB proliferate, eating up sugars and releasing CO_2 and lactic acid. The pickles become salty and sour, and take on the flavours of the pickling spices.

DIRECTORY OF FERMENTS • Lactic acid bacteria 77

OSMOSIS
DRAWS WATER MOLECULES FROM THE CUCUMBER CELLS INTO THE SURROUNDING SALTY BRINE.

FLAVOURS
CONCENTRATE IN THE PICKLE AS SALT OR ACID CREATES A GRADIENT, PULLING WATER INTO THE BRINE.

Salt molecules in brine

Salt molecules osmose into the cucumber's flesh

Water concentration in the vegetable and brine gradually equalizes

OSMOSIS IN BRINE

DILL PICKLE

Flesh softens as microbes and osmosis break down cell structure

Fermentation dulls the skin as chlorophyll degrades and acids leach into the tissues

MAKE YOUR OWN

This recipe is for wet-brined whole dill pickles, using 5% salt. For half-sours, use 3.5% salt and shorten the fermentation time.

EQUIPMENT bowl • 1-litre jar
INGREDIENTS 400g cucumbers • 40g salt
• 10g fresh dill

 LAB *L. mesenteroides, L. brevis, L. plantarum, P. pentosaceus*   **5–10 DAYS**

1. **Wash the cucumbers** and dill well. In a bowl, mix the salt with 400ml of water until dissolved to make your brine.

2. **Pack the whole cucumbers** and roughly torn dill into the sanitized jar (see p59), then pour in the brine, making sure the ingredients are completely submerged.

3. **Seal the jar** and store at room temperature, away from direct sunlight. Fermentation will take 5–10 days depending on temperature. Check daily and open the jar to release any gas build-up.

4. **Once the pickles are tasty**, transfer the jar to the refrigerator to slow down the fermentation. Pickles can be stored in the fridge for several months.

Troubleshooting

• As cucumbers have a high water content they are more susceptible to surface moulds than most firm vegetables like cabbage, so it is important to keep pickles submerged below the brine.

• You may encounter soft pickles, but don't panic – this happens to everyone. They are still edible and great for chopping up to add to different condiments, such as mayonnaise.

• To ensure your pickles stay crunchy, you can add tannin-rich ingredients to your brine, such as fig, vine, or oak leaves, or a tea bag (see box, opposite). You can also try removing the nub at the blossom end of each cucumber; there is a higher concentration of pectinase (see p74) at the flowering end of the fruit.

UMEBOSHI

Salted Japanese plums can be fermented in many different styles. Some include shiso leaves (*Perilla frutescens*), some are sun-cured, some are aged for years; some are dry ferments, some are brined – all are delicious.

This traditional Japanese pickle is made by packing small, sour, unripe ume plums (*Prunus mume*), which are closely related to apricots, in salt. The primary microbial actor in umeboshi is *Lactobacillus*, which increases the acidity and provides their characteristic mouth-puckeringly sour flavour.

As well as their intense sourness, umeboshi are deeply salty, fruity, and sometimes bitter or slightly sweet. They are delicious eaten in simple *onigiri* (rice balls wrapped in nori seaweed sheets), which allows the character of umeboshi to sing. The umeboshi liquid should also be preserved, as it is fantastic used as a seasoning for plain rice and in salad dressings.

EARLY RECORDS FROM THE HEIAN PERIOD (794–1185 CE) OUTLINE CEREMONIAL AND MEDICINAL USES OF UMEBOSHI.

SALT VARIABLES

There is huge variability in the amount of salt used to make umeboshi. Some recipes use as little as 8 per cent salt, while others go up to 20 per cent. Fruit contains more sugar and acid than vegetables, so a higher salt percentage is used to inhibit the microbes that cause spoilage. Higher salt percentages are robust but inhibit *Lactobacillus*, lengthening fermentation time. This additional ageing can lead to more complex, nuanced flavours. At lower salt percentages *Lactobacillus* can proliferate more quickly, speeding up fermentation and resulting in a sourer flavour. But lower salt also allows moulds to grow more easily, making low-salt ferments more challenging.

Stages of fermentation

With the ume packed in salt, water is drawn out of them via osmosis. They ferment in their own brine with the help of *Lactobacillus*.

RED SHISO LEAF   **UNRIPE UME PLUM**

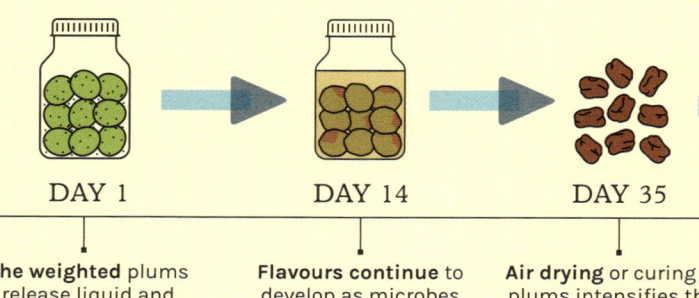

DAY 1 — The weighted plums release liquid and *Lactobacillus* starts fermentation.

DAY 14 — Flavours continue to develop as microbes break down sugars and create lactic acid.

DAY 35 — Air drying or curing the plums intensifies their flavour. Fermentation is now complete.

DIRECTORY OF FERMENTS • Lactic acid bacteria 79

How salt content controls microbial action

Lower salt in umeboshi allows the LAB to be more microbially active. Higher salt restricts this activity, rendering the umeboshi closer to salt preservation.

8% SALT

Low-salt umeboshi
Fruity, sharp, and lively, with brighter acidity and a less overpowering salt presence.

20% SALT

High-salt umeboshi
Rich, deep, and savoury, with a lingering, briny intensity.

UME
STONES CONTAIN AMYGDALIN, WHICH CAN RELEASE CYANIDE. FERMENTATION HELPS REDUCE ITS PRESENCE.

ANTI-MICROBIAL
RED SHISO LEAVES BRING VIBRANT COLOUR AND HERBAL DEPTH TO UMEBOSHI.

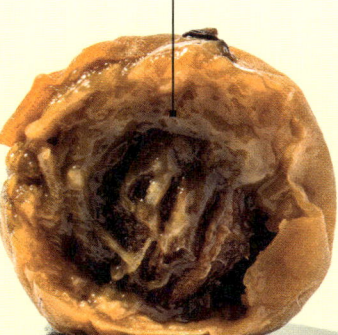

FERMENTED UMEBOSHI

MAKE YOUR OWN

This recipe forgoes the multi-step process used in traditional umeboshi, making it far more accessible as a home project. To scale the amount up or down, weigh your ume and shiso, then add 10% salt.

EQUIPMENT resealable plastic bag • tray • plates • jar
INGREDIENTS 1kg unripe ume plums • 5 red shiso leaves (optional) • 100g sea salt

 LAB *T. halophilus, L. plantarum, L. brevis* | **5–6 WEEKS**

1. **Gently wash** the ume and shiso leaves (if using), taking care to remove any stems.
2. **Place the plums and leaves** plus the salt in a thick resealable bag, then seal it, excluding as much air as possible. Massage everything together.
3. **Place the bag on a tray** and weigh it down with a few plates (about double the weight of the ingredients).
4. **Massage the bag** every day for the first couple of weeks until the contents are saturated with liquid.
5. **Leave to ferment** for a further 3 weeks, then drain the liquid and reserve it for use in seasonings or salad dressings.
6. **Separate the ume** onto a tray and leave in a dry place with good ventilation for 3 days, turning each day.
7. **Store** in a jar in the fridge, or leave at room temperature to further develop their flavour.

Troubleshooting

• The most likely problem you'll face is getting hold of the ume in the first place. Thankfully, there are many non-traditional but viable and delicious alternatives such as apricots and young damson plums.

• It's important to avoid bruising the fruit, as this can encourage mould growth, so take care when handling.

• You can use a glass jar instead of a plastic bag as a fermentation vessel – just be careful to weigh down the fruit properly.

HOT SAUCE

Fermentation preserves fresh chilli peppers and develops their flavour complexity. A whole new world of possibilities opens up when you make your own.

Bird's eye/Thai chilli
50,000–100,000 Scoville heat units

Habanero and Scotch bonnet
100,000–350,000 Scoville heat units

Sivri
10,000–25,000 Scoville heat units

Jalapeño
2,500–8,000 Scoville heat units

CAPSAICIN DOES NOT DEGRADE DURING FERMENTATION, BUT OTHER COMPOUNDS EMERGE TO BRING COMPLEXITY.

Chillies have been eaten for thousands of years in South America, but they made their way into world cuisines following the Columbian exchange in the fifteenth century. The precursor to modern-day hot sauces didn't come until much later, in the nineteenth century, when tabasco chilli peppers were turned into a sauce in Louisiana.

There are now many styles of hot sauce and almost as many techniques to make them as there are makers. The ingredients that are available and popular in the region where the sauce is being produced will define the final product, with fruity Scotch bonnet in the Caribbean, sharp jalapeño and smoky chipotle in Mexico, thin, vinegared buffalo in the Southern US, and sweetened, garlicky condiments in South East Asia making up a few of the broader categories.

Anaerobic system

Carbonic maceration is a winemaking technique that can also be applied to hot sauce fermentation. The ferment is transferred to a sealed keg and oxygen purged from the environment by forcing in CO_2 to create an anaerobic (oxygen-free) system, almost completely removing the risk of contamination by microbes other than LAB.

WHOLE CHILLIES

Whole chillies and salt are added to the keg and sealed inside.

WHY FERMENT HOT SAUCE?

Some hot sauces are produced without fermentation, using vinegar, salt, and cooking for preservation, while others use these preservation techniques after fermentation to make the final product more shelf-stable. Processing after fermentation (particularly using heat) can denature or evaporate flavour compounds and aromatics. A simple cooked vinegar hot sauce can be delicious, but it will always lack the extra depth of flavour that fermentation produces.

FLAVOUR FACTORS

The flavour pillars of a fermented hot sauce are the pungent heat and sweetness from the fresh chillies, salt, and acidity from lactic acid. During fermentation, lactic acid bacteria (LAB) break down the sugars present in chilli peppers, producing umami compounds along with acid, which combine with the hot, pungent capsaicin and other fruity, grassy, and earthy aroma compounds in the chillies. The balance of these flavours in your sauce will vary depending on the chilli you choose (any variety will work), additional flavouring ingredients, time, temperature, salt ratio, and moisture content.

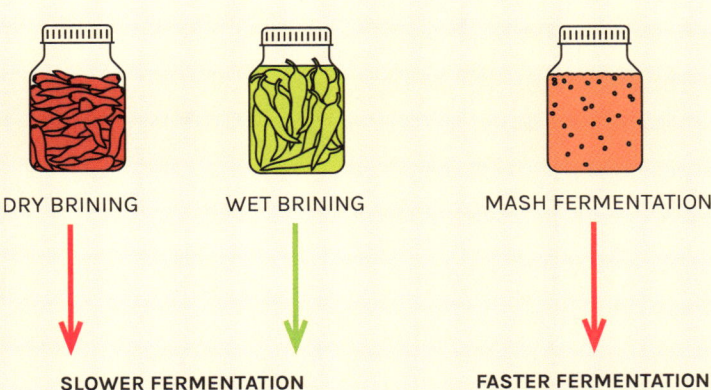

DRY BRINING | **WET BRINING** | **MASH FERMENTATION**

SLOWER FERMENTATION
Dry or wet brined methods are slower, as the microbes have to get through the exterior surface of the chilli to get to the cells, resulting in bruising and breaking.

FASTER FERMENTATION
The fastest method, due to the increased surface area of the chillies, resulting in minimal restriction to the movement of the microbes and enzymes.

FLAVOURS CONTINUE TO DEVELOP AND ACIDITY INCREASES AFTER BOTTLING.

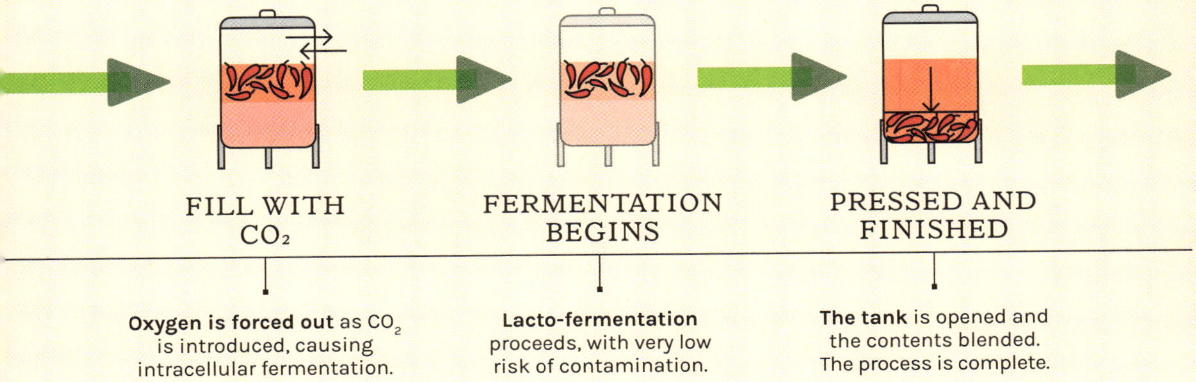

FILL WITH CO_2
Oxygen is forced out as CO_2 is introduced, causing intracellular fermentation.

FERMENTATION BEGINS
Lacto-fermentation proceeds, with very low risk of contamination.

PRESSED AND FINISHED
The tank is opened and the contents blended. The process is complete.

MAKE YOUR OWN
MASH-FERMENTED HOT SAUCE

This method makes mash-fermented chillies that are processed into a hot sauce.

EQUIPMENT
- food processor
- 500ml lidded jar
- funnel
- bottles

INGREDIENTS
- 500g chillies
- 10g salt

LAB *L. plantarum*, *L. brevis*, *L. mesenteroides*, *P. pentosaceus*

7–14 DAYS

② **Transfer the chilli mash** to a clean jar, then add the salt and mix into the mash until it has dissolved.

① **Select your chillies**, avoiding any with soft sections or mould. Any kind of chilli can be used, depending on your taste. Finely chop them or pass them through a food processor to form a mash (you may wish to wear gloves to protect your hands from the capsaicin). Remove the seeds and pith if you prefer; retaining them can add extra heat, but also a little bitterness in some cases.

③ **Seal the jar** and store at room temperature, away from direct sunlight. Fermentation will take 7–14 days, depending on temperature – the ideal temperature is 18–20°C (64–68°F).

④ **Check daily** – you should quickly start to see bubbles forming in the jar. Release any gas build-up by opening the lid briefly, and shake the jar every few days to mix.

⑤ **Taste occasionally**, and once the mash has reached the desired level of acidity, pass through a food processor or blender. Bottle and store in the fridge for up to 6 months.

HOT SAUCE VARIABLES

SALT
Vary the salt percentage to make your sauce more or less salty. This will also impact how quickly fermentation progresses (more salt makes it slower; less makes it faster).

LIQUID
Alter the ratio of liquid to chilli (the brine is usually around 2 per cent salt) to dilute or thicken your final sauce.

FLAVOURINGS
Add complex flavours with fruit, vegetables, herbs, and spices. Tropical fruits like pineapple and mango work well, as do sweet root vegetables like beetroot, umami miso paste, and fresh garlic.

TIME
Fermented chilli mash will be ready to use right away but can be aged almost indefinitely, with the flavour changing and developing throughout the process. This is unusual compared to other lacto-ferments, which tend to reach a flavour peak and then start to soften and become less tasty. The longer you ferment chillies, the more acidic they will get, and the more time the microbes have to produce different flavour compounds, adding complexity.

Troubleshooting

• Kahm yeast (see p62) is a perennial problem for most high-water-content ferments, forming a silvery film on the surface during fermentation. It is benign and can be safely scraped off. It can, however, lead to softening, discolouration, and loss of flavour. Use "magic spray" (see p59) to prevent its return.

• Slow or no fermentation can occur if conditions are very cold. Anything below room temperature will slow things down, particularly below 10°C (50°F). Microbial action doesn't fully "stop" until you hit freezer temperatures, but it is effectively arrested below 5°C (41°F). Higher than 25°C (77°F) and it will start to ferment very quickly and produce a lot of gas.

• Unknown surface moulds are a bad sign and best practice is to discard the project and start again.

• Without pasteurization or chemical stabilization the sauce is still very much alive after bottling and still produces carbon dioxide. This can cause sauce bottles to pop like champagne when opened. Avoid this by keeping bottled sauce in the fridge; the cold temperature (below 5°C/41°F) drastically slows fermentation, reducing CO_2 build-up.

KIMCHI

Kimchi dates back over 2,000 years, and is rooted in the need to preserve vegetables during Korea's long, harsh winters. It is now celebrated worldwide for its robust flavours, health benefits, and culinary versatility. A key part of Korean cuisine, making kimchi is a ritual central to Korean communities.

The word "kimchi" comes from a contraction of the words *dimchae* or *chimchae*; *dim* or *chim* means "to dunk" and *chae* is the abbreviated word for *chaeso*, meaning "vegetables". In its primary format, kimchi was made from vegetables (usually napa cabbage or radish) dunked in salt brine, the same method used in Eastern European lacto-fermentation (p74).

CULTURAL IMPORTANCE

Kimchi is far more than just a dish in Korea; it's a symbol of resilience, community, and tradition. The annual *kimjang* season, a UNESCO-recognized cultural heritage practice, is a time when families and neighbours come together to prepare large batches of kimchi for the winter (see p15). This collective effort

ANTIFUNGAL AND ANTIBACTERIAL GARLIC, GINGER, ONION, AND CHILLIES DEVELOP RESILIENT MICROBES IN KIMCHI.

GOCHUGARU CHILLI FLAKES BRING MILD HEAT, SWEETNESS, AND COMPLEX SMOKY FLAVOURS.

SPRING ONION · DAIKON RADISH · CARROT · GINGER · NAPA CABBAGE · NASHI PEAR · GARLIC · FISH SAUCE · GOCHUGARU

BAEK KIMCHI **BAECHU KIMCHI**

The traditional clay pots used for storing and fermenting food in Korea are called *onggi*. The porous clay allows air to circulate, which helps the fermentation process.

Kimchi transparency

As the *Lactobacillius* breaks down the structure of the cabbage during fermentation, its dense fibre network becomes looser, allowing light to pass through it unhindered. As a result, the cabbage becomes translucent.

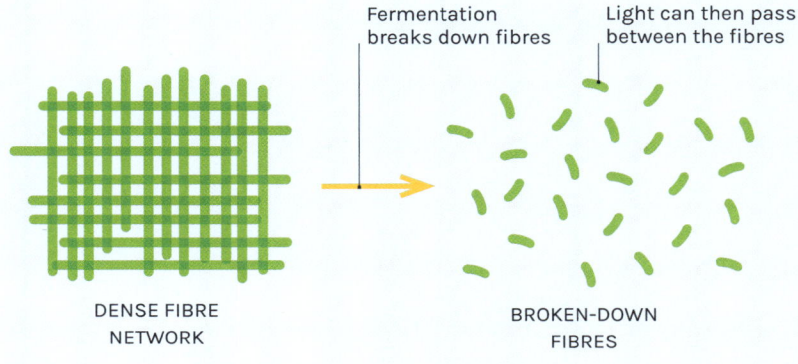

fosters community bonds and reflects Korea's agrarian roots.

Kimchi also plays a symbolic role in Korean activism. Historically, eating was part of what differentiated Koreans from spies during wartime. It was also an act of resistance towards the Japanese occupation. A garden full of porous, breathable clay pots called *onggi* that housed all of the Korean ferments would be treasured by each household and often handed down for generations.

HEALTH BENEFITS

Lactic acid bacteria (LAB) in kimchi contribute to gut health by introducing probiotics, with the peak of probiotic benefit at around day 10. Recent studies suggest that kimchi's LAB may even have anti-inflammatory and antimicrobial properties. Anticandida properties have also been found in kimchi, making it a preventative against yeast infections.

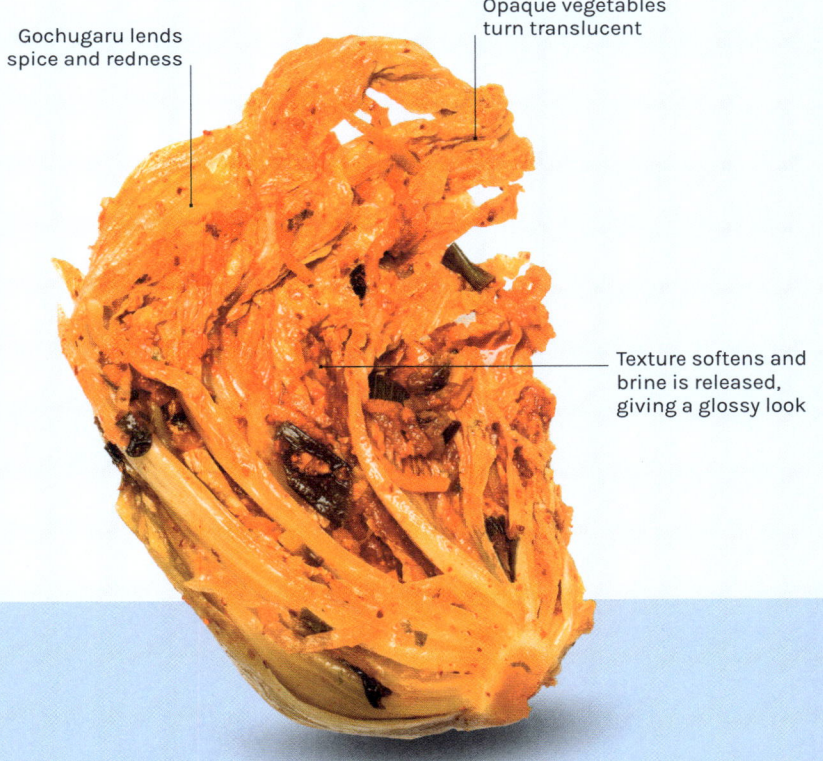

NAPA CABBAGE KIMCHI

KIMCHI IN FOCUS

Kimchi is an umbrella term encompassing over 200 varieties, each with its unique regional and seasonal twist. Each type reflects the diversity of Korea's landscape, climate, and culinary traditions, showcasing the adaptability and creativity of Korean food culture.

Kimchi was developed over centuries by Korean women experimenting with different combinations and discovering that garlic, ginger, and onion make a great base for fermentation. They understood the nature of the ingredients so well that they knew which spices would allow them to reduce the quantity of salt when it became expensive. Their creativity further blossomed when they started adding fruits for sweetness, chillies for the iconic kick, and fish sauce to bring umami.

Today, kimchi remains a quintessential part of any Korean meal, often referred to as one of the *banchan* (side dishes) that accompany rice. Its centrality to Korean identity is evident in the phrase "kimchi culture", which denotes Korea's unique culinary heritage.

In the traditional Korean fermentation process of making kimchi, vegetables are salted, seasoned with spices, and left to develop complex flavours over time. Extra ingredients like green onions and radishes can be included to boost texture and taste. And that process can result in a vast array of dishes. While napa cabbage and radish are the most common bases, kimchi can also incorporate ingredients like mustard greens, perilla leaves, or seafood. Each type has its own particular flavour profile, ranging from spicy and tangy to mild and refreshing.

27.6 GRAMS
OF KIMCHI ARE CONSUMED PER DAY, ON AVERAGE, IN KOREA.

Elements of flavour

AS KIMCHI FERMENTS, THE INGREDIENTS DEVELOP A BOLD BALANCE OF FLAVOURS AND TEXTURES.

SPICE/CAPSAICIN
FROM KOREAN RED PEPPER FLAKES (GOCHUGARU).

SOUR/TANGY
FROM LACTIC ACID PRODUCED DURING FERMENTATION.

UMAMI/SAVOURY
DERIVED FROM INGREDIENTS LIKE SALTED SHRIMP OR FERMENTED FISH SAUCE.

ALLIUM/SULFUROUS
FROM GARLIC, ONIONS, AND GINGER.

CRUNCHY AND JUICY
FROM NAPA CABBAGE AND RADISHES.

Kimchi fridges

Specialist kimchi fridges are a household staple in Korea. These storage units separate the smell from other foods, and the temperature and humidity are perfectly set for maturing kimchi. Many have compartments for different types of kimchi, and adjustable fermentation modes.

MATURE
KIMCHI (1–3+ MONTHS IN THE FRIDGE) IS EXCELLENT FOR COOKING IN SOUPS, FRIED RICE, OR STEWS.

BAECHU KIMCHI
(NAPA CABBAGE KIMCHI)
The most iconic version, made with napa cabbage, gochugaru, garlic, ginger, and fish sauce.

BAEK KIMCHI
(WHITE KIMCHI)
A non-spicy version made without chilli flakes, popular for its light, refreshing taste.

CHONGGAK KIMCHI
(PONYTAIL RADISH KIMCHI)
Uses whole young radishes with greens attached, offering a spicier, sharper flavour.

YEOLMU KIMCHI
(YOUNG RADISH KIMCHI)
A summer kimchi made from tender radish greens and light seasoning.

KKAKDUGI
(CUBED RADISH KIMCHI)
Made with diced daikon radish, this type is crunchy and slightly sweet.

OI SOBAGI
(CUCUMBER KIMCHI)
A stuffed-cucumber version, typically made during the summer, known for its refreshing crispness.

> **GAM-CHIL-MAT** IS THE KOREAN WORD FOR SAVOURY UMAMI FLAVOUR.

MAKE YOUR OWN
CAULIFLOWER LEAF KIMCHI

This recipe is a creative, zero-waste twist on kimchi. Incorporating a family paste recipe from Gwangju, known for its bold Jeolla-style flavours, this kimchi is packed with heat, umami, and a satisfying crunch that sets it apart from traditional napa cabbage varieties.

EQUIPMENT
- bowls
- food processor
- large lidded storage jar

INGREDIENTS (makes approx. 1kg)
- 500g cauliflower leaves (roughly trimmed and washed)
- 15g fine sea salt (3% cauliflower leaf weight)
- 50g spring onions, cut into 3-4cm pieces
- 50g carrots, julienned
- 100g daikon radish (mooli), julienned

FOR THE KIMCHI PASTE
- 5 cloves garlic • 3cm fresh root ginger
- 1 small onion • ½ apple or pear (around 100g)
- 1 tbsp rice flour • 3-6 tbsp gochugaru (Korean red pepper flakes), to taste • 2 tbsp fish sauce or soy sauce
- 1 tsp sugar (optional)

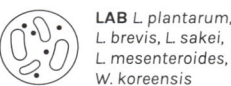

LAB *L. plantarum, L. brevis, L. sakei, L. mesenteroides, W. koreensis*

3–6 DAYS

2 **Meanwhile, prepare the paste ingredients.** Mince the garlic and ginger, and set aside. Next, blend the onion and apple (or pear) in a food processor. Finally, make a rice porridge by combining the rice flour with 5 tablespoons of water, and cooking over a low heat until thickened. Leave to cool, then combine all the paste ingredients in a bowl and mix thoroughly until an even purée forms.

1 **Cut the cauliflower leaves** into bite-sized pieces. Place in a bowl, sprinkle with the sea salt, then massage gently, and leave for 2-4 hours to draw out moisture. Flip occasionally.

3 **Add the paste mixture** to the drained cauliflower leaves, spring onions, carrots, and radish. Then, with clean hands (or gloves), massage together so the vegetables are coated evenly.

DIRECTORY OF FERMENTS • Lactic acid bacteria 89

Troubleshooting

- If your kitchen is cool, fermentation may take longer (a week), while warmer temperatures will speed it up (three days). If your vegetable pieces are smaller, it will take less time to salt as well as to ferment.

- To prevent kahm yeast (see p62) from settling on the surface, store in an airtight container and put a weight on top of the kimchi to submerge it under the brine.

- If your kimchi goes soft, blend or mash it into a hot sauce.

④ **Transfer the kimchi** to a sterilized glass jar, pressing down firmly to minimize air pockets. Leave about 2–3cm of space at the top to allow for expansion during fermentation.

⑤ **Loosely seal the jar** and leave it at room temperature (18–22°C/64–72°F) for 3–6 days. Burp the jar daily by opening the lid to release gases and press the kimchi down to submerge it in its own brine.

⑥ **Taste the kimchi regularly**, and after 2–5 days, when it has reached the desired tang, transfer to the fridge to slow the fermentation. Store for 1–3 months, ideally at 1–2°C (34–36°F) with minimum air exposure in a kimchi fridge. Storing at 4–6°C (39–43°F) in a regular fridge will also work, although the kimchi will sour more quickly.

YOGURT

A product of milk fermentation, yogurt has transcended cultural boundaries and formed an integral part of diets around the world for millennia. Its origins can be traced back to central and western Asia, where natural fermentation processes led to the discovery of its unique properties.

Microbes

Thermophilic LAB are responsible for turning milk into yogurt. Common strains used are *L. bulgaricus*, *S. thermophilus*, *L. acidophilus*, *L. plantarum*, and *L. rhamnosus*.

Milk, the primary ingredient of yogurt, is composed of water, fat, protein, carbohydrates (mainly lactose), vitamins, and minerals. Roughly 80 per cent of milk's protein content is casein, while the remaining 20 per cent is whey. This composition not only provides the nutritional benefits associated with yogurt, but also plays a critical role in its texture.

The thick creaminess of yogurt develops through fermentation. The milk is heated and then specific strains of lactic acid bacteria (LAB), such as *Lactobacillus bulgaricus* and *Streptococcus thermophilus*, are added. These bacteria eat up the lactose in milk, producing lactic acid as a byproduct.

MILK

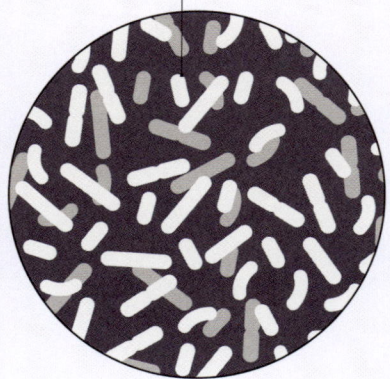

Thermophilic spherical cocci form in pairs or short chains

Rod-shaped bacilli grow well in low pH

STREPTOCOCCUS THERMOPHILUS

Gives yogurt its smooth texture and creamy taste. It also prepares the environment for *L. bulgaricus* to do its work.

LACTOBACILLUS BULGARICUS

One of the two main cultures used to make yogurt, *L. bulgaricus* ferments lactose into lactic acid, thickening the milk.

The accumulation of lactic acid lowers the pH, resulting in the milk's acidification. This causes the casein proteins to coagulate, forming the gel-like matrix that gives set yogurt its thick texture. It holds this structure until stirring breaks it up, making it runny.

LAB AND TEMPERATURE

Thermophilic (heat-loving) LAB are responsible for converting warm milk to yogurt. Certain strains do a better job than others, which is why the starter and its source are important. When making yogurt, milk is first heated to 82°C (180°F) which unfolds the proteins, helps kill any unwanted bacteria, and evaporates some of the water. The milk is inoculated with starter culture; most yogurt bacteria inoculate best at warm temperatures of 40–45°C (104–113°F). The yogurt is then incubated at 38–45°C (100–113°F). As the LAB grow and produce acid, the milk proteins coagulate, helping the yogurt to set.

> **CASEIN PROTEINS** IN SET YOGURT FORM A GEL MATRIX, CREATING A THICK, SCOOPABLE TEXTURE.

YOGURT

Varieties of yogurt

Dahi/curd A traditional Indian fermented milk product with a slightly tangy taste.

Mishti doi A sweet, caramel-like Indian yogurt made by fermenting evaporated milk and palm jaggery or sugar.

Yoğurt Turkey is one of the oldest yogurt-producing cultures. Plain, unsweetened versions are eaten daily with meals.

Greek-style yogurt is made by straining regular yogurt to remove whey, resulting in a thicker texture.

Matzoon and matsoni Matzoon from Armenia and matsoni from Georgia are both fermented dairy products similar to yogurt, with a smooth texture that is softer than Greek yogurt.

Kiselo mlyako The name for this Bulgarian fermented dairy product means "sour milk". It is made using *L. bulgaricus*, which was first isolated in the area but is now used around the world.

Labneh Somewhere between a yogurt and a cheese, this is made by removing the whey from plain yogurt and is a staple in Lebanon, Syria, and Israel.

Raib A popular Moroccan yogurt drink made by fermenting milk with sugar and often flavoured with orange blossom water.

Nunu A spontaneously fermenting cow's-milk yogurt drink enjoyed in West Africa.

Amasi A thick, curdled cow's milk popular in South Africa. It looks similar to cottage cheese, although it has a stronger flavour.

Skyr A strained, high-protein, rennet-based yogurt-cheese from Iceland.

Filmjölk A buttery, drinkable yogurt from Sweden, often paired with muesli or fruit.

Viili A thick, smooth, stringy yogurt from Finland. The texture is caused by exopolysaccharides.

MAKE YOUR OWN
YOGURT

Making yogurt is straightforward and can give you a healthier, richer product than store-bought versions. The more fat in the milk, the thicker the yogurt will be, and you can always add a little cream to make it thicker. The texture will also be affected by the time and temperature.

EQUIPMENT
- saucepan
- incubator (see p55)
- thermometer (optional)
- whisk
- sieve
- jug
- ceramic, terracotta, or glass container

INGREDIENTS
- 500ml whole milk
- 50ml fresh cream (optional)
- 15ml yogurt starter (see box opposite)

 LAB *L. bulgaricus*, *S. thermophilus*, *L. acidophilus*, *L. plantarum*, *L. rhamnosus*

16 HOURS

② **Wait for the milk to cool to 45°C (113°F).** Without a thermometer you'll know it is the correct temperature if you can stick your finger in the milk for 10 seconds without it being uncomfortable. If it cools down too much simply heat it back up to 45°C (113°F). Prepare your incubation chamber.

① **Heat the milk** (and cream, if using) to at least 82°C (180°F) while stirring so it doesn't catch on the bottom of the pan. If you don't have a thermometer, heat the milk until you start seeing steam rise and bubbles forming round the sides of the pan.

③ **Once the milk** is at the correct temperature, work quickly. Add the yogurt starter and whisk it into the milk to distribute it.

DIRECTORY OF FERMENTS • Lactic acid bacteria 93

④ **Pour the mixture** into a jug, straining the milk through a sieve to break up any bubbles and catch any solids.

⑥ **Leave** in the fridge for 8 hours to set and thicken before eating. Strain through a muslin cloth for 2–4 hours in the fridge to produce a thicker Greek-style yogurt. The yogurt will keep in the fridge for up to a week.

⑤ **Transfer to a container and place in an incubator** or oven at its lowest temperature. Cover and incubate at 38–45°C (100–113°F) for 5–8 hours until it wobbles like jelly.

Heirloom starters

Try to get your hands on an heirloom starter if you can; this will get better and stronger with more use, as you're getting a bigger and more diverse population of bacteria and yeasts, and the benefits that come with it. You may be able to get a starter from someone else who is making their own yogurt, or from an online marketplace or health-food store. Shop-bought plain yogurt labelled "live culture" can also be used as your starter (but avoid flavoured or sweetened yogurt).

Troubleshooting

• If your yogurt is too runny, let it incubate for a few more hours. Use more starter in your next batch. If it doesn't set at all, you may have added the starter to the milk when it was too hot.

• If your yogurt is too sour, it has overfermented. Incubate it for fewer hours in your next batch.

• Yogurt can become stringy and yeasty if there has been microbial contamination. It isn't dangerous, but it isn't very nice to eat. Discard and try again.

KEFIR

This fermented drinking yogurt originated some 2,000 years ago in the mountains of the Caucasus. Created from a symbiotic culture of "kefir grains", which look like little bits of cauliflower, it turns milk into a powerhouse of different microbes and bioactive components.

It is believed that kefir was discovered by shepherds who noticed that the milk they kept in goatskin bags took on a fizzy, tangy characteristic that not only tasted good, but also had health benefits. Clumps of microbes (kefir grains) were present in this milk and people began to cultivate them. Kefir grains are a type of biofilm (see p142), consisting of a variety of microorganisms held together in a gluey substance called kefiran. With up to 40 different strains of bacteria and yeasts present in milk kefir, the fermentation process releases bioactive compounds, as well as encouraging the growth of lactic acid bacteria (LAB) and helpful yeasts and other species. It also creates short-chain peptides – short proteins that can stimulate the immune system – and a number of volatile flavour compounds that are responsible for kefir's distinctive taste.

FERMENTATION BACTERIA

No two sets of kefir grains have the same microbial content because they pick up species from their local environment and handler. However, some are commonly present, most

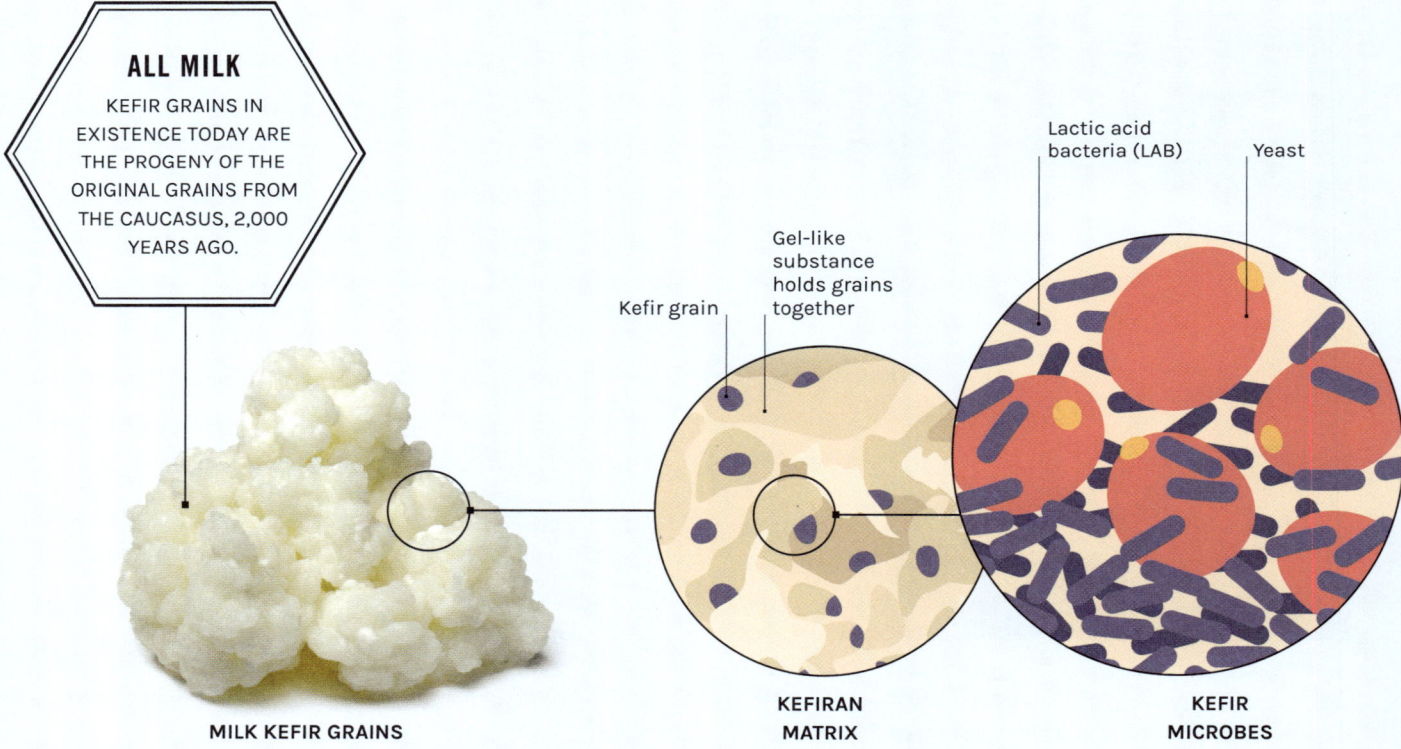

ALL MILK
KEFIR GRAINS IN EXISTENCE TODAY ARE THE PROGENY OF THE ORIGINAL GRAINS FROM THE CAUCASUS, 2,000 YEARS AGO.

MILK KEFIR GRAINS

Kefir grain
Gel-like substance holds grains together

KEFIRAN MATRIX

Lactic acid bacteria (LAB)
Yeast

KEFIR MICROBES

notably the kefiran producers *Lactobacillus kefiri* and *L. kefiranofaciens*. Microbes including *Streptococcus thermophilus* and *L. bulgaricus*, yeasts *Saccharomyces* and *Kluyveromyces*, and *Enterococcus durans* and acetic acid bacteria are also frequently found.

THE SCIENCE BEHIND THE PROCESS

When making yogurt, the milk is denatured to open up the structure of the milk proteins and kill off other microbes. This is not an essential step for kefir – the fermentation happens quite happily at a cool room temperature, which makes kefir easy to make. When kefir grains are added to milk the lactic acid bacteria they contain use the lactose (sugar) in the milk to produce lactic acid. As lactic acid is produced, it lowers the pH in the jar until the acidity is such that the structure of the milk protein changes and forms a curd. Yeast ferments sugars into ethanol and carbon dioxide, which adds a slight fizziness to the finished product. Further bioactive compounds such as kefiran and amino acids are also produced.

Kefir can be made with animal milk or soya milk, with differing results. Cow's milk gives a firmly set curd that becomes like a drinking yogurt when disturbed – the thickness is governed by the fat content, with high-fat milk making a thicker, more unctuous kefir. Goat's milk has a different protein structure and the resulting kefir barely thickens, though it tastes delicious – rather like liquid goat cheese. Some plant milks can also be used to make kefir. Soya milk contains a whole range of amino acids within its proteins, and can form curds when acidified.

HEALTH BENEFITS

Regular consumption of kefir is associated with health benefits including reduced inflammation, improved insulin sensitivity, therapeutic effects on osteoporosis, improved cholesterol, positive effects on the gut microbiota, regulation of appetite and enhanced recovery from infection, and lowered blood pressure.

WATER

KEFIR GRAIN MICROBES ARE SO GOOD AT MAKING DEXTRAN THAT THEY ARE USED AS A THICKENING AGENT IN COMMERCIAL FOOD PRODUCTION.

WATER KEFIR GRAINS

What is water kefir?

Water kefir is made with a different type of kefir grain, which uses sugar water instead of milk as its source of energy. Water kefir grains are also a biofilm or SCOBY (see p192), but while milk kefir grains are held together by kefiran, water kefir grains are held together by dextran, an exopolysaccharide produced by strains of LAB – usually *Lactobacillus hilgardii* and *Leuconostoc mesenteroides*.

Water kefir contains many different microbes, although there are usually fewer species present than in milk kefir – between 7 and 15. Also, as the substrate is less nutritious than milk, fewer types of bioactive compounds are produced. However, it can be a good choice for people who are allergic to milk proteins, severely lactose intolerant, or don't like the flavour of soya milk.

MAKE YOUR OWN
KEFIR

Making kefir at home is simple, cost effective, beneficial to the environment, and, research suggests, better for your health than mass-produced commercial kefir. With each batch your grains will grow, doubling every couple of weeks. As they grow, split them off and share them with your friends, freeze them for a rainy day, or dehydrate them to make a type of kefir "Parmesan". You can also feed excess grains to your pets, or eat them yourself, blended into a smoothie. Use homogenized cow's milk to get new kefir grains working. After that, you can use other milks, too (see box, below).

EQUIPMENT
- 4 × glass jars (2 × small, 2 × large), clip-top or lidded
- sieve
- paper towel (optional)
- rubber band (optional)

INGREDIENTS
- 1 tsp milk kefir grains
- 850ml whole homogenized cow's milk (350ml to acclimatize the grains; 500ml to make a full batch)

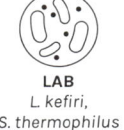
LAB
L. kefiri,
S. thermophilus

Yeasts
S. cerevisiae,
K. marxianus,
E. durans

AAB
A. aceti

4–8 DAYS

① **Place the kefir grains** in a small jar and add about 50ml of the milk. Seal and leave at room temperature until the milk has set firm. This might take up to 72 hours. If it doesn't set, drain off the milk and repeat.

② **When the kefir has set** strain through a sieve into a small jar, retaining the grains. Keep the kefir sealed in the fridge and consume to acclimatize yourself to it. Next, add 100ml of the milk to the grains, seal, and again leave to set.

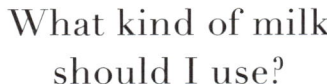

What kind of milk should I use?

Although you can use goat or soya milk for your kefir grains, whole homogenized cow's milk gives the best results. When the grains are up and running you can change the milk as often as you like and try goat, sheep, mare, soya, semi-skimmed, skimmed, UHT, Jersey, or unhomogenized (avoid the thick cream until grains are established) milks.

③ **When the kefir has set** strain off into another vessel, or the one with the previous kefir in. Then add 200ml of the milk to the kefir grains in a large jar, seal, and again leave to set for up to 72 hours.

④ **When the milk has set** strain off the kefir. Now your grains are ready to make 500ml of kefir in a large jar, using the same method as before. For optimal flavour use a clip-top jar with room for plenty of airspace, or, for a stronger, tarter kefir, cover with a paper towel and a rubber band instead of a lid. If the kefir separates, don't worry; upon straining it will recombine. Once made, your kefir will keep in the fridge for up to a week.

Troubleshooting

• When it's very warm or very cold your kefir might not set, or it might set very quickly and separate. Try to find the most temperate spot in your house – leave it for longer if it's cold or watch for it changing sooner if warm.

• Milk from different sources can affect the grains – they need to get used to it. When using unhomogenized milk, sometimes the fat settles around the grains and prevents them from setting the milk. If this happens, gently stir the kefir a couple of times and leave for a few hours. If using unhomogenized milk, try to leave out the very creamy part at first, introducing it little by little – the culture will learn to cope.

• If the kefir grains are floating on the top of the jar, or there is a lot of gas, or it's not setting, there may be an imbalance – sometimes the yeasts outgrow the LAB. In this case, go back to the beginning – make a tiny batch in a 50ml quantity with a lid on the container, which will help to suppress the yeast and let the LAB grow.

• If the kefir has separated into tiny curds, smells nothing like kefir, or is bitter, it's likely the milk has gone off before the kefir could get going. Throw it away, wash the grains, and start again in a small volume.

• The only occasion when kefir can't be saved is when it has been abandoned in the fridge for months and fridge moulds have got in, turning it black or green. Throw it away and go back to your frozen grains, starting again with a small volume.

Adding kefir to your diet

Introduce kefir into your diet gradually, starting with a teaspoon and building up to two teaspoons, then a tablespoon, then 50ml, and doubling until you are having around 125ml daily. You can eat it as is, or add a little lemon, lime, or orange zest.

CHEESE

Cheesemaking encompasses numerous microbial interactions. Milk is inoculated with bacterial cultures, aged with moulds and yeasts, and transformed by the enzyme rennet in a process harnessed by our Neolithic ancestors, making dairy nutrients safe, preservable, transportable, and digestible.

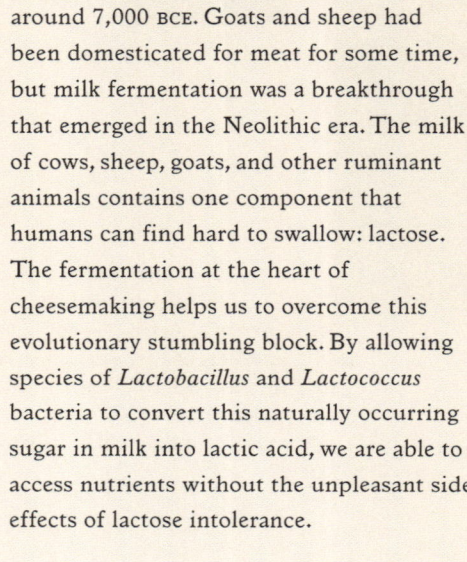

MILK IS AN IMPORTANT SOURCE OF FAT, PROTEIN, AND VITAMINS SUCH AS CALCIUM.

Keeping dairy animals dates back to around 7,000 BCE. Goats and sheep had been domesticated for meat for some time, but milk fermentation was a breakthrough that emerged in the Neolithic era. The milk of cows, sheep, goats, and other ruminant animals contains one component that humans can find hard to swallow: lactose. The fermentation at the heart of cheesemaking helps us to overcome this evolutionary stumbling block. By allowing species of *Lactobacillus* and *Lactococcus* bacteria to convert this naturally occurring sugar in milk into lactic acid, we are able to access nutrients without the unpleasant side effects of lactose intolerance.

FROM MILK TO CHEESE

Once the starter has been added to the milk the lactic acid bacteria (LAB) get to work immediately, converting lactose into lactic acid. If sufficient acidity is reached (pH 4.6), the proteins in milk will start to cling to each other in small clusters of curd, a process known as acid coagulation. This produces fragile, crumbly curds for fresh cheeses like quark or feta.

THE ROLE OF RENNET

The enzyme rennet (derived from the stomachs of calves, kids, or lambs) is used as a coagulant, transforming liquid milk to a solid blob of milk jelly (junket). This type

Cheese production

All the components needed for cheese are present in raw milk. Native bacteria are boosted with additional cultures.

MILK

HEAT THE MILK

Milk is heated to help curd formation and control bacteria growth.

ADD THE STARTER

The starter is added to ferment lactose into lactic acid.

ADD THE RENNET

Rennet is added to help coagulate the protein in the milk.

CUT THE CURDS

Curds are cut into smaller pieces to release more whey.

Lactic and rennet (enzymatic) coagulation

In lactic coagulation, LAB ferment lactose into lactic acid, creating soft, fragile curds that can be used to make cream cheese. In rennet coagulation, an enzyme called chymosin breaks down clusters of protein, leading to firmer curds used to create harder cheeses.

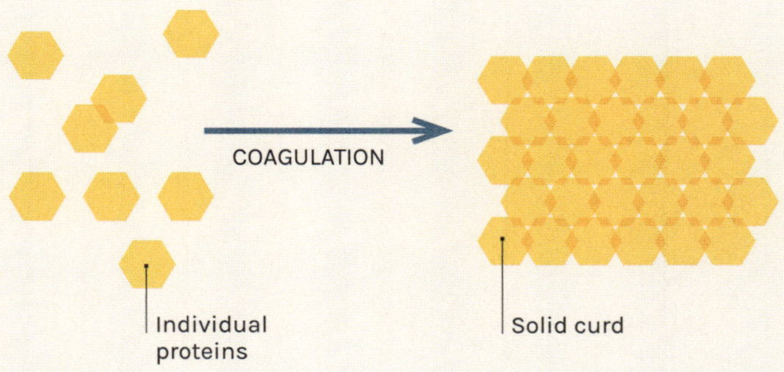

COAGULATION

Individual proteins → Solid curd

of coagulation forms a robust curd suited to many cheese types, including Cheddar, Gouda, and Swiss cheese.

MOULDS AND YEASTS

Many soft cheeses rely on the controlled growth of moulds and yeasts to create a rind that will ripen the paste. The moulds are sometimes introduced at the same time as the starter culture but are not active until the cheese starts to mature. They may also be present in the natural microflora of a maturing cave, or encouraged by carefully washing the rind with a brine solution.

Blue cheeses rely on a secondary fermentation; *Leuconostoc* will ferment citrate into carbon dioxide, creating small openings in the curd.

RENNET WAS SOURCED FROM THISTLES, FIG SAP, GROUND IVY, AND EVEN SNAILS IN CENTURIES PAST.

ROQUEFORT IS AGED IN CAVES TO PRODUCE BLUE MOULD AND STRONG, TANGY FLAVOURS.

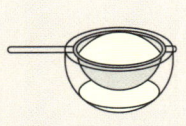
COOK AND DRAIN THE CURDS
The curds are gently heated, then the whey is drained away.

MOULD AND PRESS CHEESE
The curds may be pressed and moulded to remove moisture.

AGEING
Cheeses are aged to develop their flavour and texture.

CHEESE IN FOCUS

While cheese has only four basic ingredients – milk, starter, rennet, and salt – there are thousands of varieties, each one the result of differing techniques and harnessing selected bacteria that will influence its size, shape, texture, flavour, and appearance.

Most cheesemaking starts with the addition of starter cultures to milk to ferment the lactose to lactic acid, which lowers the pH level in preparation for the addition of rennet. The rennet then acts as a coagulant and forms the curd mass. After this basic process, the decisions made by the cheesemaker really start to influence the resulting style of cheese.

FROM CURD TO CHEESE

The size of the curd defines the firmness of the cheese. Larger, walnut-size curd pieces handled gently retain moisture, resulting in soft cheeses. Finer curds give semi-hard cheeses and for the hardest of all cheeses, the curd will be cut down to the size of a rice grain. It may then be stretched, washed, scalded, cheddared, or scooped into moulds where the whey can drain away.

Salt may be sprinkled on the outside of the fledgling cheeses, or larger pieces may be slipped into a salty brine bath overnight. This adds flavour and slows down the activity of the starter culture, controlling the acid production and allowing other desirable bacterial strains to establish themselves.

THE AGEING PROCESS

The length of time a cheese takes to age is defined by its moisture content; soft cheeses can be ready within weeks, while the hardest cheeses can take years to mature. During this time they will be subject to further enzymatic processes, which alter the texture and flavour, creating complexity. Every cheese has a peak, and the expertise of a cheese grader or affineur is to distribute it at the moment of cheesy perfection.

MOZZARELLA
Age profile 2–3 days
Style Fresh **Milk** Buffalo or cow
When the curd is formed, it is heated in hot water, then kneaded to stretch it. This aligns the protein threads, giving a satisfying stringy melt when cooked.

VALENÇAY
Age profile 4 weeks
Style Soft **Milk** Raw goat
The yeast rind on this cheese is easily recognizable by its wrinkled, brain-like pattern created by Geotrichum candidum. Valençay is also sprinkled with charcoal to help neutralize acidity.

GOUDA
Age profile 3–36 months
Style Hard **Milk** Cow, sheep, or goat
When curds have been cut, a little whey is drained off and replaced with hot water to wash the curds. This limits lactic acid production, resulting in sweeter-tasting cheese.

ROQUEFORT
Age profile 3–9 months
Style Blue **Milk** Raw sheep
The blue mould Penicillium roqueforti is naturally present in the Combalou caves in the village of Roquefort-sur-Soulzon, where the cheeses are aged.

EMMENTAL
Age profile 4–24 months
Style Hard **Milk** Cow
After the cheese is moulded with Propionibacterium freudenreichii, a secondary fermentation converts lactate into CO_2 to create the trademark bubbles through the paste.

CRUNCHY
FLAVOUR-RICH TYROSINE CRYSTALS FORM WHEN PROTEASES BREAK DOWN CASEIN DURING AGEING.

MOULD
PENICILLIUM ROQUEFORTI FORMS DEEP CHANNELS INTO CHEESE, CREATING BLUE SPOTS AND VEINS.

CHEDDAR

Age profile 3–24 months
Style Hard **Milk** Cow

The texture and flavour of this cheese is due to "cheddaring". Drained curd is chopped into large blocks, which are stacked on top of each other in the vat.

CAMEMBERT DE NORMANDIE

Age profile 4 weeks
Style Soft **Milk** Raw cow

The white, bloomy *Penicillium candidum* (*camemberti*) mould on the rind is responsible for ripening the cheese. Tiny filaments grow into the paste and break down the proteins to soften it.

TALEGGIO

Age profile 1–3 months
Style Washed rind **Milk** Cow

The cheese's surface is painted with a brine several times as it ripens to encourage yeasts and *Brevibacterium linens* moulds to thrive, creating a sticky, stinky, pinkish rind.

Filaments of *P. candidum* (*camemberti*)

HOLES

IN SWISS-STYLE CHEESES ARE CALLED "EYES", AND IF A CHEESE FAILS TO PRODUCE THEM IT IS TERMED "BLIND".

Penicillium candidum

This mould appears as a fluffy white rind on cheeses like Brie and Camembert. It adds creamy texture and mild, mushroomy flavours.

MOULDS AND MORE

Mould fermentation	**104**
How was mould domesticated?	**106**
Culinary moulds	**108**
Koji	**110**
Soy sauce	**118**
Black garlic	**124**
Miso	**126**
Tsukemono	**132**
Doubanjiang	**134**
Gochujang	**136**
Tempeh	**140**
Nattō	**142**
Fermented tofu	**144**
Garum	**146**

MOULD FERMENTATION

Moulds are a broad group of fungi whose thread-like growth and powerful enzymes make them essential to natural ecosystems – and uniquely suited to fermentation. Unlike yeasts and bacteria, moulds are multicellular, building branching networks that reach deep into and around substrates.

Mould networks start with hyphae: long, tubular filaments that grow outwards from spores. As hyphae spread, they secrete a suite of enzymes (see p36) that break down complex molecules outside the mould's body. This external breakdown, called extracellular digestion, allows the mould to absorb the resulting sugars, amino acids, and other nutrients through its cell walls. It's a strategy that enables moulds to tackle tough materials like lignin in wood, collagen in dry-aged meat, or starches and proteins in cereals and legumes.

Over time, the hyphae weave into a dense structure known as mycelium. This is what we typically see when we observe mould: a fluffy or felt-like mat spreading across the surface. Each species forms a distinct pattern of growth.

Penicillium camemberti, for example, produces a uniform surface bloom on Brie, while *P. roqueforti* grows in veins through blue cheese (see p100). In tempeh, *Rhizopus oligosporus* forms a thick, white matrix that binds soya beans together in a cohesive block (see p140).

For moulds to thrive, they need specific environmental conditions. Most species are aerobic, meaning they require oxygen to grow. Temperature plays a crucial role, too. *Aspergillus oryzae*, for example, thrives at around 30°C (86°F), while *Penicillium* species prefer cooler, cave-like conditions. High humidity supports hyphal growth, but too much moisture can favour bacterial growth.

Given the potential risk of other microbial growth, moulds evolved to be highly competitive. They don't

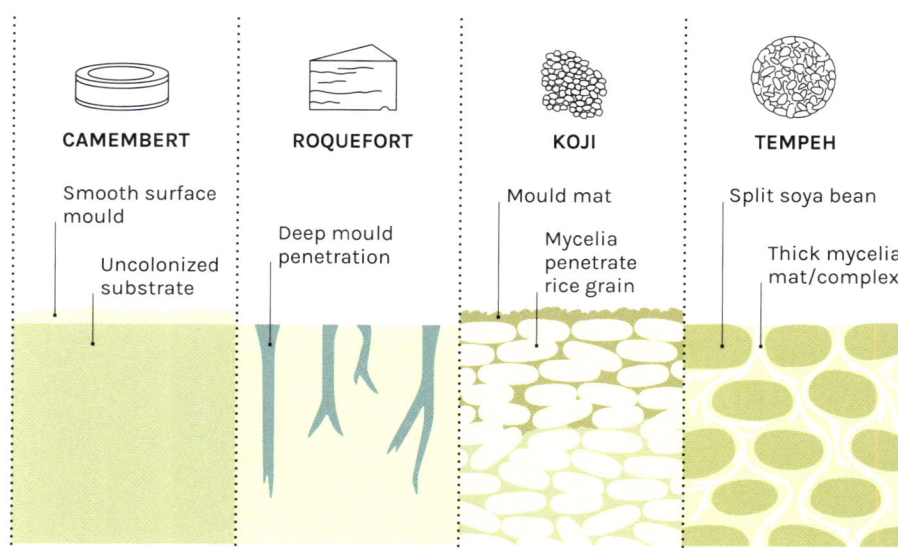

Fungal mycelium spreads across or through substrates differently depending on species. Each shows a distinct growth pattern, from the snowy bloom on Camembert to the dense internal webbing of tempeh.

CAMEMBERT
- Smooth surface mould
- Uncolonized substrate

ROQUEFORT
- Deep mould penetration

KOJI
- Mould mat
- Mycelia penetrate rice grain

TEMPEH
- Split soya bean
- Thick mycelial mat/complex

just grow quickly; they have developed strategies that make it harder for other microbes to survive. Their sprawling mycelium physically blocks access to nutrients, and some species even secrete antimicrobial compounds. *P. chrysogenum*, for example, famously produces penicillin.

Mould metabolism also generates heat. In high-density growth, such as in tempeh or koji (see p110) production, this exothermic growth can raise the temperature of the fermenting mass, further deterring unwanted microbes and accelerating enzyme activity.

Each spore (conidium) is genetically identical to the parent organism, allowing rapid colonization of suitable environments. Spores are incredibly lightweight and resilient, designed to travel by air or water, or to hitch a ride with animals. When they land on a compatible surface with the right moisture, temperature, and nutrients, they germinate, sending out new hyphae to begin the growth cycle again. In some moulds, sexual reproduction can also occur under environmental stress, resulting in spores with greater genetic diversity and adaptability, but this is very uncommon in controlled food fermentations.

CHEESE
MOULDS MAY HAVE FIRST BEEN DOMESTICATED IN COOL CAVES, SHAPED BY WILD MICROBES.

HUMANS
LEARNED TO CULTIVATE SPECIFIC MOULDS, OFTEN AIDED BY CHEESE MITES SPREADING SPORES.

Making more mould

Moulds reproduce via microscopic spores that function like seeds. Mostly, these are formed asexually in structures called conidia, which develop at the tips of aerial hyphae (conidiophores). These look like tiny dandelion heads poking through the mycelial surface, giving moulds their powdery appearance.

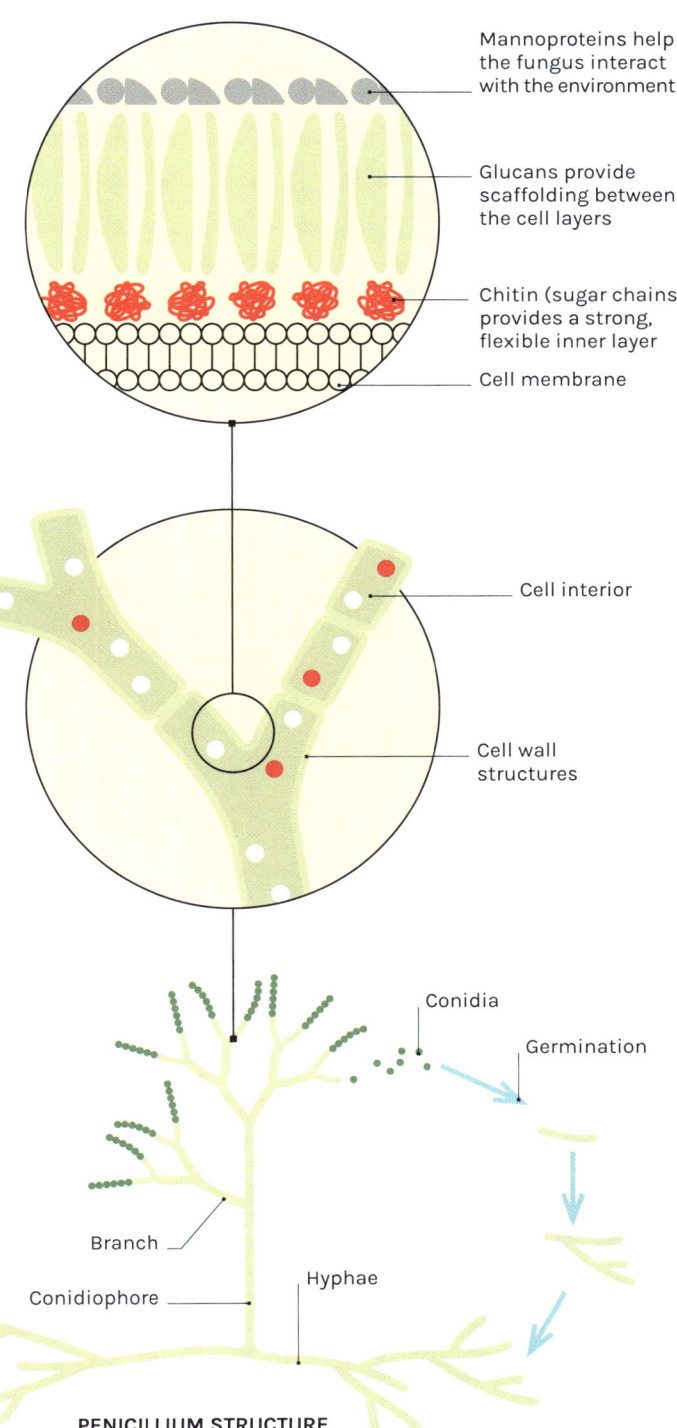

HOW WAS MOULD DOMESTICATED?

Originally, all moulds existed in the wild. Through observation, repetition, and selection, humans have shaped them into domesticated fermentation specialists.

CAMEMBERT WAS ONCE GREEN, RIPENED WITH WILD PENICILLIUM THAT PRODUCED BLUE-GREEN MOULDS.

Domestication is usually associated with plants and animals (see timeline, right), but moulds have also been shaped by human activity. *Aspergillus oryzae* and *Penicillium camemberti* are no longer wild organisms. They've undergone significant genetic and behavioural changes that make them better suited to human environments, and less competitive in nature.

Mould domestication has been mostly indirect, through sustained, generational use: reinoculating successful batches or sharing cultures, which favours growth traits unconsciously. Over time, this selection has favoured mutations that improved performance in fermentation, especially traits like rapid growth, consistent sporulation (producing spores), low toxin production, and desirable flavour or colour.

A. oryzae, the mould behind koji, is one of the earliest and most extensively domesticated fungi. Genetic studies show that it evolved from a close relative of *A. flavus*, a wild mould that produces the potent poison aflatoxin. Through generations of use in saké, miso, and soy sauce, strains were selected that grew well on grains, secreted amylases and proteases (see p36), and lacked toxic secondary metabolites. Modern *A. oryzae* has lost entire gene groups for toxin production. It has also adapted to high-starch substrates,

How serial passaging works

Though not exclusive to fungi, serial passaging is the process of repeatedly transferring microbes to fresh media over time, allowing selection for specific traits.

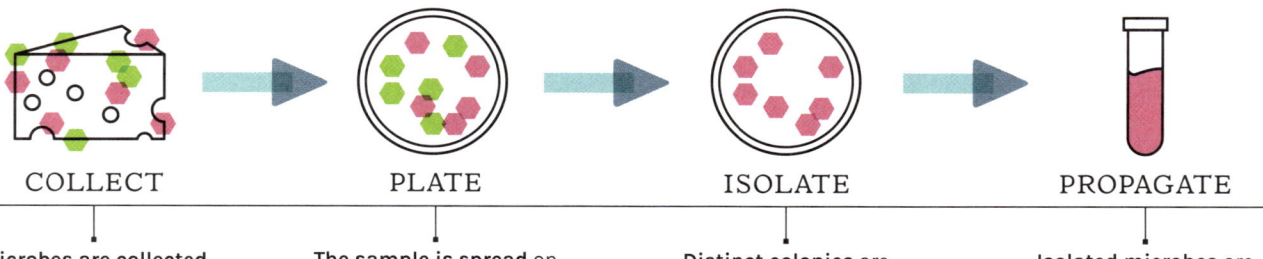

COLLECT — Microbes are collected from a ferment or environment using sterile tools and a buffer solution.

PLATE — The sample is spread on nutrient agar to encourage colony growth from individual cells.

ISOLATE — Distinct colonies are selected and plated again to isolate a single strain.

PROPAGATE — Isolated microbes are grown in fresh media to increase biomass for use in fermentation.

Cultural adaptation

In Japan, koji strains were adapted to local grains, humidity, and seasonal rhythms, producing distinct regional variants now maintained by specific breweries or miso makers. In Europe, cheese moulds evolved differently in Normandy caves, Alpine cellars, and Welsh dairies. These adaptations were shaped by climate, tools, and taste. A single species of mould often hides a mosaic of local domestications, each shaped by human preference and microbial chance.

grows best at 30–35°C (86–95°F), and is dependent on human environments to thrive. Under normal conditions, it now no longer produces airborne spores, reducing the risk of contamination in mixed fermentations.

P. camemberti likely evolved from wild *P. biforme* or *P. fuscoglaucum,* both commonly found in soil and in cave environments. In soft-ripened cheese production, strains that formed a white, uniform surface bloom with a mild aroma were repeatedly favoured. Over time, these traits stabilized. Domesticated *P. camemberti* produces fewer pigments, sporulates less aggressively, and exhibits a slower, more even growth pattern – ideal for rind development.

MODERN SELECTION

Serial passaging – growing a mould repeatedly on the same substrate – selects for faster growth, better sporulation, and stronger enzyme activity. Individual colonies with useful traits can also be isolated and cloned. Some laboratories use UV light or chemical mutagens to force random mutations, then screen for improvements. Long-term consistency is now often ensured through spore banks and cryopreservation. More rarely, genome editing has been explored in industrial contexts; it's generally avoided in traditional work. These high-tech methods are a modern extension of observation and selection.

Timeline of domestication

- **c. 13,000 BCE**
  Dogs domesticated from wolves (likely in multiple locations)

- **c. 9500 BCE**
  Domestication of wheat and barley in the Fertile Crescent of the Middle East

- **c. 9000 BCE**
  Domestication of rice in the Yangtze River basin

- **c. 8000 BCE**
  Goats and sheep domesticated in western Asia

- **c. 7500 BCE**
  Domestication of maize in Mesoamerica

- **c. 6000 BCE**
  Domestication of pigs and chickens in East Asia

- **c. 3000 BCE**
  Fermentation with wild *Penicillium* species in blue cheese caves (e.g. Roquefort)

- **c. 2000 BCE**
  Use of *Monascus purpureus* in red rice fermentation in China

- **c. 1000 CE**
  Earliest documented use of *Aspergillus oryzae* in Japan (koji-making)

- **c. 1600 CE**
  Selective use of *Penicillium roqueforti* in Roquefort cheese caves

- **c. 1600–1700 CE**
  Records suggest tempeh fermentation with *Rhizopus oligosporus* was common in Java

- **c. 1700 CE**
  Probable origin of *P. camemberti* from *P. biforme*

- **c. 1800s**
  Industrial standardization of *A. oryzae* and other fermentation moulds

- **c. 1920s**
  Selection of pure white *P. camemberti* strains for Brie and Camembert

CULINARY MOULDS

The unique ability that moulds have to grow across and into food, breaking down complex molecules as they go, makes them perfect candidates to make food more bioavailable, useful – and, of course, delicious.

Put simply, moulds are a biological strategy, defined by the type of structure they form and a similar set of behaviours. Genetically, koji mould is closer to brewer's yeast than tempeh – but tempeh and koji behave far more similarly to each other than to yeast. However, where food fermentation is concerned, we can talk about moulds as a single category.

Within culinary moulds there exist different genera, within each genus exists individual species, and within species exist individual strains. On each step down the evolutionary ladder there is more subtle variance in microbial behaviour, which has allowed humans to select for very specific traits.

PROMINENT MOULDS IN FERMENTATION

ASPERGILLUS
Aspergillus moulds are known for their exceptional enzymatic power and adaptability. Species like *A. oryzae* have been used for centuries in East Asian fermentations to lay the biochemical foundation for products like miso, shoyu, saké, and amazake. The mycelium grows primarily on the surface of grains or beans, forming a visible white coating that marks active fermentation. The *Aspergillus* forms compact, radial colonies and produces conidia (see p105) on highly branched conidiophores, giving it a fluffy surface. It thrives in warm, moist, aerobic environments, often generating significant heat during growth. One of its defining features is its ability to secrete a wide spectrum of enzymes – amylases, proteases, and lipases – into its environment, making it extraordinarily efficient at transforming complex substrates like rice, barley, and soya beans.

RHIZOPUS
The *Rhizopus* genus includes fast-growing, heat-tolerant moulds commonly used in Southeast Asian fermentations. *R. oligosporus* is the primary species involved in making tempeh (see p140), where it forms a dense, white mycelial mat that binds soya beans into a firm cake. *Rhizopus* is classified as a zygomycete, meaning it reproduces both sexually (via zygospores) and asexually through sporangia (rounded structures atop upright stalks or sporangiophores). It has broad, ribbon-like hyphae that grow rapidly under warm, humid, aerobic conditions. *Rhizopus* grows throughout and between the substrate, generating both structural cohesion and biochemical transformation. It secretes enzymes such as phytases (these reduce anti-nutrients, which affect the body's absorption of nutrients), as well as proteases and lipases that predigest soy proteins and fats, enhancing digestibility and flavour.

Industrial uses

Some mould species have unique abilities, for example *A. niger* produces citric acid as a byproduct of sugar metabolism, especially when key nutrients like iron or manganese are limited. This metabolic quirk is thought to help the mould absorb minerals from its environment. Under these stress conditions, the mould floods its surroundings with citric acid, acidifying the substrate and deterring competitors. Industrial fermentation mimics this process, feeding *A. niger* high-sugar, low-nutrient media to produce citric acid on a commercial scale.

PENICILLIUM

Penicillium camemberti and *P. roqueforti* (see p100) are critical to traditional European cheesemaking. Moulds within the genus tend to grow best in cool, humid, oxygen-rich environments. They produce bushy conidiophores that give rise to chains of dry, fragile conidia, responsible for the powdery green, blue, or white surfaces seen in ripened cheeses. Unlike *Aspergillus* and *Rhizopus*, which grow mainly on grains and legumes, *Penicillium* can thrive on dairy protein substrates. It secretes proteases and lipases that drive ripening, texture softening, and the formation of volatile aroma compounds characteristic of cheese such as Brie, Camembert, Roquefort, and Stilton. *P. camemberti* grows mainly on the surface, forming a tight rind, while *P. roqueforti* is inoculated internally and penetrates the cheese via air channels. Some species, such as *P. chrysogenum*, also produce bioactive compounds such as penicillin, highlighting the genus's antimicrobial potential. Domesticated strains have been selected for colour, flavour profile, and safety, making them essential players in mould-ripened cheese production.

The structural differences in the three key culinary moulds *Aspergillus*, *Rhizopus*, and *Penicillium* affect how each one spreads, sporulates (makes spores), and interacts with its particular substrate.

KOJI (ASPERGILLUS) — Round vesicles with radiating spores; Unbranched conidiophore; Hyphae

TEMPEH (RHIZOPUS) — Tightly packed sporangia ready to sporulate; Sporulation; Root-like rhizoids at the base

STILTON (PENICILLIUM) — Branching conidia chain of spores; Brush-like conidiophore

KOJI

Koji is a mould ferment from Japan. It's made by growing koji-kin (mould spores) on a substrate of rice, wheat, barley, or soya beans. Koji is the first stage of fermentation from which a plethora of subsequent ferments are made.

The *Aspergillus* family of moulds is responsible for koji fermentation. Before koji, wild species of *Aspergillus* were captured alongside *Rhizopus, Bacillus subtilis*, lactic acid bacteria, and yeasts on cooked beans and grains to form blocks of fermentation starter. These became products like qū balls in China and meju blocks in Korea.

During the Japanese Nara period (710–794 CE) *Aspergillus* was deliberately cultivated, predominantly by saké brewers, to create specific flavour profiles in saké. Most modern koji production involves "pure culture" fermentation (where only one species of *Aspergillus* is used); the most common used today is *A. oryzae*.

ENZYMES

Much of the process of growing koji is tailored to produce certain enzymes that will optimize results for the second stage of fermentation. The enzymes needed for making saké are different from those needed to make miso. There are three main ways to alter the quantity and variety of enzymes of the final koji:

- **Substrate** This determines much of the enzymatic content. Substrates richer in starch will lead to higher amylase activity, while more protein-rich substrates will lead to higher protease activity.
- **Temperature** By controlling the core temperature of the koji during growth, we can influence the production of enzymes. Higher temperatures (38–43°C/100–109°F) produce more amylase, and lower temperatures (28–38°C/82–100°F) produce more protease.
- **Strain** The strain is selected for its enzyme-producing abilities. Some are more adapted to produce protease, some amylase, and some to produce both equally.

How koji is made

Starchy, polished white rice used as a substrate produces high levels of amylase; a protein-rich base such as soya beans will give higher protease levels.

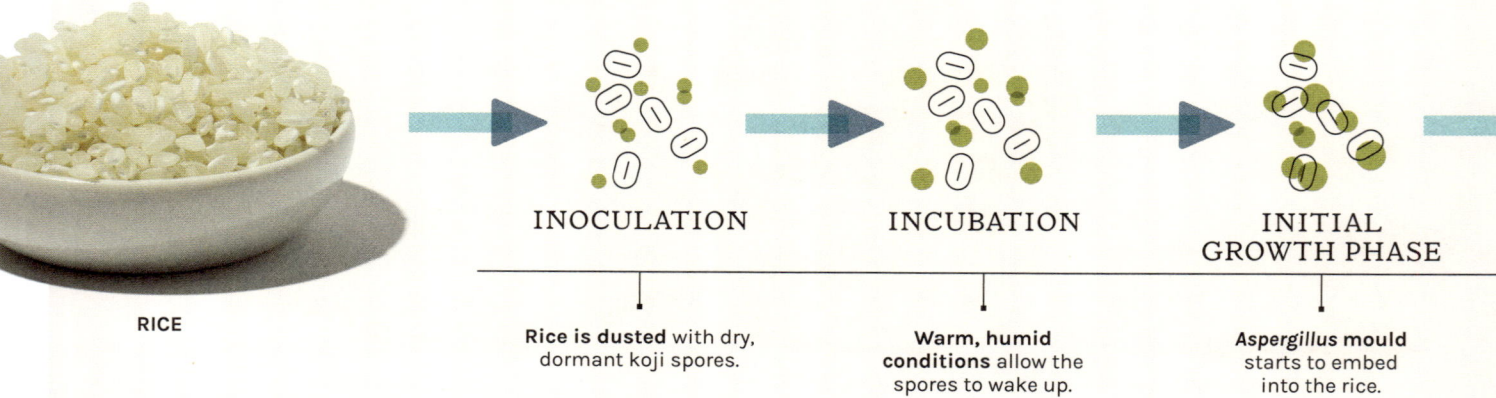

RICE → **INOCULATION** → **INCUBATION** → **INITIAL GROWTH PHASE**

Rice is dusted with dry, dormant koji spores.

Warm, humid conditions allow the spores to wake up.

***Aspergillus* mould** starts to embed into the rice.

DIRECTORY OF FERMENTS • Moulds and more

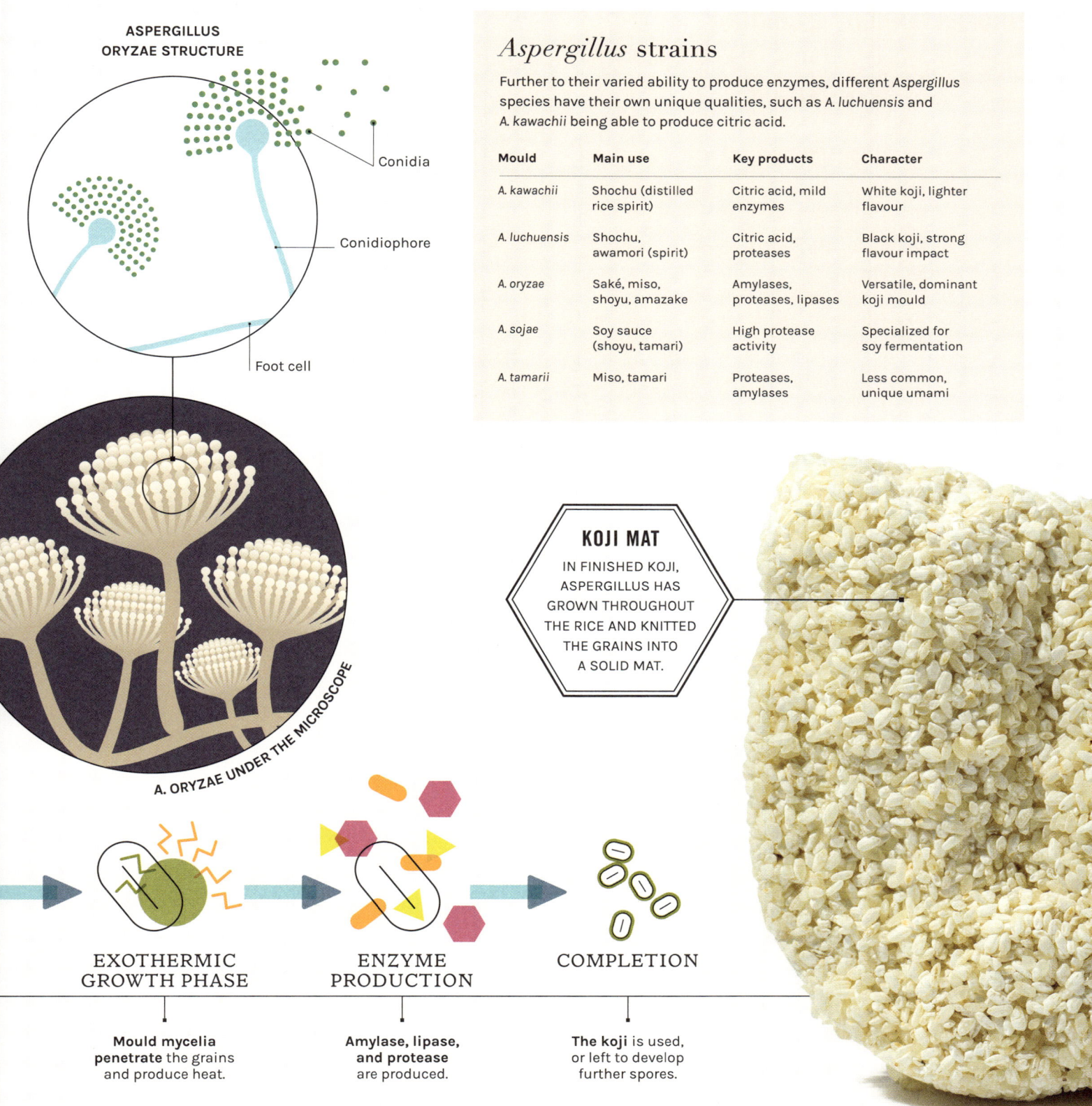

ASPERGILLUS ORYZAE STRUCTURE
- Conidia
- Conidiophore
- Foot cell

A. ORYZAE UNDER THE MICROSCOPE

Aspergillus strains

Further to their varied ability to produce enzymes, different *Aspergillus* species have their own unique qualities, such as *A. luchuensis* and *A. kawachii* being able to produce citric acid.

Mould	Main use	Key products	Character
A. kawachii	Shochu (distilled rice spirit)	Citric acid, mild enzymes	White koji, lighter flavour
A. luchuensis	Shochu, awamori (spirit)	Citric acid, proteases	Black koji, strong flavour impact
A. oryzae	Saké, miso, shoyu, amazake	Amylases, proteases, lipases	Versatile, dominant koji mould
A. sojae	Soy sauce (shoyu, tamari)	High protease activity	Specialized for soy fermentation
A. tamarii	Miso, tamari	Proteases, amylases	Less common, unique umami

KOJI MAT
IN FINISHED KOJI, ASPERGILLUS HAS GROWN THROUGHOUT THE RICE AND KNITTED THE GRAINS INTO A SOLID MAT.

EXOTHERMIC GROWTH PHASE
Mould mycelia **penetrate** the grains and produce heat.

ENZYME PRODUCTION
Amylase, lipase, and protease are produced.

COMPLETION
The koji is used, or left to develop further spores.

UNDERSTANDING TECHNIQUE

The technique on pages 113–115 will work in most circumstances when using rice, but it's important to understand what the parameters are and what they do.

Soaking
When the grain substrate is soaked it absorbs all the water it requires for cooking, generally around 30–60 per cent additional mass. (Steaming doesn't add any further water.) The length of the soak is based on the absorption rate of the grain. Certain grains absorb water faster than others, leading to lower soaking times.

Steaming
The steaming time is controlled by the rate at which starches gelatinize – this is the process by which they absorb water and lose their organized structure, increasing the surface area of available starch for koji to grow on. When a perfectly cooked grain of rice is squeezed it will have some resistance on the outside and a rubberiness inside. When a few grains are rubbed together, they should form into a cohesive stretchy ball without lumps. The Japanese term for this is *gaiko-nainan* – firm outside, soft inside.

Cooling temperature
Koji, even in its spore form, will struggle and start to die off in temperatures above 46°C (115°F). So it is important that the substrate is cooled well below that prior to inoculation.

Mixing regimen and completion time
Mixing serves to aerate, improve the coverage, and, critically, lower the temperature of the koji. Koji growth is exothermic (it gives off heat) and if left alone it can produce enough heat to kill itself. Therefore mixing is required. Traditional methods call for four mixes in order to tightly control the growth and internal temperature of the koji, though for this simplified method two mixes are sufficient.

Koji hydration and gelatinization

Soaking hydrates rice evenly, while gelatinization during steaming makes the grains soft internally and rigid externally. This prepares them for colonization by mould.

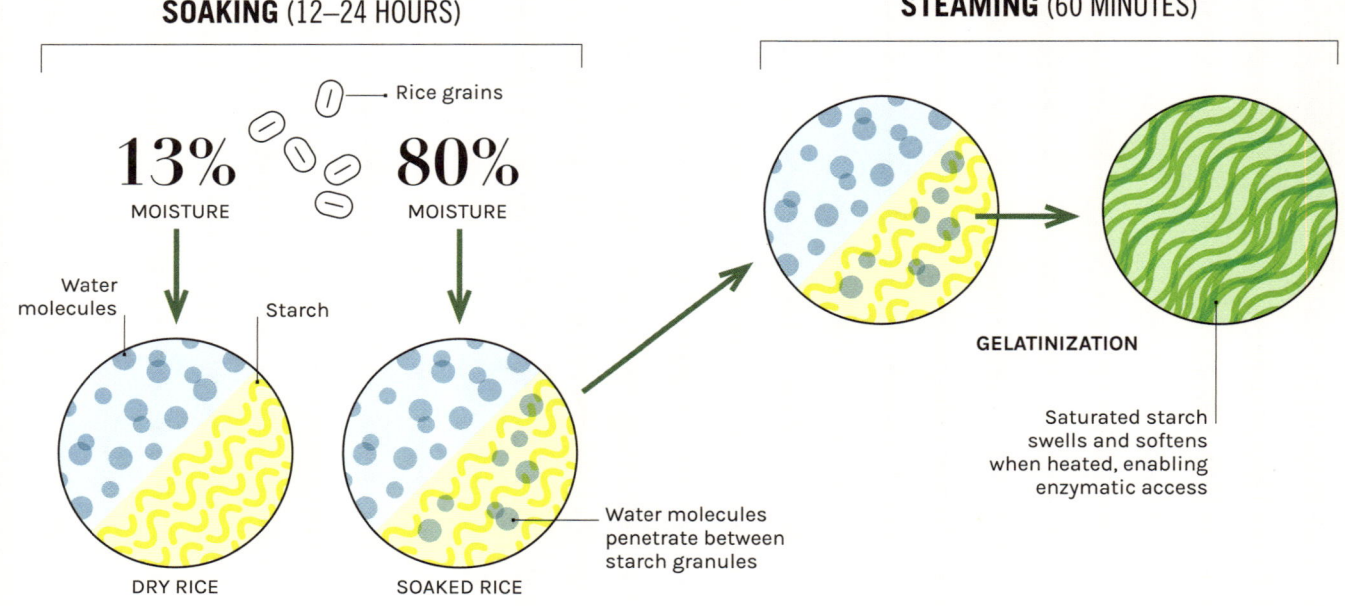

MAKE YOUR OWN
RICE KOJI

This is a shortened and simplified technique for short-grain rice koji that dispenses with many of the intricacies of a traditional method. Select any non-glutinous short-grain rice – sushi rice is ideal. Temperature and humidity will need to be controlled so an incubator (see p55) of some description is required (a bread proofer is perfect). Rice koji is an achievable home ferment, but does require precise measuring, and careful checking of temperatures as fermentation progresses.

These steps will make around a kilo of a versatile koji that can be used to make miso, soy sauce, tamari, saké, and most other koji-based ferments. Different types of rice, grains, legumes, or other substrates can behave quite differently to short-grain rice, so the parameters may need adjusting – look at the technique tips on the next page for more advice. Think of this recipe as a template to adapt through your own research and experimentation.

EQUIPMENT
- large bowl
- sieve and tea strainer
- steamer
- thermometer
- tray
- incubator (see p55)

INGREDIENTS
- 500g uncooked rice
- 1g koji spore starter (widely available online and at Asian supermarkets)

Moulds
A. oryzae

Enzymes
Amylase, protease

48 HOURS

REHYDRATION
WHEN USING DRIED KOJI IN A RECIPE THAT CALLS FOR FRESH, A GOOD RULE OF THUMB IS TO REHYDRATE IT AT A 1:0.3 RATIO OF DRIED KOJI TO WATER.

DRIED KOJI

1:0.3 RATIO

WATER

 Rinse the rice thoroughly until the water runs clear. Then transfer to a large bowl and add at least double the rice's weight in water. Soak the rice for 12–24 hours.

After soaking, transfer the rice to a sieve and allow the water to strain out for 15–30 minutes.

③ **Transfer the strained rice** to a steamer and steam for 45–60 minutes, then allow to cool to below 30°C (86°F). Now weigh the cooked rice. (It should be around double the dry weight, so 1kg in this case.)

⑤ **Mix the inoculated rice** and then spread evenly in the tray to a depth of around 4cm. Then transfer the tray to your incubation chamber and incubate at around 30°C (86°F) and 70% humidity.

④ **Transfer to a tray (or trays if needed) and inoculate** at a ratio of 1:1000 spores to cooked rice (so 1g spores for every kilo of cooked rice – always round up if in doubt). Dust the spores over the rice using a tea strainer.

⑥ **After 22 hours, remove from the incubator,** break apart and mix. The rice will be matting together into a block and giving off its own heat. Return to the incubator for another 8 hours and then break apart and mix again.

DIRECTORY OF FERMENTS • Moulds and more 115

7. **The koji should be complete 44–48 hours** after initial incubation. The rice will have formed into a solid mat of koji ready to be crumbled for immediate use or storage.

8. **Store in the fridge for 2 weeks,** or the freezer for a year. Dehydrated, it will keep for up to 2 years.

Troubleshooting

Koji can be vulnerable to contamination by pathogens such as *Bacillus cereus* and harmful moulds, so it's essential to follow good practice, stay attentive throughout the process, and observe the substrate closely. While koji fermentation is generally safe when managed well, it is more complex than many other ferments. If something seems off or you're unsure, it's always better to compost it and start again. Below are some common problems and explanations for why they may crop up:

• If there is a yellow, green, or black powdery surface, the koji has grown for too long, or been too hot, fully matured, and sporulated. The koji will no longer be at its enzymatic peak and may have some off flavours, but it is still usable. The colour of the mould should correlate to the type of *Aspergillus* used. If it doesn't, or it is pink, there has been contamination and the batch will need to be discarded and composted.

• If the final koji feels wet or mushy, it is likely that it was soaked or cooked for too long, and it should be discarded. An overly high moisture content can significantly impair *Aspergillus* growth and could potentially harbour pathogens.

• Occasionally due to a temperature spike, incorrect inoculation, too much moisture, or plain bad luck, *B. subtilis* (nattō, see p142) bacteria can colonize your batch. This is apparent from a distinct ammonia smell or a slimy texture. It is far more likely to be a problem in legume kojis. While a *B. subtilis* population isn't pathogenic, it makes the koji unusable.

• Patchy or uneven growth can occur as a result of improper mixing. The koji is still usable, but it won't be your best. If the koji is too dry it is likely that the incubation environment wasn't humid enough. Again, it is usable but not ideal.

KOJI IN FOCUS

Koji is a toolkit. Once grown, it can be used immediately to create a range of powerful secondary ferments, such as those below. From the savoury depth of shio koji to the sweetness of amazake, these are the building blocks for everyday umami and kokumi.

These three ferments – shio koji, mirin, and amazake – offer some of the most immediate and practical uses of koji, making them ideal entry points for beginners. Each one is simple to make, yet rich in flavour and function, revealing the incredible transformative potential of koji.

SHIO KOJI

Shio koji is a traditional Japanese marinade and flavour enhancer. Not only is it packed with umami and sugars, it is rich with enzymes from the koji, which will go to work on whatever ingredient is being used, intensifying them.

This is a salt-brined enzymatic ferment made by combining fresh koji with water and 6–10 per cent salt by weight. Over 5–10 days, the protease and amylase enzymes produced by *Aspergillus oryzae* diffuse from the mould hyphae into the brine, creating a solution rich in active enzymes. The enzymatic action continues when applied to proteins and vegetables, making it a powerful marinade that breaks the ingredient down into its fundamental flavour compounds. It can be used as is, or alternatively it can be blended smooth, or filtered to create a clarified liquid seasoning.

MIRIN

Mirin is a sweet liquid seasoning made from glutinous rice, rice koji, and shochu. It is the base of sushi rice seasoning, making it one of the key flavour pillars of Japanese cuisine. Traditional mirin is brewed over months (or even years), and its alcohol content sits closer to a low wine than a condiment.

Over months of fermentation and resting, mirin develops a rich sweetness balanced by subtle acidity (primarily lactic and succinic acid traces), along with a deepening amber hue. Its sugar content (typically 40–45 per cent) is not from added sugar but entirely from the enzymatic transformation of starch.

AMAZAKE

Amazake is a sweet, enzyme-dense porridge. It can be used in place of sweeteners and marinades, as a drink, or reduced into syrup. It's a short, non-alcoholic enzymatic ferment where koji's amylases are used to saccharify starches at a thermostable "sweet spot" of around 55°C (131°F). At this temperature, *A. oryzae* enzymes remain active while microbial proliferation is limited, resulting in a clean, sugar-rich mixture.

ALPHA-AMYLASE IS A LIQUEFACTION ENZYME IN KOJI – IT TURNS GELATINIZED STARCH INTO A LIQUID.

Koji substrates

In traditional Japanese koji-making for miso, shoyu, and saké there are three main ingredients: rice, barley, and soya beans. Each offers different qualities, nutritional profiles, and flavours.

RICE KOJI

Made with *Aspergillus oryzae*. Rich in amylase. Used in saké, amazake, shio koji, and most misos. Sweet, light, enzymatically potent.

STARCH	PROTEIN
75–80%	6–8%

BARLEY KOJI

Typically made with *A. oryzae* or *A. sojae*. Earthy and nutty. High in amylase and moderate protease. Used in mugi miso and shoyu.

STARCH	PROTEIN
60–65%	10–12%

SOYA BEAN KOJI

Made with *A. sojae* or *A. tamarii*. High protease activity. Used for tamari and hatcho miso. Deep umami, dense, and savoury.

STARCH	PROTEIN
15–20%	35–40%

These substrates are often blended to balance enzymes and flavour – rice for subtle flavours and sweetness, and fermentation speed; barley for texture and aroma; soya beans for depth and protein breakdown.

Enzymatic profiles can be adjusted by substrate (for example, barley or millet) or other fermentation parameters.

MAKE YOUR OWN SHIO KOJI

This recipe combines koji, water, and salt to create a basic, versatile shio koji. After fermentation the grains will still be intact. The paste can be blended for a smoother texture or clarified by filtering.

1. **In a sanitized glass jar** (see p59), combine koji and water in a ratio of 1:1, then mix in 6% of the total weight in salt (so 100g koji, 100g water, 12g salt).

2. **Seal the jar** and leave to ferment at room temperature for 7 days, mixing daily.

3. **Store the finished shio koji** in a sealed container in the fridge for 2 months.

MAKE YOUR OWN MIRIN

Traditional mirin has a long and rich history, with many different types and techniques behind it. This version is a short-cut, a quick and simplified method designed to be achievable in a home kitchen, but still rich in flavour and enzyme-driven character. Expect it to shift from light gold to deep amber over time, with notes of raisin, soy, and dried fruit developing as it matures.

1. **Cook and then cool glutinous rice.** Then, combine the cooked rice with koji and vodka at a ratio of 1:1:2.

2. **Transfer the mixture** to a sanitized jar (see p59), then leave in the dark at room temperature to age for 3-12 months.

3. **When it reaches your desired flavour**, filter and bottle. Store at room temperature. After bottling, the mirin will continue to develop and the colour will darken. It will keep for years.

MAKE YOUR OWN AMAZAKE

This method makes a sweet, thick amazake usable for a sweetener, flavour enhancer, or marinade. Flavour and consistency variations can be made by using a different starch source, altering the ratios, and fermenting at room temperature after incubation.

1. **Combine koji, water, and cooked rice** in a ratio of 1:1:2 – ideally in a rice cooker or yogurt maker.

2. **Keep it at around 55°C (131°F)** for approximately 12 hours. A rice cooker on a warm setting is perfect for this.

3. **Transfer to a sanitized jar** (see p59) and store for 1 month in the fridge.

SOY SAUCE

A general term that encompasses many different soy-based condiments found across Asia, soy sauce refers to a seasoning produced by fermenting a mash of soya beans, grains (typically wheat), salt, and water with specific microbial cultures – primarily *Aspergillus oryzae*, lactic acid bacteria, and yeast. The result is an enzymatically broken-down, umami-rich liquid composed of amino acids, simple sugars, organic acids, and aromatic compounds.

Aspergillus oryzae and *A. sojae* are the main mould types used to make soy sauce. There are many isolated strains of these moulds, which each lend different qualities to the final sauce. The strain of mould can affect the kinds of enzymes created during fermentation, which in turn changes the concentrations of sugar or umami present. The strain of mould also affects fermentation time, as well as the amount of sediment produced (allowing for easier clarification and pressing). Some commercial manufacturers use lab-grown strains of bacteria and yeast in the brine to ensure complete consistency of the finished soy.

Not all methods use "pure-culture" inoculation. Traditional Chinese and Korean styles favour wild inoculation, making use of *Aspergillus* floating in the environment, which lands on the cooling ingredients and proliferates. When this happens, a far more diverse collection of microbes take up residence in the paste, including different strains of *Aspergillus*, lactic acid bacteria (LAB), yeasts, and moulds – for example, *Bacillus subtilis* (nattō bacteria; see p142), *Rhizopus* (tempeh mould; see p140), and *Mucor* species. This "wild" method can lead to inconsistencies in the products but creates a rich and varied regional "microbial terroir".

How soy sauce is made

Cooked soya beans are mixed with roasted wheat and *Aspergillus* mould. After fermentation with salt, the mash is pressed, filtered, and pasteurized. The result is a deeply savoury, umami-rich seasoning, whose flavour evolves over months or years.

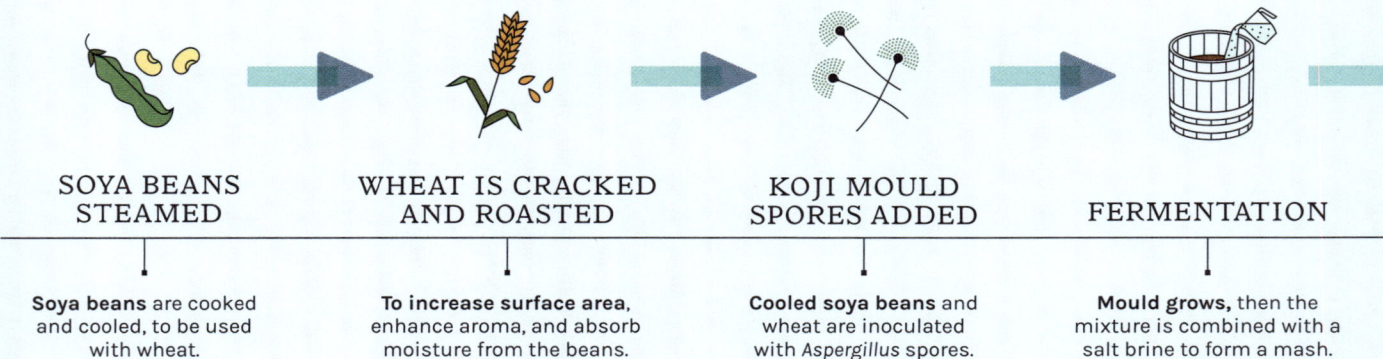

SOYA BEANS STEAMED
Soya beans are cooked and cooled, to be used with wheat.

WHEAT IS CRACKED AND ROASTED
To increase surface area, enhance aroma, and absorb moisture from the beans.

KOJI MOULD SPORES ADDED
Cooled soya beans and wheat are inoculated with *Aspergillus* spores.

FERMENTATION
Mould grows, then the mixture is combined with a salt brine to form a mash.

DIRECTORY OF FERMENTS • Moulds and more

All traditional methods share the complexity provided by the diverse microbes that are involved in the fermentation. The various microbes will break down large molecules differently, providing a wider array of flavour compounds. Traditional soy sauce fermentation will produce many flavour compounds, such as glutamic acid, peptides, and nucleotides, which all work together to produce umami (see p22) and kokumi (see p24) tastes. The longer fermentation time in these traditional methods also allows other microbes and the Maillard reaction (see p124) – when amino acids and sugars react slowly over time – to produce their own unique blend of flavour compounds and to deepen the colour.

Modern industrial techniques like acid hydrolysis can produce soy sauce in a matter of days. This process breaks down the ingredients using hydrochloric acid, which reduces the complex ingredients to just glutamic acid, providing a one-note umami experience. Traditional brewing, however, can take months or even years, with moulds, yeasts, enzymes, and bacteria all working together to produce a finished sauce with vibrant, layered, unique flavours.

SOYA BEANS
CAN BE YELLOW, BLACK, OR DEFATTED; EACH BRINGS UNIQUE FLAVOURS TO THE FINAL SAUCE.

SOYA BEANS

SHIRO
(WHITE) SHOYU IS A LIGHT SAUCE MADE WITH MOSTLY (OR ONLY) WHEAT, LENDING SUBTLE SWEETNESS AND GENTLE UMAMI.

SHIRO SHOYU

BARREL-AGED SOY SAUCE

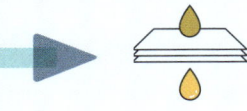  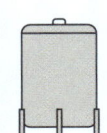  

FILTRATION — **PASTEURIZING** — **BOTTLING**

The mix is pressed and filtered to extract a rich sauce.

Heat stabilizes flavour, extends shelf life, and halts microbial activity.

Shoyu is bottled to preserve flavour, colour, and aroma.

SOY SAUCE IN FOCUS

Soy sauce comes from an ancient precursor ferment, jiang, which is also the progenitor of miso (see p126), fish sauce (see p146), doubanjiang (see p134), gochujang (see p136), and many other Asian ferments. It began as a method to ferment and preserve a wide array of foods, with the word jiang simply meaning "paste", but developed into the silky, umami, salty liquid we know as soy sauce.

To make *jiang*, ingredients (ranging from soya beans to wheat to fish to sesame seeds) were salted, mashed, and packed into vessels along with whatever ambient microbes were in the environment. As the technique developed it was refined into soy-based pastes. As these ferment, liquid is released that pools at the top of the paste. This is likely to be the point at which soy sauce diverged from pastes: since the liquid that forms was found to be delicious, methods began to develop specifically to make the sauce without the paste. These sauces were refined again into different variations, using different ratios of ingredients, different strains of *Aspergillus*, and different fermentation times to provide certain qualities, such as increased sweetness or thickness.

GANJANG
Korea

Blocks of cooked barley and soy (*meju*) are dried slightly on warm floorboards, then hung outside for weeks to develop cultures. The blocks are submerged in brine in traditional *onggi* pots for fermentation.

Soy vessels

All traditional soy sauce methods use specific fermentation vessels. In Japan, cedar barrels called *kioke* are used; in Korea it is clay pots called *onggi*. They are rarely sterilized – some not for over 100 years – so they develop their own microbiome, which contributes to the final product's "microbial terroir". These vessels have become a rarity in soy sauce production, however. When fifth-generation shoyu maker Yasuo Yamamoto, of brewery Yamaroku Shoyu, sought out new cedar barrels for his soy sauce in 2011, he found only one manufacturer left in Japan, so he decided to learn to make them himself.

TAMARI
Japan

The fifth and oldest type of shoyu doesn't use any wheat, only soya beans. Deliberate tamari brewing developed from the liquid pooling on top of miso in around 1300.

JIANGYOU
China

Made by forming loose, cooked wheat and soy balls (*douban*), which are stacked on straw mats for weeks to culture mould before being mixed with brine and fermented in clay pots.

KOIKUCHI
IS THE MOST POPULAR AND WELL-ROUNDED DARK SOY SAUCE. USUKUCHI IS MORE GENTLY FLAVOURED.

TAMARI
IS A GLUTEN-FREE FORM OF SOY SAUCE, AS IT IS MADE WITHOUT WHEAT.

KECAP

IS MADE FROM SOYA BEANS, PALM SUGAR, AND SPICES. IT IS THICK, SWEET, AND SYRUPY.

KECAP

SHIRO (WHITE SOY SAUCE)

BARREL-AGED SOY SAUCE

TAMARI

KOIKUCHI

Soy family tree

Originating as a broad category of fermented pastes, ancient jiang gradually diverged into regional styles – from pastes to liquids – each adapting to local ingredients, climates, and culinary preferences.

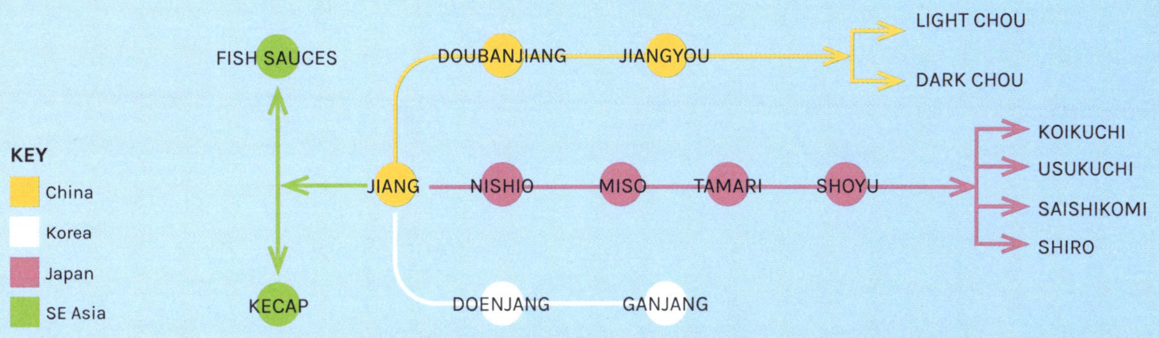

KEY
- China
- Korea
- Japan
- SE Asia

Soy family tree branches:
- FISH SAUCES ↔ KECAP
- JIANG → DOUBANJIANG → JIANGYOU → LIGHT CHOU / DARK CHOU
- JIANG → NISHIO → MISO → TAMARI → SHOYU → KOIKUCHI / USUKUCHI / SAISHIKOMI / SHIRO
- JIANG → DOENJANG → GANJANG

MAKE YOUR OWN
KOJI TAMARI

Koji tamari is a simple method that makes a sweet and light sauce. Either homemade or shop-bought dried koji can be used; if using dried koji, rehydrate it by adding 30% of its weight in water. To scale the recipe up or down, use a ratio of 1 part koji: 1 part cooked soya beans: 2 parts water: 10% salt. Note that soya beans will double in weight when cooked.

EQUIPMENT
- large bowl
- saucepan
- large jar
- muslin cloths
- rubber band
- storage bottle

INGREDIENTS
- 100g dried soya beans
- 200g rice koji (see p110) or 140g dried koji + 60ml water
- 80g salt

Moulds — *A. oryzae*
LAB — *T. halophilus*
Yeasts — *Z. rouxii*
6 MONTHS

2 **Simmer the beans** in fresh water for 3–4 hours, until soft. Drain, reserving the liquid, then allow the beans to cool.

1 **Wash then soak the soya beans** overnight in a clean bowl, then drain off the water.

3 **Combine the koji**, cooked soya beans, and salt with 400ml of water in a large jar. Cover the container with a muslin cloth and secure it with a rubber band. Store in a cool, dark place.

DIRECTORY OF FERMENTS • Moulds and more 123

④ **Stir every 2 days** for the first 2 weeks, then ferment for a further 22 weeks, mixing weekly.

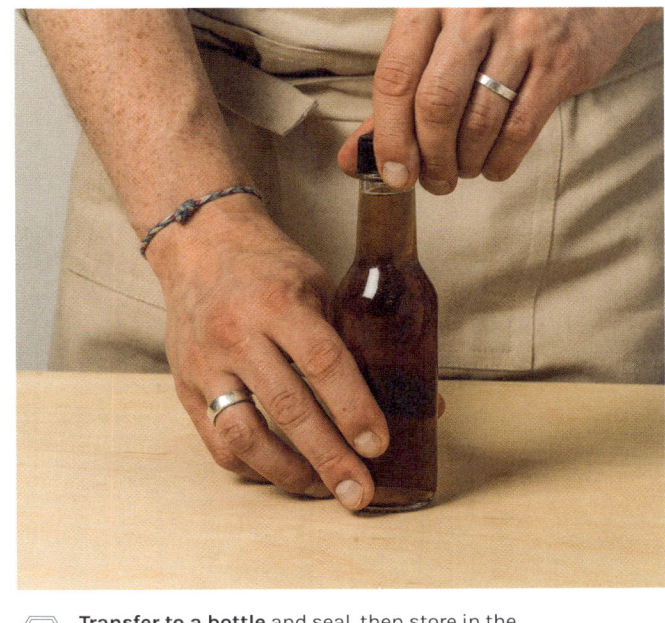

⑥ **Transfer to a bottle** and seal, then store in the fridge for up to a year.

⑤ **The liquid will have darkened** significantly. Strain as much liquid as possible through a clean muslin cloth. (Reserve the solids; they can be used like other fermented bean pastes.)

THE RICE KOJI TAMARI SHORTCUT

Koji tamari uses the enzymes from rice koji and the high protein from soya beans in a comparatively low-salt environment to produce a lighter and sweeter sauce in a fraction of the time the traditional method takes. You are essentially expediting the process with the addition of rice koji and soya beans, instead of solely soya beans, which speeds up the process.

Troubleshooting

• If a speckled white layer of kahm yeast (see p62) starts to form, skim it off as soon as possible, and ensure the brine is mixed every 2 days until kahm no longer forms. You can also use some "magic spray" (see p59) to prevent it from returning. The yeast itself is harmless, but it can produce ethyl acetate if left for more than a week, and this volatile molecule gives unpleasant acetone-like flavours and aromas.

BLACK GARLIC

Black garlic is the sweet, rich, soft, umami result of the Maillard reaction and enzymatic degradation over time. While not strictly an example of fermentation (as microbes aren't involved), the ageing process of black garlic shares many similarities with fermentation.

The Maillard reaction

As food is heated, amino acids react with reducing sugars, causing browning. This chemical reaction typically starts at above 140°C (284°F), but can occur at lower temperatures over longer time periods.

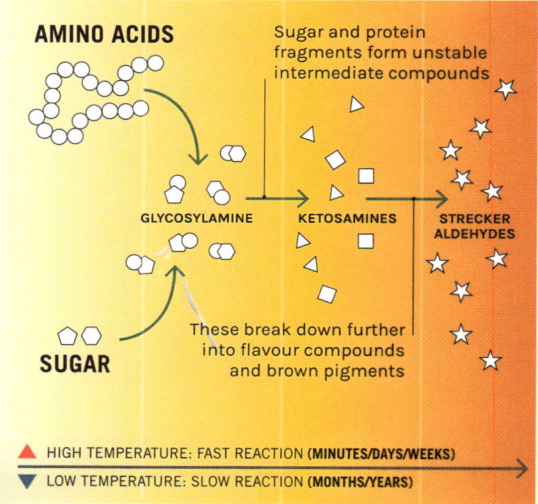

RAW GARLIC BLACK GARLIC

ENZYME TEMPERATURE

Enzymes related to blackening are less efficient below 65°C (149°F), while temperatures above 75°C (167°F) can cause them to denature, resulting in scorched, bitter garlic.

HUMIDITY LEVEL

High humidity prevents the garlic from drying out, leaving enough fluid for the enzymes to move around within the cloves, and for chemical reactions to occur.

MAILLARD REACTION

The Maillard reaction will proceed at ambient temperatures, albeit very slowly, so even during storage the garlic will continue to blacken, developing its flavour.

REDUCING SUGARS

Reducing sugars contain an "active" group allowing them to behave as a reducing agent and donate electrons to other molecules. In garlic these are glucose and fructose.

To make blackened garlic, fresh garlic bulbs are aged in a temperature- and humidity-controlled environment, a technique rooted in East Asian cooking. This is one of the most transformative methods, with enzymatic activity and the Maillard reaction turning fresh garlic into something almost unrecognizable. The black colour comes from compounds called "melanoidins" created during ageing. Unlike fermentation, this is a chemical rather than biological process, with enzymes – not microbes – driving the reaction.

ENZYMATIC DEGRADATION

Enzymes including alliinase and invertase are present within fresh garlic cloves. Alliinase breaks down the pungent sulfur compounds in fresh garlic when the cloves are crushed, cut, or, as in this case, aged. The low to moderate heat breaks down the starch in the garlic into sugars, and invertase converts the sucrose into glucose and fructose (the reducing sugars in garlic). Ageing garlic begins with this short period of enzymatic activity, which creates the molecules required for the Maillard reaction to proceed (see opposite). This process causes the garlic to blacken, soften, and mellow in flavour, developing slowly over the course of weeks to months at around 70°C (158°F). The Maillard reaction also produces unstable compounds, which are quickly rearranged, decomposed, degraded, and reformed into myriad new flavour compounds.

The chemistry of flavour

The following chemical families present each bring a different flavour profile to black garlic:

- **Pyridines** Nutty, earthy
- **Furans** Fresh coffee, buttery
- **Aldehydes** Sweet, almond, chocolate, beefy

Each chemical family is made up of many individual compounds, with their own character. In black garlic, aroma compounds combine in different ways to give a complex flavour and that unmistakable "cooked" quality.

MAKE YOUR OWN

If you don't have access to an incubator or a specialist garlic blackener, try using a rice/pressure cooker on a "keep warm" setting or a very rough set-up of reptile mats and tube heaters around a Tupperware box wrapped in tea towels.

EQUIPMENT incubator (see p55)
INGREDIENTS whole, unpeeled bulbs of garlic

Enzymes Alliinase, invertase

4–8 DAYS at 70°C (158°F)

1. **Select dry garlic bulbs** that are free from mould or soft spots. Brush off any dirt.
2. **Place the bulbs** in the incubation chamber. The temperature inside the chamber should be stable at 70°C (158°F), and humidity should be around 80%.
3. **Check every few days** to monitor the temperature and humidity levels. To check humidity with a home set-up, just open the chamber. If there is a little visible condensation on the surfaces inside, the humidity is fine. If it's completely dry or water is pooling, see the Troubleshooting tips below.
4. **After 4 weeks** the black garlic is ready. Alternatively, you can continue to incubate for up to 8 weeks for greater depth of flavour.
5. **Store in a dry place** at room temperature for up to a year. As blackening garlic removes most of the harsh pungency of fresh garlic, it can be paired effectively with sweet foods like chocolate and ice cream, as well as savoury dishes.

Troubleshooting

- When using improvised incubator set-ups, humidity can become an issue, lowering over time and drying out the garlic or building up and pooling in the chamber. If you notice the humidity dropping, add a damp towel to the incubator or tightly wrap the cloves in foil. If water is pooling anywhere, leave the top of the incubator slightly ajar until it dries out a little.

- Fuzzy mould will develop if the garlic bulb gets damp during storage. If this happens, the garlic should be discarded or composted.

MISO

This traditional Japanese umami-rich paste is typically made with a combination of soya beans, rice, barley, salt, and koji (see p110). It can be used to enrich soups, marinades, dressings, and stews, adding depth, saltiness, and a rounded, savoury backbone.

SOYA BEANS
PROVIDE PROTEIN AND FAT, WHICH BREAK DOWN INTO SAVOURY FLAVOUR AND CREAMY TEXTURE.

STEAMED RICE
FEEDS KOJI MOULD, GENERATING ENZYMES THAT UNLOCK SWEETNESS AND UMAMI.

BARLEY
ADDS SWEETNESS AND AROMA. ITS HUSKINESS IMPARTS A NUTTY DEPTH AND TEXTURAL BITE.

PEAS AND LENTILS
CAN BE USED TO INCREDIBLE EFFECT, WITH GREEN PEAS HAVING HUGE UMAMI POTENTIAL.

Miso differs from other fermented bean pastes (doubanjiang, see p134; and gochujang, see p136) in two key ways. First, a pure culture is almost always used as a starter, rather than wild fermentation. Second, the ingredients are limited to rice, barley, soya beans, and salt.

Koji is grown on one of these ingredients, then they are combined in different ratios to form the varieties of miso found across Japan. As a general rule, the more rice or barley, the sweeter the miso; the more soya beans, the more savoury the miso.

FERMENTATION MECHANISM
Koji is the predominant driver in miso, being responsible for the majority of the flavour development. The enzymes it provides break starches into sugars and proteins into the amino acid umami source. Koji is far from the only contributor, though. *Lactobacillus*, salt-tolerant (halotolerant) yeasts, and the Maillard reaction (see p124) play important roles, too.

Lactobacillus produces lactic acid – albeit in lesser amounts than in other lacto-ferments – giving miso a slight tang, while halotolerant yeasts create alcohol, again in lesser amounts, which help to stabilize the microbial system and exclude unwanted microbes. They also produce aromatic compounds, such as acetates, phenols, and aldehydes, giving miso its final layer of complexity.

Ultimately, the different proportions of ingredients used, koji type, liquid content, fermentation vessel, and ambient ecology all contribute to the concentrations of the various microbes that proliferate in the miso.

Artisanal producers rely on "backslopping", using a small quantity of a previous batch of miso to inoculate the subsequent batch with the desired yeasts and *Lactobacillus*. The unique microbial profile of the wooden kioke barrels (see p130) used also contributes. In a commercial setting, reliable lab-grown cultures of *Lactobacillus* and yeasts will be used to ensure the desired consistency.

Amino pastes

The term "amino paste" refers to any miso-like product that is made using similar methods to traditional misos, but with different ingredients. The name refers to the high content of umami-producing amino acids in the paste. Many fermenters use the terms miso and amino (or tasty/umami) paste interchangeably, but the distinction is generally made when the ingredients are non-traditional.

Key miso varieties

There is a huge variance in miso types across Japan. The three main types are rice-based misos all over the country, soya-bean-based misos in the central area where Kansai and Chubu meet, and barley-based misos in Kyushu.

SOYA BEANS + KOJI + SALT

SHIRO IS PALE, SWEET, AND QUICK TO FERMENT. HIGH IN RICE CONTENT, IT HAS A DELICATE, MELLOW PROFILE.

MUGI IS MADE WITH BARLEY. CHUNKY AND AROMATIC, ITS LONG FERMENT YIELDS EARTHY NOTES AND RUSTIC CHARM.

HATCHO IS DENSE AND DARK. FERMENTED WITH ONLY SOYA BEANS FOR YEARS, IT IS COMPLEX AND UMAMI-RICH.

WHITE (SHIRO) MISO — Rice koji, Soya beans, Salt

BARLEY (MUGI) MISO — Barley koji, Soya beans, Salt

HATCHO MISO — Soya beans, Salt

MAKE YOUR OWN
WHITE SOYA BEAN MISO

This white miso is made using a fast-fermenting method, which will only take six weeks to finish, resulting in a sweet, rich, umami miso. It's worth taking a bit of extra time to ensure that everything is correct before you start, otherwise many potential pitfalls will only be identified beyond the point at which they can be rectified. Measure twice, ferment once! That being said, even when things go wrong something usable can be recovered. To scale the recipe up or down, use a ratio of 1:1 cooked soya beans to koji, with 8% salt.

EQUIPMENT
- large bowl
- sieve
- large jar

INGREDIENTS
- 100g dried soya beans (200g cooked weight)
- 200g rice koji (or 140g dried koji + 60ml water)
- 32g salt, plus extra for salting and topping

Moulds
A. oryzae

Yeasts
Z. rouxii

LAB
T. halophilus

6 WEEKS

② **Combine the beans, koji, and salt** and mash into a paste. Add a little reserved liquid if the paste is dry.

① **Wash and then soak** the soya beans overnight. Strain, and then simmer in fresh water for 3–4 hours. Once the beans are soft, strain, reserve the liquid, and allow to cool.

③ **Lightly salt** an empty sanitized jar and pack it tightly with the paste.

DIRECTORY OF FERMENTS • Moulds and more 129

⬡5 **Scrape off the salt topping** (this can be used as umami salt), and taste to check you are happy with the flavour. Miso can be stored for years. If stored in the fridge, it will hold the flavour it had when it finished fermenting. If stored ambiently, it will continue to change and develop.

Troubleshooting

• If the miso has been exposed to extreme temperature fluctuations, the yeasts in the system can become stressed and produce an unpleasant acetone aroma. Removing the paste from the fermentation vessel, aerating it to dissipate these volatile compounds, and keeping it in the fridge can solve the problem. The same technique can be used if the miso becomes overly alcoholic in flavour.

• If the miso starts to dry out, not enough liquid was present at the start of the process. It's still completely usable, although fermentation will have likely halted so the flavour will no longer develop. Next time, try adding a little more of the reserved cooking liquid to the paste, and proportionately more salt so the ratios remain the same.

• Slimy miso can be a problem and is generally caused by a *Bacillus subtilis* (nattō; see p142) infection. While still edible, it isn't pleasant, so discard and compost.

• Unknown moulds can be deleterious and without expert advice it is hard to identify them. If you are unsure, discard the project and compost.

⬡4 **Generously salt the top of the paste,** then seal the container and leave in the dark at room temperature to ferment for 6 weeks. The colour should start to darken after 4 weeks.

MISO IN FOCUS

It is likely that miso's ancient progenitor paste, jiang, came to Japan from multiple locations in China and Korea between c. 555 and c. 700 CE, coinciding with the arrival and spread of Buddhism in these regions.

The ancient precursor to miso is *jiang*, a preserving paste made to store surplus game, meat, or seafood. As soya farming became widespread, soya beans were more commonly used, and regions began to specialize in their own pastes. Miso, doubanjiang (see p134), and gochujang (see p136) all share this common heritage.

Etymologically, miso has Chinese roots. The Chinese character for *jiang* (the ancestor to miso) arrived in Japan around 700 CE and was pronounced "*hishio*". Over time this pronunciation developed into "*misho*", eventually settling into the contemporary character and pronunciation we have today – miso.

The technique that is now commonly used in hatcho miso production, miso-dama, was most likely introduced from Korea. Whereas the more commonly used direct inoculation method most likely came from China.

Interestingly, a fermented paste that didn't go on to evolve into miso did exist in Japan, prior to the introduction of more technologically involved processes from China and Korea. These will have been miso-like pastes, which utilized animal products, sea salt, and spices, without the use of pure culture inoculation, which would have resembled the early forms of *jiang* found in China. Some very specific forms of this parallel still exist today, such as *shiokara*, a strongly flavoured seafood paste made with different ingredients and by various methods, depending on the animal product used. *Shottsuru* is a fish sauce made in a similar method to Southeast Asian fish sauces or ancient Roman garum (see p14 and p146).

Kioke barrels

The kioke is the traditional barrel used to age miso. For some artisanal miso producers the character of the kioke is as important as the ingredients. They are constructed using Japanese cedar wood and bound with pleated bamboo.

Miso-dama

Miso-dama is a method of growing koji for miso where soya beans are cooked and mashed, formed into balls, then inoculated with koji spores. These are then mixed with salt and water and packed into kioke. This method is most commonly used in the production of hatcho miso.

HATCHO MISO (PURE SOYA BEAN MISO)
Historic miso from Aichi. Pure soya beans, aged over two years. Intensely savoury and low in sweetness.

SHIRO MISO (WHITE MISO)
Light, sweet Kyoto-style miso. High rice content, and short fermentation of weeks to a few months.

AWASE MISO (MIXED MISO)
A blend of red and white misos. Balanced flavour, for general use.

MUGI MISO (BARLEY MISO)
Rustic miso from Kyushu/Shikoku. Made with barley and soya beans, and aged for 1–2 years. Rich and earthy.

SHINSHU MISO (YELLOW MISO)
Pale yellow miso from Nagano. Soya beans and rice, medium salt, fermented for several months to a year.

AKA MISO (RED MISO)
Dark red miso from central Japan. Long-fermented soya bean base, with deep umami and saltiness.

TSUKEMONO

Tsukemono, or Japanese pickled vegetables, are a core element of Japanese cuisine, from the traditional to the modern, and showcase a variety of preservation methods that illustrate the diverse culinary practices of the country.

ASAZUKE
AND AMAZUZUKE RELY ON SALT OR ACID WITHOUT ACTIVE FERMENTATION.

MISOZUKE
AND NUKAZUKE INVOLVE MICROBIAL FERMENTATION THAT TRANSFORMS FLAVOUR AND TEXTURE.

In Japan, nearly all meals include *tsukemono* – they are a fundamental part of the dining experience, not only as a palate cleanser with a delightful crunch, but also as an aid to digestion. *Tsukemono*, which translates as "pickled things", is the catch-all term for the pickles of Japan and encompasses countless preservation traditions. As in many cultures, preserving foods via salt, acid, and mould was once a means of survival in Japan. Today, *tsukemono* are ubiquitous, seen everywhere from convenience-store *onigiri* rice balls and train-station bento boxes, to high-end *omakase* restaurants, with applications increasing globally as chefs and home fermenters connect the dots between traditional processes and new ingredients.

TSUKEMONO VARIETIES

Conveniently, most *tsukemono* types are named after their preservation medium. And the beauty of all varieties, from the simple to the more involved, is that the preservation method can work with a wide array of vegetables, reflecting Japanese cuisine's focus on seasonality.

Asazuke and *amazuzuke* These are some of the simplest (and entry-level) varieties. *Asazuke* are lightly pickled in salt, and *amazuzuke* in sweet vinegar. These are relatively quick pickles, either with brine occurring naturally due to the addition of salt (in the former) or adding an acidic brine (in the latter) for short- to medium-term preservation.

MISOZUKE

SAKURAZUKE (PINK RADISH)

TAKUAN (DAIKON RADISH)

Preservation beds

Nuka-doko beds are living substrates where bacteria and yeasts thrive in rice bran. When stirred daily, they can remain active for decades, preserving vegetables through safe, acidic fermentation.

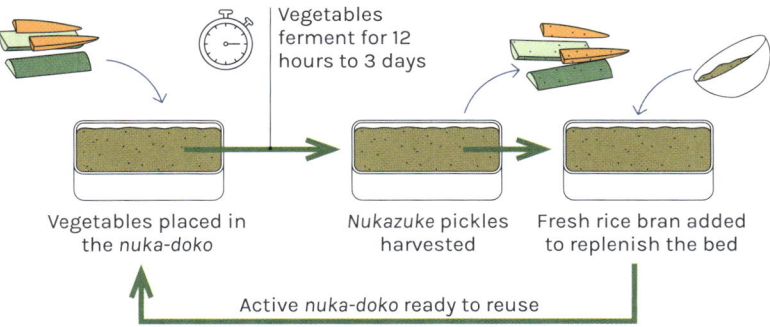

Doko **preservation beds** For other *tsukemono* varieties, vegetables are submerged in a preservation bed (called *doko*), which both imparts flavour and provides a microbially safe environment for preservation due to its salt content. These beds use different ingredients to preserve the vegetables. *Nukazuke*, for example, are vegetables pickled in a *nuka-doko* – a bed of fermented rice bran (*nuka* is a byproduct of rice production), while *misozuke* are vegetables pickled in a bed of miso (see right).

KYURIZUKE (CUCUMBER)   **TAKANA (MUSTARD LEAVES)**

MAKE YOUR OWN MISOZUKE

Adapt the miso and aromatics in this recipe to suit your taste. Any variety of miso can work, with darker types imparting a saltier flavour and lighter varieties a sweeter flavour. Any combination of the aromatics listed will work, too.

EQUIPMENT large mixing bowl • food-safe or glass container with lid
INGREDIENTS Aromatics thumb-sized piece of kombu (cut into thin strips) • 8 garlic cloves (10g, left whole) • 10–15g ginger, grated • 1 dried red chilli pepper (whole) • a few pieces of lemon peel
Vegetables 150g miso (see p126) • 15ml mirin • around 100–200g vegetables of your choice, e.g. radishes (halved); carrots (cut into batons); daikon radishes (sliced); cucumber (cut into batons)

LAB *L. plantarum*, *T. halophilus*, *Pediococcus* spp.   **1–2 WEEKS**

1. **First, make the *miso-doko* preservation bed.** Mix the miso, mirin, and aromatics in a large bowl until fully combined.

2. **Transfer the mixture** to the lidded container, then add the vegetable pieces (all cut to a similar size), ensuring they are fully submerged.

3. **Seal the container and leave to pickle.** Depending on the vegetables, the time can vary from a few hours to a few days (e.g. 1–2 days for cucumbers or radishes; 1–2 weeks for whole carrots). Temperature can also vary: the container can be left in the fridge, or at room temperature; if the latter, the process will accelerate, but more attention may be needed to avoid potential spoilage. Taste the pickles at intervals until they have a flavour you like.

4. **When the vegetables are pickled to your liking,** wipe off any excess *miso-doko* with kitchen paper (if you want; this will be salty but can be nice to eat depending on your taste) and enjoy.

Troubleshooting

- The preservation bed can be reused multiple times without a problem. However, if it begins to smell yeasty, taste sour, or grow mould, it has likely spoiled and should be discarded.

DOUBANJIANG

Doubanjiang is a sauce made from fermented bean paste that originates from China. The most popular and well-known version of doubanjiang is the spicy Sichuanese version that is made using split broad beans and chillies.

This Chinese paste is similar to miso (see p126), but the mould is grown directly on the bean. There are versions of thick bean sauce in the north of China that are yellowish in colour, featuring soya beans, and another in the south that is thick, sweetened, and dark brown. There are many regional variations that may contain fermented wheat flour, soya beans, broad beans, and even watermelon.

Sichuan-style doubanjiang has a strong spiciness, balanced by nutty umami from the broad beans. The classic dish associated with it is mapo tofu (tofu simmered with minced beef, doubanjiang, and Sichuan peppercorns) – a marriage of flavours central to Sichuanese cuisine. Southern- and northern-style doubanjiangs are sweeter or saltier but still deeply umami: an ideal base for sauces or marinades.

MAKING DOUBANJIANG

The most famous variety of doubanjiang is made in Pixian, Sichuan's sauce capital, and is fermented in sunlight over a minimum of two years. The pots of fermenting sauce are opened and stirred daily, then smoothed carefully and covered when it rains. The makers believe that a combination of humidity, sunshine, time, and agitation results in the perfect paste.

CHILLIES ARRIVED IN CHINA IN THE SIXTEENTH CENTURY, GIVING SICHUAN DOUBANJIANG ITS SIGNATURE HEAT.

PROTEIN-RICH BROAD BEANS ARE BROKEN DOWN BY PROTEASE TO FORM A COMPLEX, UMAMI PASTE.

ERJINGTIAO CHILLI

BROAD BEANS

FRESH RED CHILLIES

DIRECTORY OF FERMENTS • Moulds and more 135

MAKE YOUR OWN

While you may not be able to reproduce the specific conditions of Pixian, you can make your own version of doubanjiang paste at home using a ready-made starter.

EQUIPMENT mixing bowls • large saucepan • baking tray • tea towel • 2 × 2-litre jars with lids • fermentation weights • blender • baking parchment

INGREDIENTS 250g dried broad beans, peeled • 20g rice flour • 1g koji starter (or follow guide per kilo in the manufacturer's instructions) • 150g salt (100g for brine; 25g for chillies; 25g for blending) • 500g fresh red chillies

 **Moulds** *A. oryzae*   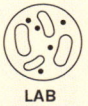 **LAB** *L. plantarum, T. halophilus*   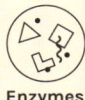 **Enzymes** Protease    **Yeasts** *Z. rouxii*   **9–11 WEEKS**

1. **Soak the broad beans** in a bowl overnight (they should double in weight, to approximately 500g). Boil in a large saucepan for 3 minutes, then drain and leave to cool.

2. **Preheat the oven** to 180°C (350°F/Gas 4). Spread the rice flour on a baking tray and cook for 5 minutes, then cool.

3. **Mix the koji starter and cooked rice flour,** then massage into the beans, covering them evenly. Cover the bowl with a clean, wet tea towel and leave at 30–36°C (86–97°F), out of direct sunlight, on a rack so air can circulate underneath. In 2–3 days the beans will start to grow mould. When it turns yellow remove the cloth and place the bowl in direct sunlight to dry the beans for 24 hours.

4. **Wash the beans** gently under the tap and drain, then place in a large jar. Mix 100g of the salt with 1 litre of water to make a 10% brine, then pour into the jar until the beans are just covered. Seal with the lid and leave at room temperature to ferment for 3 weeks. Burp the jar and stir the beans weekly.

5. **Meanwhile, wash the chillies,** trim off stems, and cut in half. While still damp, toss in a bowl with 25g salt until well covered. Place in a jar and press down firmly with weights, then seal and ferment at room temperature for 3 weeks. Check every other day to burp the jar.

6. **After 3 weeks, drain the beans,** reserving the brine. Then blend the chillies with the beans, using some brine if needed to create a thick paste.

7. **Mix 25g salt into the paste,** then return the paste to a jar. Place a piece of parchment paper on the surface to protect the paste from oxidation, then seal and ferment at room temperature for a further 6–8 weeks.

8. **Check the paper** every week or two and replace if necessary. Spray the paper's surface and sides of the jar with vodka or another neutral spirit to keep them clean. Put the jar in the sun occasionally to deepen the sauce's colour but remember to bring it in again so it doesn't dry out. Store the finished paste in the fridge; it will keep for as long the top of the jar remains clean. Transfer to smaller jars as you use the sauce to minimize air exposure.

Troubleshooting

- When growing koji, keep an eye on the beans. If they get too hot, they will suffer, so break them up and spread them in a thin layer. If too cold, they will take longer to mould, so pile them up and cover with cloth.

Regional styles

Doubanjiang is part of a family of regional bean pastes spanning Sichuan and beyond. The different styles reflect local tastes and ingredients.

 **Classic** Broad bean and chilli paste, aged in sunlight for years.

 **Tianmianjiang** Sweet paste made from wheat flour with soya beans and salt.

 **Huang jiang** Milder, yellowish soya bean pastes, with less heat, more umami.

DOUBANJIANG

RICE PORRIDGE   RICE SYRUP   MEJU POWDER   RED CHILLI POWDER

GOCHUJANG

One of the yardsticks of Korean gastronomy, gochujang embodies the intricate balance of flavours – sweet, salty, spicy, and umami – that define the cuisine. This iconic fermented chilli paste has wooed chefs, cooks, and food enthusiasts the world over with its vibrant flavours.

Like achaar in India, miso in Japan, and tahini in the Middle East, gochujang runs through the veins of Korean culture. The magic of gochujang starts with a few simple ingredients: rice (or rice flour), chilli peppers (*gochu*), fermented soya beans (*meju*), rice syrup, barley malt powder, salt, and water. A thick, glutinous rice porridge fuels the microorganisms and gives the paste (*jang*) body, with the chillies adding heat and colour, and *meju* pumping the mix full of microbes that will transform a dull and flavourless paste into something exquisite over the course of 6 to 12 months, or longer.

MAKING GOCHUJANG

The typical ingredients to make gochujang are used in specific proportions (see chart opposite). A thick porridge is made first with the rice and

Stages of fermentation

Once the chilli powder, glutinous rice, malt, salt, and water have been combined, the mixture is aged to develop rich umami flavours. During this time, natural fermentation enhances the complexity of the sauce, influenced by sunlight and seasonal temperatures. The paste gradually thickens and deepens in flavour, until ready to eat.

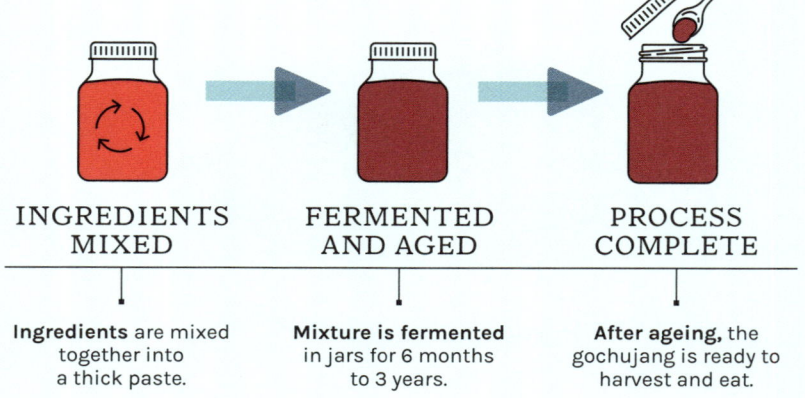

INGREDIENTS MIXED — Ingredients are mixed together into a thick paste.

FERMENTED AND AGED — Mixture is fermented in jars for 6 months to 3 years.

PROCESS COMPLETE — After ageing, the gochujang is ready to harvest and eat.

DIRECTORY OF FERMENTS • Moulds and more

INGREDIENTS PROPORTIONS

Red chilli powder, rice, and water dominate in the ratios of ingredients in a traditional gochujang recipe, but each ingredient is essential to the process.

KEY
- 14% red chilli powder
- 9.5% glutinous rice or rice flour
- 5% meju powder
- 7.5% salt
- 7.5% barley malt powder
- 9.5% rice syrup
- 47% water

water, and the rest of the ingredients are then mixed in, after which the paste is packed into *onggi* – traditional earthenware crocks used for all types of fermentation. During the fermentation process, bacteria including *Bacillaceae* (*Firmicutes*), followed by yeasts (*Candida* and *Zygosaccharomyces*) and fungi (*Aspergillus* and *Rhizopus*), break down the ingredients to produce the rich, spicy flavour gochujang is known for. The first mouthful of the sticky paste coats your palate in a warm rush of chilli heat while tickling your taste buds with a honeyed sweetness just as the umami kicks in.

From Korean fried chicken, soups, stews, and marinades, to dips and even drinks (such as a gochujang Bloody Mary), gochujang can be used in place of chillies in many recipes to give an extra dimension of flavour.

CAPSAICIN IN CHILLIES HELPS BOOST METABOLISM AND REDUCE INFLAMMATION.

GOCHUJANG IS A NUTRIENT-RICH INGREDIENT THAT CONTAINS VITAMIN C, IRON, AND PROBIOTICS.

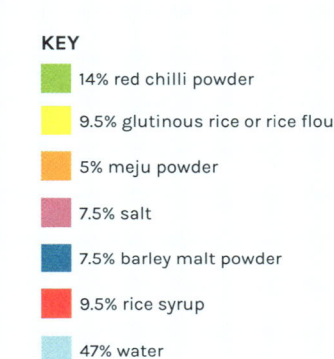

GOCHUJANG PASTE

HISTORICAL TIMELINE OF GOCHUJANG

57 BCE
EARLY REFERENCES
Gochujang has roots dating back to the Three Kingdoms period (57 BCE–668 CE). Early forms of fermented condiments likely evolved during this era.

1800s
JOSEON DYNASTY
The first written record of gochujang appears in the nineteenth-century cookbook *Siuijonso*, highlighting its firmly rooted role in Korean cuisine.

1900s
MODERN EVOLUTION
Industrialization and advancements in food processing lead to the commercial production of gochujang, making it more accessible.

2000s
GLOBAL POPULARITY
The rise of the Korean Wave (*Hallyu*) in the early 2000s boosts global interest in Korean culture, including gochujang. In the 2010s, Korean fried chicken and other dishes featuring gochujang gain popularity internationally, with gochujang becoming a staple in cross-cultural cuisine.

2025
PRESENT DAY
Gochujang is celebrated worldwide for its rich flavours and versatility, influencing culinary trends across various cultures.

MAKE YOUR OWN
GOCHUJANG

Making gochujang at home can be a rewarding process but requires patience as the traditional method, explained below, takes six months. The longer you leave it to ferment, the deeper the flavour will become. You can also play around with the sweetness by adjusting the rice or honey used.

EQUIPMENT
- mixing bowls
- muslin cloth
- 2-litre jar or crock pot
- tea towel
- cling film or baking parchment

INGREDIENTS (makes approx. 1kg gochujang)
- 75g malt barley flour
- 95g glutinous rice flour (or rice)
- 50g fermented soya bean powder (*meju*)
- 140g Korean red chilli powder (*gochugaru*)
- 75g sea salt
- 95g malt or rice syrup

Moulds — *A. oryzae* | Bacteria — *B. subtilis, B. licheniformis* | Yeasts — *Z. rouxii* | **6–12 MONTHS**

MEJU (FERMENTED SOYA BEAN POWDER) CAN BE SUBSTITUTED WITH THE SAME QUANTITY OF KOJI RICE.

EXPERIMENT WITH DIFFERENT CHILLI VARIETIES UNTIL YOU FIND YOUR FAVOURITE.

14% CHILLIES

GOCHUGARU ADDS HEAT AND COLOUR

① **Mix the malt barley flour** with 470ml of water and leave for about 6 hours, allowing the malt to dissolve. Strain the liquid through a muslin cloth to remove the solids.

② **In a large saucepan**, combine the rice flour with the strained barley water and cook over a medium heat, stirring constantly until it thickens to a porridge consistency. Transfer to a bowl and let it cool completely.

DIRECTORY OF FERMENTS • **Moulds and more** 139

⬡5⬡ **Once filled, sprinkle a layer of salt** on the surface and lay a piece of cling film or parchment flat on the surface, making sure there are no creases or air pockets. Sprinkle salt on top of the cling film or baking parchment for added safety against unwanted microbes.

⬡6⬡ **Seal and leave the jar in a warm spot** where the temperature remains consistent, for at least 6 months, but the longer the better.

Troubleshooting

• Be sure to open your gochujang every few months to check that no mould is growing on the top. If this happens, simply scrape it off and add a fresh layer of salt.

⬡3⬡ **Mix the porridge** with the fermented soya bean powder, red chilli powder, salt, and syrup, then stir the mixture until well combined. It should be a thick, glossy paste.

⬡4⬡ **Transfer the paste** to a sanitized 2-litre jar or crock pot. Add the mixture one spoon at a time and spread it evenly, then tap the jar gently on a rolled-up tea towel to eliminate any bubbles and make sure the paste settles.

TEMPEH

Tempeh is a mould-based soya bean ferment originating from Java, Indonesia. It has a deep, nutty flavour and is produced in solid blocks or cakes with a firm texture.

The driver in the tempeh-making process is a fungus family called *Rhizopus*, most commonly *R. oligosporus* and *R. oryzae*. Although there is some debate as to the precise origin of the process, it is likely to have been discovered when cooked soya beans were stored in *waru* (*Hibiscus tiliaceus*) leaves. These leaves have trichomes – little filaments or hairs – on their underside, which foster a dominant population of *R. oligosporus*. In this way, the leaves themselves provided the initial inoculation to kick-start the fermentation process.

After the soya beans have been cooked and inoculated, the *Rhizopus* spores begin to germinate in warm, humid conditions. They shoot out roots called hyphae, which form a mycelial mat. This mass of interwoven hyphae penetrates the beans and forms a dense mesh in the spaces between them, binding them together into solid blocks of tempeh.

In order for the *Rhizopus* to grow it feeds on the beans by emitting enzymes that break down larger molecules into smaller ones so they can be absorbed into the mycelia and provide energy to the fungus.

FERMENTATION
INCREASES THE VITAMIN CONTENT, SWEETNESS, AND UMAMI TASTE OF TEMPEH.

ENZYMES
PRE-DIGEST THE BEANS, BREAKING DOWN PROTEINS INTO AMINO ACIDS, ADDING UMAMI TASTE.

SOYA BEANS
PROVIDE THE SUBSTRATE FOR THE RHIZOPUS TO FEED ON.

SOYA BEANS

Tempeh production

Tempeh is made with only a few ingredients – soya beans, vinegar, and spores – creating a flavoursome plant-based food staple.

SOAK
The soya beans are soaked and drained, then vinegar is added.

COOK
The beans are boiled for around 45 minutes.

INOCULATE
Spores are dusted over the beans and they are incubated.

DIRECTORY OF FERMENTS • Moulds and more 141

Mould growth

Once the beans are cooked and inoculated, they provide the ideal environment for the *Rhizopus* mould to grow.

MOULD STRUCTURE

Branching hyphae grow rapidly, releasing spores

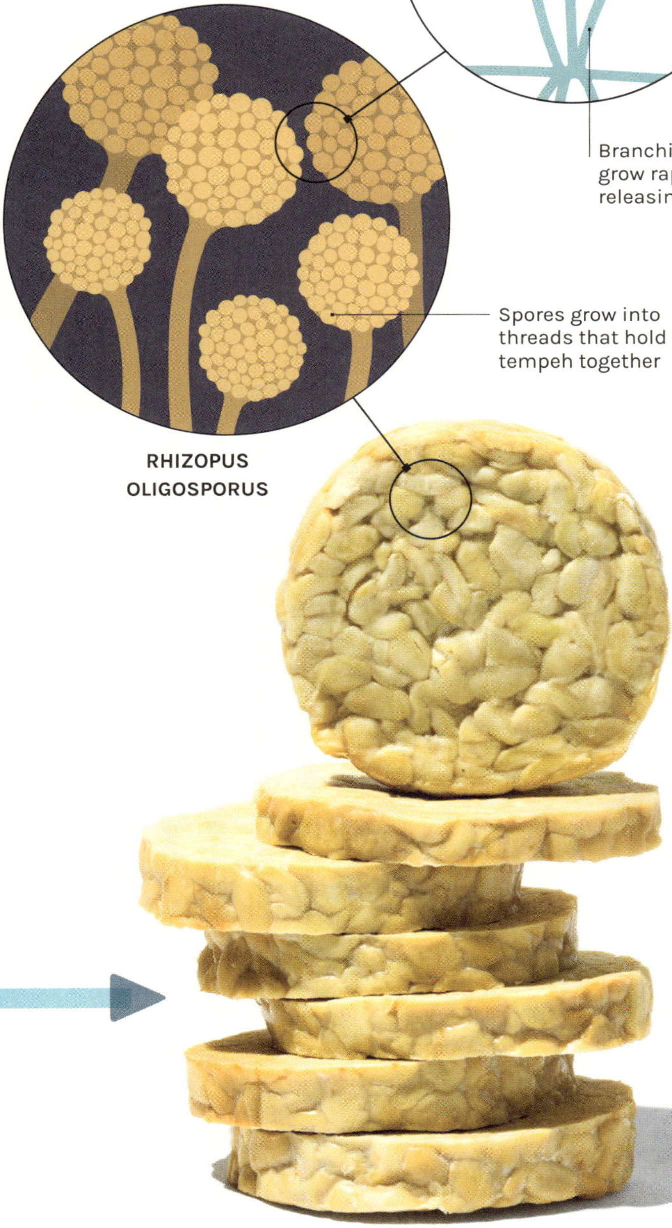

Spores grow into threads that hold the tempeh together

RHIZOPUS OLIGOSPORUS

TEMPEH

MAKE YOUR OWN

If you don't have an incubator, a dehydrator, bread proofer, or an insulated box with a small heat mat will do. You can buy tempeh spore starters online or from speciality Asian supermarkets.

EQUIPMENT incubator (see p55) • zip-lock bag • toothpick • thermometer
INGREDIENTS 500g dry soya beans • 10ml vinegar • 1g tempeh spores

Moulds *R. oryzae, R. oligosporus*

Enzymes Protease, amylase, lipase

24–36 HOURS

1. **Rinse then cover** the beans with 1 litre of water, then add the vinegar and leave overnight.

2. **Strain the beans** and refresh the water. Rub the beans to crack them and remove the shells.

3. **Strain and refresh** the water again. Boil the beans for 45 minutes or until cooked but still firm. Empty onto a tray and blot with a paper towel.

4. **Inoculate with the spores** by carefully and evenly dusting over the surface, then mix.

5. **Place in a zip-lock bag;** it should be 3-4cm in depth when laid flat. Seal, then poke holes at 2cm intervals across the surface with a toothpick.

6. **Incubate at 30°C (86°F)** until the tempeh is producing its own heat. This will normally be after 18-24 hours. After that, keep the tempeh cool. At all times the internal temperature should stay between 28-32°C (82-90°F).

7. **The tempeh will be finished** after a further 6-12 hours, when it has formed a firm cake knitted together with white mycelia. Store in the fridge for up to a month, or in the freezer for up to a year.

Troubleshooting

• If black mould forms, the tempeh has over-fermented. It is still edible, though more pungent.

• If the tempeh is slimy, it is likely a *Bacillus subtilis* infection due to unsanitized equipment, incorrect inoculation rate, or overheating. Compost and restart.

• Smells of ammonia or rot mean the beans are decomposing due to overheating or not enough spores. Compost and start afresh.

NATTŌ

Nattō is a traditional Japanese "superfood" made of fermented soya beans. During fermentation, the beans develop a slimy texture with a slight ammonia and umami flavour. This makes it a challenging food for Western palates, but in Japan it is a breakfast staple.

NEBA NEBA IS THE JAPANESE TERM DESCRIBING SLIMY FOODS LIKE NATTŌ AND OKRA.

NATTŌ

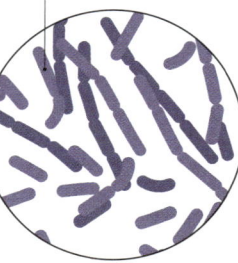

B. subtilis produces spores

BACILLUS SUBTILIS BIOFILM

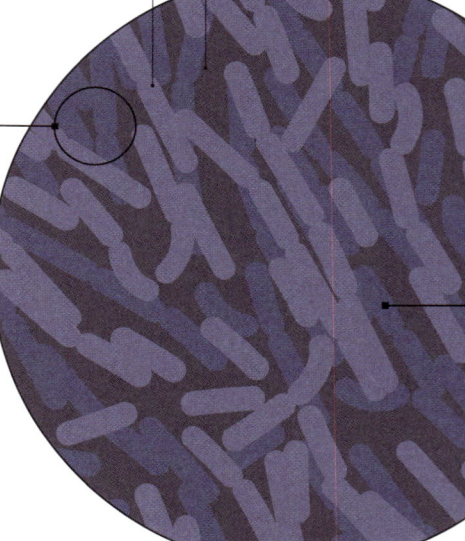

An intricate matrix of cells form the biofilm

Rod-shaped bacterial cells knit together

BIOFILM STRUCTURE

NUTRIENTS IN SOYA BEANS ARE SIGNIFICANTLY MORE BIOAVAILABLE ONCE FERMENTED INTO NATTŌ, AND ANTINUTRIENTS ARE REDUCED.

Bacterial biofilm

The slimy biofilm that holds nattō together serves as a bacterial transport system, allowing microbes to spread and share materials.

Nattō sits as a bit of an outlier in the fermentation world. Though it shares ingredients and flavour profiles with some mould-based ferments, the driver of fermentation here is *Bacillus subtilis* – a spore-forming, alkaline-loving, biofilm-producing bacteria – usually considered a contaminant. However, in the right conditions, it can be used to create delicious, healthy food, breaking down proteins into ammonia and amino acids, generating deep savoury flavours.

During fermentation, the alkaline formation process breaks down proteins in the beans, making them more bioavailable. The *B. subtilis* bacteria create a biofilm, a suspension of densely packed nutrients, which gives the finished ferment its sticky, slimy texture. Fermentation increases the levels of nutrients in the beans, including vitamins K1 and K2, potassium, copper, iron, and calcium. The most unique health-giving quality, however, belongs to nattō's namesake, the enzyme nattokinase, which can break down blood clots.

It's likely that nattō was first discovered by accident, while cooked soya beans were stored in rice straw. The practice of making nattō became standardized in Japan during the Heian period (794–1185), with households making their own, as an easy way to maximize the nutrition from an affordable protein source.

RESILIENT
B. SUBTILIS CAN SURVIVE EXTREMES OF HEAT, COLD, WET, DRY, AND EVEN THE VACUUM OF SPACE.

Variations

There are many other fermented legume foods that utilize *B. subtilis*. These are generally wild ferments, when the bacteria is found ambiently, such as *kinema* (from Nepal and the Himalayan regions) and Korean *cheonggukjang* – both made with soya beans – and *dawadawa* (from West Africa), which is made with African locust bean seeds. You can apply the method described here to other pulses, which will result in different textures and flavours.

MAKE YOUR OWN

Nattō is a cultured ferment, so it requires a starter. Dried packets of nattō starter, similar to yeast, are widely available. If scaling the amount up or down, use a ratio of 1:500 spores to cooked beans.

EQUIPMENT tray (at least 4cm deep) • thermometer • cling film/tin foil • toothpick • incubator (see p55)
INGREDIENTS 500g soya beans • 1g nattō spores

 Bacteria *B. subtilis*  **Enzymes** Nattokinase, protease, cellulase   **1–2 DAYS**

1. **Soak the soya beans overnight,** then boil for around 2 hours, or pressure cook for about 45 minutes until soft. Drain the cooked beans and transfer to your tray.

2. **While the beans are hot,** around 80°C (176°F), inoculate with the nattō spores and mix well.

3. **Spread the inoculated beans** in an even, 4cm-thick layer in the tray. Cover with cling film or tin foil, then make holes across the surface, roughly 3cm apart, with a toothpick. Incubate at 30°C (86°F) for 20 hours.

4. **After 20 hours,** the nattō is ready to eat. Transfer to a sealed container and store in the fridge for up to 4 weeks. The flavour develops in the first week. Fresh nattō will keep in the freezer for 6 months.

Troubleshooting

• If the beans aren't slimy after the fermentation period there has likely been poor or no microbial growth. Ensure your equipment is properly sanitized and enough inoculant is used.

• Precise temperature and timing isn't completely essential – a little variance around 30°C (86°F) and the 20-hour duration shouldn't be a problem.

• If an intense ammonia aroma and flavour is created (which some people prefer), fermentation went on for too long or took place at too high a temperature.

• A white crust can form on the top of the nattō if conditions in the tray are too dry. This isn't harmful, but can alter the texture and flavour. Avoid this by making fewer holes in the cling film or foil covering, to improve the seal and allow less moisture to escape.

FERMENTED TOFU

Tofu, which originates from China, is a plant-based, protein-rich food that has become a staple around the world. It is relatively easy to make, healthy, and, when fermented, has an umami flavour and creamy texture that make it highly versatile.

Fresh tofu is made by soaking, pressing, boiling, and coagulating juice from ground soya beans, and can either then be refrigerated, frozen, dried, smoked, or preserved through fermentation.

There are two main types of fermented tofu. *Doufuru* (or *furu*) is mould-based and varies by region depending on the starter and seasoning. Mould enzymes break down the texture of the tofu and, combined with salt, rice wine, and spices, it becomes a creamy, richly flavoured condiment, similar to cheese.

Chou doufu is fermented in a brine of soya beans, rotten bamboo shoots, fermented meat or shrimp, or amaranth leaves or stems, then aged to develop its flavours. Often eaten deep-fried as street food, it is pungent, thanks to its vegetable-based alkaline brine – hence its nickname "stinky tofu".

Wild fermentation is still widely practised in East Asia, especially for mould-based ferments. Wild ferments like *mao doufu* ("hairy tofu"), which has the *Mucor* mycelium growing on the surface, are likely to include many hundreds of different microbes, and the right environment encourages *Mucor*, *Aspergillus*, and *Rhizopus* growth, which helps in secondary fermentation.

FRESH TOFU IS PROTEIN RICH AND VERSATILE, TAKING ON THE FLAVOURS OF WHATEVER YOU COOK IT WITH.

FRESH TOFU

SOUTHERN STYLE (NANRU)

From Fujian province and very popular with the Hakka people. Using red yeast rice and a brine of rice alcohol and salt, this version is bright red and has a sweet, umami flavour.

TAIWANESE STYLE (FURU)

Salt-cured tofu chunks are fermented in a rice alcohol brine with koji beans and koji rice. The koji lends sweet flavours, a beautiful texture, and a caramel-brown colour.

DIRECTORY OF FERMENTS • Moulds and more 145

Koji fermentation

Fermented tofu today can be made using lab-conditioned koji instead of wild fermentation. The benefit of this method is its predictability, resulting in reliable taste and flavour.

A furry coating of *Actinomucor elegans* mould forms on the surface of the tofu.

The furry tofu is submerged in an alcohol and salt brine with grains of rice koji.

As the tofu ages, its texture softens and its colour and flavour deepens.

FERMENTED TOFU CAN BE STORED IN ITS SALTY BRINE FOR MONTHS, OR EVEN YEARS.

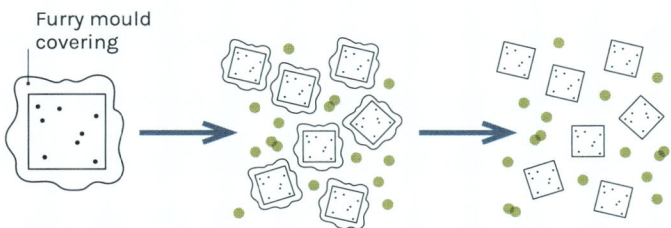

SICHUAN STYLE (MAO DOUFU)

The furry moulded tofu is fermented dry after being dipped in rice alcohol, salt, and spices. This contains the classic flavours of Sichuanese cuisine: flower pepper and chillies.

CANTONESE STYLE (FUYU)

The most minimalist style. Mould (*Actinomucor elegans*) is typically grown directly onto the surface, then the fuzzy tofu is fermented in a brine of rice alcohol (20%) and salt.

MAKE YOUR OWN
CANTONESE-STYLE FERMENTED TOFU

You can buy *Mucor* starter culture online to make this tofu. Alternatively, you can substitute the *Mucor* starter with 1g of koji starter and mix it with 20g pre-cooked rice flour instead of water.

EQUIPMENT mixing bowls • steamer • large container or jar with lid
INGREDIENTS 280g firm tofu • 1 tsp *Mucor* powder • 500ml 20% ABV alcohol (traditionally rice wine) • 40g salt

 Moulds A. elegans, M. racemosus, M. purpureus, A. oryzae

 Enzymes Protease, amylase, lipase

5–8 WEEKS

1. **Cut the tofu** into bite-size pieces, cook for a couple of minutes in boiling water, then drain and leave to dry.

2. **Mix the *Mucor* powder** and 80ml of cooled, boiled water in a bowl, stirring to remove lumps.

3. **Dip the tofu pieces** into the starter and water mixture, making sure they are fully coated.

4. **Place the tofu in the steamer**, leaving space between each piece. Cover, and leave in a well-ventilated, warm place, 27–30°C (81–86°F), for 3 days until the tofu is covered with a thick fuzz of mould. You can remove the lid during this time to check on the progress of the growth.

5. **Dip each piece of furry tofu in the alcohol**, then stack them in the container or jar.

6. **Mix the alcohol and salt** (8%) until dissolved to make a brine, then add to the jar to cover the tofu. Seal tightly, and leave to ferment for 5–8 weeks at room temperature. Invert the jar every couple of days at the beginning of the process to make sure all the tofu is well covered. Check weekly, and burp the jar to release any built-up gas. Refrigerate after fermentation and store in the brine for up to 2 years. You can eat it straight from the jar or use it as a condiment or seasoning for meat and vegetables.

Troubleshooting

• The texture will continue to get softer after fermentation, and eventually it will turn into a paste. This is nothing to worry about; it's still delicious.

GARUM

Originating in ancient Greece, garum – fish sauce – is, for cooks and chefs, liquid gold. Traditionally an enzymatic ferment made only with fish, modern recipes often use koji to drive the fermentation process.

Garum was first developed by the ancient Phoenicians around 2,500 years ago as a byproduct of fish preservation. The resultant liquid was used as a seasoning at a time when spices were a rare and expensive commodity. The Greeks called this sauce *garos* and the Romans adopted this as garum.

This ancient condiment, rich in umami and amino acids, is a fundamental element of Southeast Asian cuisines. In Vietnam, fish sauce, or *nuoc-mam*, is typically made from anchovies, with a clear, reddish-brown colour and a bright, slightly sweet taste. Thai fish sauce, known as *nam pla*, often uses different types of fish and is a darker-hued sauce with a punchier aroma. In the Philippines, fish sauce, or *patis*, is usually lighter in colour and milder in flavour.

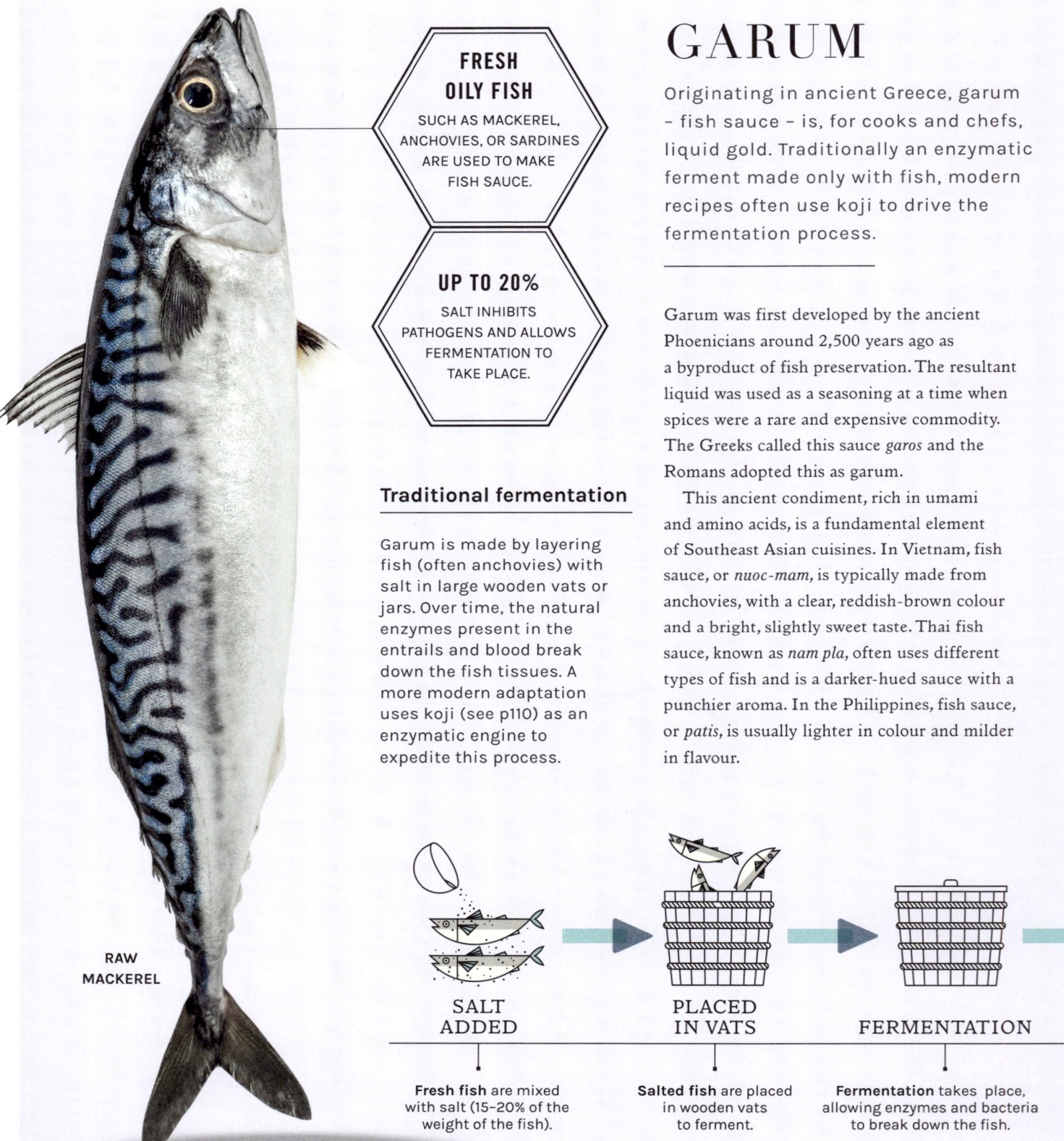

FRESH OILY FISH SUCH AS MACKEREL, ANCHOVIES, OR SARDINES ARE USED TO MAKE FISH SAUCE.

UP TO 20% SALT INHIBITS PATHOGENS AND ALLOWS FERMENTATION TO TAKE PLACE.

RAW MACKEREL

Traditional fermentation

Garum is made by layering fish (often anchovies) with salt in large wooden vats or jars. Over time, the natural enzymes present in the entrails and blood break down the fish tissues. A more modern adaptation uses koji (see p110) as an enzymatic engine to expedite this process.

SALT ADDED — Fresh fish are mixed with salt (15–20% of the weight of the fish).

PLACED IN VATS — Salted fish are placed in wooden vats to ferment.

FERMENTATION — Fermentation takes place, allowing enzymes and bacteria to break down the fish.

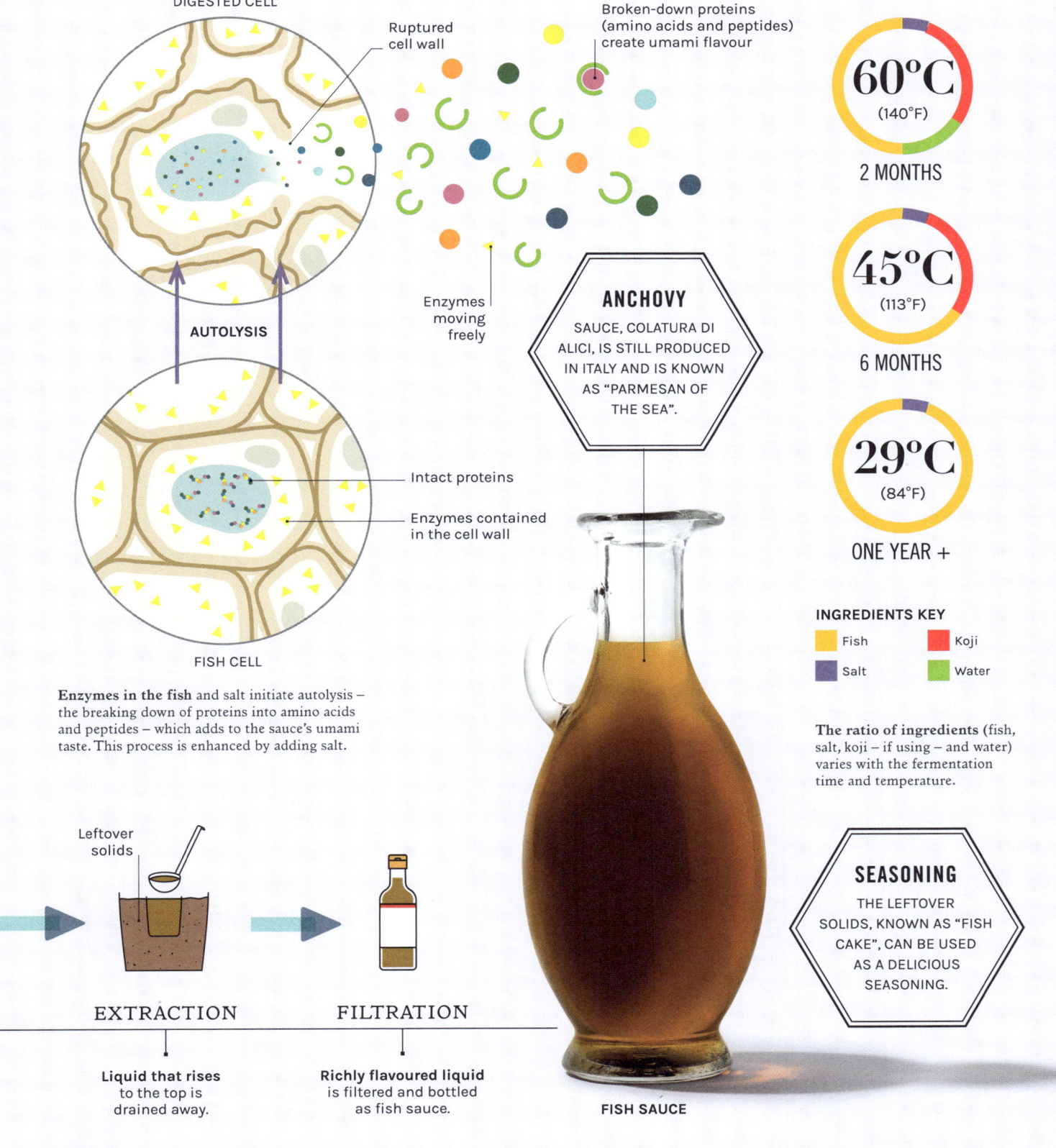

YEASTS

Yeast fermentation	**150**
Utilizing yeast	**152**
Idli and dosa	**154**
Bread	**156**
Wine	**162**
Beer	**168**
Cider	**172**
Mead	**174**
Saké	**176**
Ginger bug and ginger beer	**182**
Kvas	**184**
Tepache	**186**

YEAST FERMENTATION

Yeasts are a type of single-celled fungus. As they grow and reproduce, they create alcohol, carbon dioxide, and hundreds of distinct flavour compounds. Their unique biology makes it possible to produce much of the food and drink we consume.

Yeasts are split across two phyla (groups of organisms). Within Ascomycota we find the "true" yeasts such as *Saccharomyces cerevisiae* (brewer's yeast), which make up the bulk of the yeast species used in fermentation, while Basidiomycota includes microbes used for niche processes and precision fermentation.

AEROBIC OR ANAEROBIC?

All yeasts share some common qualities. Most notably, they can survive in both aerobic (with oxygen) and anaerobic (without oxygen) environments. This metabolic versatility is key to how yeasts help shape food products from bread and beer to vinegar and kombucha.

In the presence of oxygen, yeasts will undergo aerobic respiration, using the oxygen to break down sugars into carbon dioxide and water (which is ideal for breads). This process yields a high amount of energy for the yeast. When oxygen is limited or absent they are able to switch to anaerobic

How yeasts multiply

Most common yeasts reproduce by budding (see below), others by fission (dividing symmetrically down the middle). This fast, flexible growth allows colonies to multiply quickly and dominate fermentation environments, often shaping the early stages of fermentation before bacteria or secondary microbes take over.

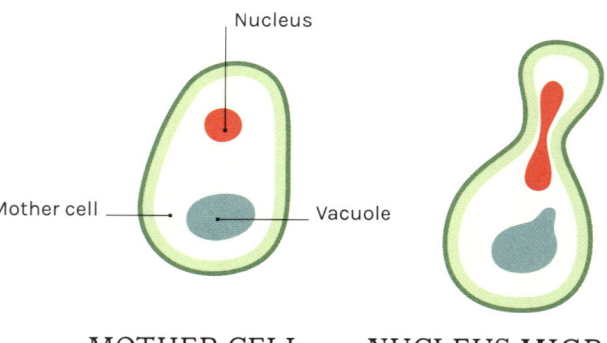

MOTHER CELL PREPARES TO BUD	NUCLEUS MIGRATES TOWARDS BUD SITE	NEW DAUGHTER CELL FORMS	NEW CELLS MATURE AND DETACH
The mother cell prepares to divide, by beginning to form a small bud.	**A daughter cell forms** off the parent, still attached by a narrow neck.	**The daughter cell** is sealed off from the parent.	**Mature daughter cells** break away, ready to begin budding themselves.

Aerobic respiration by yeast uses oxygen to break down glucose, which then releases carbon dioxide, water, and a large amount of energy.

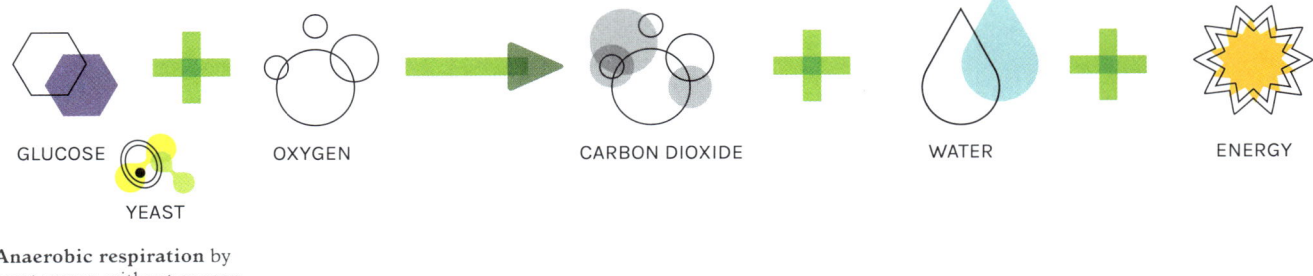

Anaerobic respiration by yeast occurs without oxygen and produces ethanol, CO_2, and a small amount of energy.

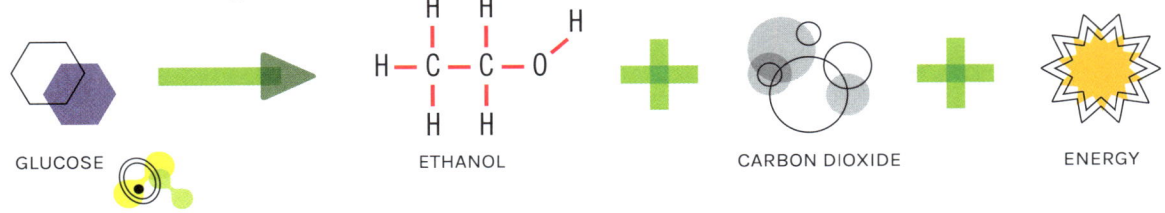

fermentation, converting sugars into ethanol and carbon dioxide (which is ideal for alcohol and kombucha) and generating less energy.

Even when oxygen is present, some yeasts can produce alcohol via a phenomenon known as the Crabtree effect. This is when the yeast (notably *S. cerevisiae*) will still choose the anaerobic pathway, provided glucose levels are high. This evolutionary quirk is part of what makes *S. cerevisiae* so dominant in alcohol fermentation: it rapidly converts sugar to ethanol, suppressing competing microbes that are less tolerant of alcohol.

Chemically, an aerobic fermentation involves glycolysis, where glucose is broken down into pyruvate molecules, which are then converted to ethanol and carbon dioxide. In aerobic respiration, however, the pyruvate continues to be broken down into water and carbon dioxide.

FERMENTING FLAVOUR

In many fermented food and drink processes, there are distinct primary and secondary fermentation stages. During primary fermentation, yeast rapidly metabolizes simple sugars, generating alcohol, carbon dioxide, and a broad suite of aromatic compounds. Secondary fermentation – which ensues once most of the initial sugars are consumed – tends to be slower and more nuanced, producing esters, acids, and higher alcohol levels that deepen the product's flavour complexity, especially when it has a long ageing process, like wine, for example.

Different yeast species, and the strains within them, can produce vastly diverse flavour profiles, even when operating under identical conditions. Many ultimately define the identity of fermented foods and drinks. For example, species of *Brettanomyces* (often used in sour beers and natural wines) produce phenolic compounds that evoke spice, smoke, or leather, while *S. cerevisiae* – the classic baker's yeast and a natural resident in sourdough cultures – contributes malty, bready aromas and subtle fruity esters.

> **YEASTS** HAVE STRAIN-SPECIFIC BIOLOGICAL TRAITS THAT FUNNEL CARBON AND NITROGEN INTO AROMA-ACTIVE BYPRODUCTS.

UTILIZING YEAST

Humans have worked with yeast for millennia – sometimes unknowingly – with increasing precision. While we often focus on the carbon dioxide that makes our bread rise, or the alcohol in our drinks, yeasts also produce an amazing array of aroma and flavour compounds.

Yeast is central to some of our most everyday food and drinks, but beyond traditional uses, we are now working with yeasts in ever more refined ways, such as tailoring strains for low-alcohol beers, precision fats, specific aroma production, or even non-food applications like bioplastics. What started with wild ferments has evolved into microbial craftsmanship, underpinned by centuries of observation.

BEER

In brewing, yeasts convert sugars from fruits, vegetables, and grains into ethanol, carbon dioxide, and an array of flavour compounds. Producers have long selected yeast strains to shape flavour, alcohol content, mouthfeel, and finish. For example, *Saccharomycodes ludwigii*, once thought of only as a spoilage organism, can ferment sugars with minimal alcohol production while still creating flavourful esters, making it ideal for low- and no-alcohol beers.

BREAD

In breadmaking, yeast's role is twofold: to create flavour and to produce carbon dioxide for rise. Whether using commercial *Saccharomyces cerevisiae* or wild sourdough cultures, yeasts behave similarly. They metabolize sugars in the flour, creating bubbles that expand gluten networks and give the bread its airy crumb (see p156). During fermentation, alongside the carbon dioxide, the yeasts produce alcohols, esters, and organic acids, contributing nutty, malty, sometimes even fruity notes to the final loaf.

Fermentation time, hydration, and temperature can all influence which flavour compounds are present in the final bread.

SCOBYs

In ferments like kombucha and kefir, yeast doesn't work alone. These form SCOBYs – symbiotic cultures of bacteria and yeast (see p192) – with each microbe producing substances that support the other. Yeasts contribute alcohol, while bacteria convert that alcohol into acids or produce polysaccharides, which make jelly pellicles (skins) that form a protective environment for the microbes.

In kefir (see p94), for example, yeasts like *S. fragilis*, *Kluyveromyces marxianus*, and others coexist with lactic acid bacteria (LAB) in dairy, in a matrix of kefiran that they build – a mass of hard, jelly-like grains. Together they produce a complex drink with a mild sparkle and creamy acidity. Similarly, kombucha's (see p196) yeasts (often

SPECIALIZED BREAD YEASTS CAN ONLY TOLERATE LOW-ALCOHOL ENVIRONMENTS.

including *Brettanomyces* and *Zygosaccharomyces*) work with acetic acid bacteria (AAB) to form a thick jelly mat. The yeast first produces alcohol and carbon dioxide before the AAB convert the alcohol to acetic acid, giving kombucha its fizz and tang.

SALTY FERMENTS

Not all yeasts thrive in sweet or starchy environments. Yeasts like *Debaryomyces hansenii* flourish in high-salt ferments such as cheese, miso, soy sauce, krauts, and kimchi. Often under-appreciated, they are in fact crucial, contributing to the breakdown of amino acids, influencing texture, and producing savoury and buttery notes.

Other yeasts

- **Saké yeasts**
Traditional yeasts like Kyokai No.7 produce a thick foam during fermentation, requiring extra space and labour. Brewers later selected non-foaming strains, like Kyokai No.701, for cleaner tanks, easier handling, and higher yields without compromising flavour. This is a perfect example of practical microbial selection shaping production efficiency.

- **Unwanted yeasts**
Kahm yeast (see p62), a common surface yeast in brined ferments, forms as a harmless silvery film. While not dangerous, it's often removed due to its off-putting appearance and its potential to create acetone-like aromas. Other wild yeasts may introduce spoilage flavours or dominate the fermentation environment.

- **Fat-producing yeasts**
Certain Basidiomycota yeasts such as *Yarrowia lipolytica* are oleaginous (able to produce fats, see p41), enabling the production of alternatives to butter, cream, and cocoa fat using precision fermentation.

COLD-TOLERANT
YEAST S. PASTORIANUS CREATES CLEAN, CRISP LAGERS WITH MINIMAL FRUITY BYPRODUCTS.

ENGINEERED
YEASTS PRODUCE BIODEGRADABLE POLYMERS – A RENEWABLE ALTERNATIVE TO PLASTICS.

HALO-TOLERANT
YEASTS THRIVE IN SALTY ENVIRONMENTS LIKE KIMCHI, ADDING FLAVOURS.

IDLI AND DOSA

Idli and dosa are breakfast staples in South Indian households. While both are made with the same ingredients of fermented rice, urad dal (split black lentils), and fenugreek seeds, these dishes are prepared and eaten in slightly different ways.

Travelling around South India, you'll find many different variants of both idli and dosa. Idli is a soft rice cake traditionally eaten for breakfast. The rice, dal, and fenugreek seeds are soaked in water, then left to ferment before being steamed in a mould. Dosa is also made from fermented and ground rice and dal but with a thinner consistency, which is then used to make crêpes that are enjoyed with a wide variety of fillings, including chutney and sambar (a spicy stew), spiced mashed potato, cheese, and onion. Both idli and dosa are rich in protein due to the lentils they contain and high in probiotics.

FERMENTING THE BATTER

The naturally occurring lactic acid bacteria (LAB) and wild yeasts that are on the surface of the rice, dal, and fenugreek seeds become active when they are soaked in water and start breaking down the starches and converting them into alcohol and carbon dioxide.

As the batter rises, the mucilage (a thick, sticky substance on the coating of the urad dal) and proteins from the dal and the seeds give the batter structural integrity by holding everything together. This helps keep the bubbles intact until it hits the heat, resulting in the perfect spongy idli or dosa. In the tropical heat of India, the batter takes about eight hours to ferment. In colder climates, it could take a bit longer.

METHI
RELEASES MUCILAGE WHEN SOAKED. THIS PROVIDES EXTRA STRUCTURE TO THE BATTER AS IT FERMENTS.

POHA
CONTAINS RESISTANT STARCH AND BEHAVES LIKE TANGZHONG IN BREADMAKING. THE RESULT IS SOFTER AND FLUFFIER.

RICE

Short, fat rices like idli rice and sushi rice have the right combination of starch molecules – amylose and amylopectin.

URAD DAL

Black lentils are high in protein and sticky. When soaked and ground they behave like whisked egg whites.

METHI

Methi (fenugreek seeds) enhance flavour via the Maillard reaction (see p124) and bring a robust microbiome to the batter.

POHA

Adding poha (beaten rice flakes) results in increased softness and fluffiness, which is especially desirable in idlis.

MAKE YOUR OWN

If you make a batch of batter once a week you can use it to make idli for the first two days, when the batter is less sour and the active fermentation helps them fluff up, and dosa on days two to five, when the slightly sour batter lends a nice tang.

EQUIPMENT 3 small bowls • blender • large mixing bowl • steamer • idli moulds (or ramekins) • cast-iron griddle (or a steel or non-stick pan) • ladle
INGREDIENTS 400g rice • 100g urad dal (split and hulled) • 15g fenugreek seeds • 100g poha (or cooked rice, optional) • ghee or vegetable oil

Yeasts
S. cerevisiae, Candida humilis

LAB
L. mesenteroides, L. fermentum

1–2 DAYS

1. **Wash the rice, dal, and seeds**, then, in 3 separate bowls, cover with water and soak for 6-7 hours. Strain off any water that isn't soaked up, retaining some.

2. **Grind the dal with the seeds** in a blender until you have a fine batter, then add to the large mixing bowl. Grind the rice and poha (if using), adding a little soaking water to make a thick batter, then add to the bowl.

3. **Leave somewhere warm**, 25-32°C (77-90°F), to ferment overnight, until the batter has grown about three times in volume and has a slight dome on the top. If you don't want to use it immediately, transfer to the fridge where it can be stored for up to a week.

4. **To cook idli**, oil your moulds lightly, pour in the batter, and steam on high for 10-15 minutes.
To cook dosa, preheat a cast-iron pan on a medium heat. Add some ghee or oil, then a ladleful of batter and spread in concentric circles. Cook for 3-4 minutes, until the bottom is golden brown. Drizzle ghee or oil across the dosa as it cooks to aid browning.

Troubleshooting

• If the batter has not increased in size enough, it is likely too cold to ferment. Use an incubator, a cupboard with a hot-water bottle inside, or an oven at the lowest temperature.

• When the batter has fermented too much, it will smell sour. You can still use it, but don't keep it long.

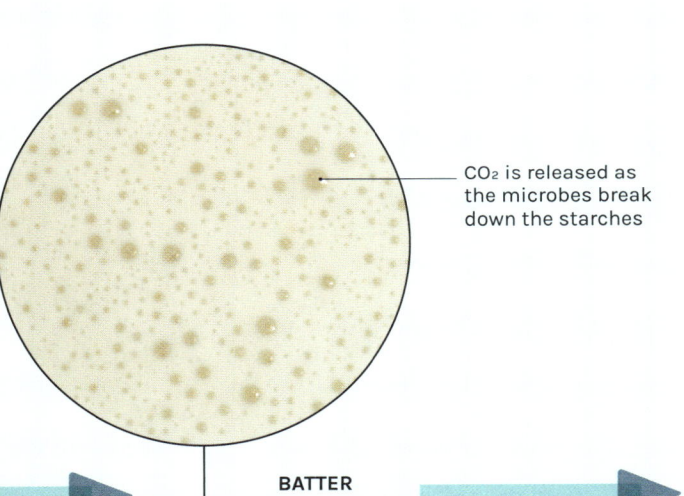

CO_2 is released as the microbes break down the starches

BATTER FERMENTATION

IDLI

DOSA

BREAD

A kitchen staple made from the simplest of ingredients, bread is one of the oldest prepared foods, and has long been integral to human civilization. At its heart is the fermentation of microbial communities, providing a natural leavening effect and bags of flavour.

Originating in the Middle East around 10,000 years ago, bread has since been on quite the journey, so that now every culture across the globe boasts its own take. The first leavened examples date back 5,000 years, giving rise to what we call sourdough bread. Flour and water were mixed together and left to spontaneously ferment, allowing a starter culture of wild yeasts and bacterial flora to naturally accumulate. This was then mixed with fresh dough and baked to obtain a lighter bread with added flavour complexity. Reinoculation of the mother culture with more flour and water allowed it to be maintained indefinitely and matured over time.

Most bread today, however, is made using isolated yeasts, namely *Saccharomyces cerevisiae* (baker's or brewer's yeast). These yeasts have been selected for their fast bulk fermentation, allowing bread to be leavened more quickly and produced on an industrial scale. Instead of the few days required to make a sourdough, breads with "fast-action" yeasts can be made in only a few hours. While this provides bread in a timely fashion, it can come at the cost of flavour complexity, texture, and nutritional value.

SOURDOUGH

Within a sourdough starter, the microbes each play different roles, but common to all is a form of fermentation. Lactic acid bacteria (LAB) convert carbohydrates into lactic acid, giving sourdough its characteristic sour taste. This also helps lower the pH of both the starter culture and bread, aiding preservation and suppressing pathogens. Also present, but to a far lesser extent, are acetic acid bacteria (AAB). They oxidize ethanol (produced

Sourdough starter culture

Flour and water are mixed, then naturally ferment from wild yeasts. It is at peak activity when bubbly and doubled in size.

- Bacteria
- CO_2 bubbles
- Starch granules
- Yeast

PRE-ACTIVATION   **BEFORE FEEDING**   **PEAK ACTIVITY**

DIRECTORY OF FERMENTS • Yeasts

Sourdough nutrition

The lactic acid produced in sourdough fermentation helps break down gluten proteins, making them more digestible and weakening their structure, creating a more open crumb. It also reduces the bioavailability of starch in the body, slowing its digestion and therefore the release of glucose into the bloodstream. As a result, sourdough has a lower glycaemic index than regular bread.

ACIDS
CREATED BY BACTERIA ACTIVATE THE ENZYME PHYTASE, WHICH AIDS ABSORPTION OF KEY MINERALS.

CARBOHYDRATE
BREAKDOWN THROUGH FERMENTATION GIVES A CHEWY TEXTURE.

from sugars by yeast) to acetic acid, which gives the bread a sharp tang and contributes to pH reduction.

Whereas LAB and AAB are important for flavour, yeasts are critical for leavening. Through enzymatic action in the yeast, fermentation converts glucose into ethanol and carbon dioxide, creating pockets of gas in the dough, which expand on baking to provide sourdough's famed open-crumb structure. Yeasts also generate various flavour compounds, such as buttery diacetyl, fruity ethyl acetate, and the ripe-banana aroma of isoamyl alcohol.

The balance of LAB, AAB, and yeast in a starter therefore determines the flavour and texture of the sourdough – and they work together in harmony.

Yeast fermentation produces CO_2 bubbles, which get trapped and expand during baking

Starch granules swell and gelatinize. Starch molecules are released and broken down into glucose

ACTIVE FERMENTATION

MAKE YOUR OWN
SOURDOUGH BREAD

To get the best results from this recipe, feed your sourdough starter ahead of time (see box below) so that it has reached peak activity when you begin. The time this takes depends on your feeding ratio, allowing you to adjust it based on when it is most convenient for you to start making the sourdough.

EQUIPMENT
- mixing bowl
- measuring jug
- tea towel or cling film
- banneton
- baking parchment
- 2 × baking sheets or Dutch oven (optional)
- scoring lame

INGREDIENTS
- 450g bread flour
- 300-320ml tepid water, as needed
- 90g sourdough starter (see box below)
- 10g salt
- ice cubes for baking

LAB
L. sanfranciscensis, L. brevis, L. plantarum, Weissella spp.

Yeasts
Wild, likely *Saccharomyces* and *Candida* spp.

AAB
Possibly *Acetobacter* and *Gluconobacter* spp.

1–3 DAYS

Making a starter culture

A sourdough starter is simple to make at home with a little patience. Mix 50g flour and 50ml water in a jar to form a thick batter, then cover with a lid and leave to ferment for 3-5 days, stirring once a day. The natural yeasts will begin to ferment, confirmed by bubbles on the surface. Now, discard half the mixture and feed the remainder with 50g flour and 50ml water, then leave for a further day. Repeat this process once a day, maintaining the ratio 1:1:1 (50g starter, 50g flour, 50ml water), until the starter is doubling in volume in a few hours. It is now active and ready to use. Going forwards, the starter should be fed once or twice a day in a ratio of 1:5:5 (10g starter, 50g flour, 50ml water) or 1:2:2 (25g starter, 50g flour, 50ml water) respectively. The best time to use it is at its peak rise after feeding. For a starter fed in a 1:2:2 ratio, this should be after 6-8 hours.

1 **Add the flour and water to a bowl**, then mix by hand to form a soft, rough dough. Cover with a tea towel or cling film and allow to sit at room temperature for 1 hour.

2 **Add the starter and salt** and work together for a few minutes until everything is fully combined and a smooth dough has formed. Cover again and leave to rest for 30 minutes.

5. **Preheat your oven to 240°C (220°C fan/475°F/Gas 9)**, with 2 baking sheets on separate shelves or, ideally, a Dutch oven placed inside for 30 minutes. Turn the sourdough out onto a sheet of baking parchment, then score the top with a deep slash down the middle with a bread lame. Using the parchment to lift it, transfer the dough onto the top preheated baking sheet or into the Dutch oven. Add a handful of ice cubes to the bottom baking sheet or put a couple into the Dutch oven before covering with the lid, then bake for 35–40 minutes, removing the lid of the Dutch oven after 25 minutes (if using). A fully baked sourdough should have a golden-brown crust, feel light when picked up, and have a hollow sound when tapped on the base. Remove from the oven and leave to cool on a wire rack.

3. **Lightly wet your hands** with water to prevent sticking, then grab one side of the dough, stretch it upwards, then fold it over towards the centre. Rotate the bowl a quarter-turn and repeat, until you have completed a full circle – this is one set. Cover and rest the dough for 30 minutes. Perform 3 or 4 more sets, resting the dough for 30 minutes between each. During this time the dough should become increasingly elastic and less sticky. After the last set, cover the dough and rest at room temperature until it has grown in size and is exhibiting large air bubbles (around 3–5 hours).

4. **Turn out the dough onto a floured surface**, flatten slightly, then pull the edges into the centre, working around the circumference. Flip the dough over and gently move it around in a circular motion, rotating and tucking the sides underneath to build up tension. Dust with flour, flip smooth-side down, and transfer to a floured banneton. Cover and proof in the fridge for 12–72 hours. A longer proofing time allows a more complex flavour and open texture to develop.

Troubleshooting

- If your dough seems loose and sticky at first, don't worry. Following the sets of stretching and folding it will soon build up its strength and elasticity.

- If your bread has not risen very high and appears dense, make sure your oven is very hot before baking, and that you have taken care to tuck the edges of the dough under itself to build up sufficient tension.

- If your starter seems inactive, test it by dropping a spoonful into a bowl of water. If it floats, it is active; if it sinks, continue feeding and allow more time for it to ripen.

BREAD IN FOCUS

Naturally fermented breads across the world hold a special place in culinary traditions. Employing unique microbial communities and made from assorted grains, the sourdough family turns out to be much larger than you first think.

Microbial diversity in a naturally leavened bread is influenced by a multitude of factors, from geographical location and fermentation conditions to flour type and hydration level. As such, despite using minimal – and often the same – ingredients, the possibilities for sourdough-making are endless. Central to all, however, is the depth of flavour and chewy texture brought about by these wild mixed cultures of yeasts and bacteria.

PAIN DE CAMPAGNE

A staple in rural France, this crusty, chewy sourdough is made with white and whole-wheat flours. With its higher nutritional content, whole-wheat flour promotes faster fermentation than white flour, so the fermentation period will need adjusting depending on the ratio.

SHOKUPAN

A light, rich bread famed for its pillowy softness and delicate crumb, shokupan (Japanese milk bread) can be made using the natural yeast ferment sakadane (see box above), which provides added flavour and the bread's airy texture.

FLATBREADS

With less reliance on gluten development for an open crumb, these breads are forgiving and can be made using a variety of grains, seeds, and tubers. Each type of flour will create a distinct starter, imparting unique flavours and characteristics, in breads such as eish merahrah and injera.

Special agents

- **Rye flours** encourage microbial diversity, influencing the levels of sour, vinegary, and fruity flavours in the final bread. In these robust breads, flavour is often enhanced with molasses, cocoa powder, or malt powder.
- **Sakadane** is a unique natural leavening agent, made from cooked rice and koji (see p110), which aids fermentation and encourages wild yeast growth. With an absence of LAB, it is not classed as a sourdough, though it functions in much the same way.

INJERA IS A TRADITIONAL ETHIOPIAN AND ERITREAN SOURDOUGH FLATBREAD MADE WITH TEFF FLOUR.

PANETTONE IS MADE WITH A STARTER CALLED LIEVITO MADRE ("MOTHER YEAST"), WHICH DEMANDS SPECIAL MAINTENANCE.

RYE BREADS

Rye flours encourage microbial diversity, influencing the levels of sour, vinegary, and fruity flavours in the resultant breads. Rich in nutrients and high in enzymatic activity, rye increases starch breakdown into sugars, fuelling the microorganisms for faster fermentation, and lending rye bread a natural sweetness.

ROBUST RYE

BREADS INCLUDE GERMAN PUMPERNICKEL AND DANISH RUGBRØD.

SAN FRANCISCO SOURDOUGH

A wheat-flour sourdough with a crispy exterior, large air pockets, and distinctive sour tang owing to the dominant *Lactobacillus sanfranciscensis*. This species of LAB was initially believed to be unique to San Francisco, but was later found to be common in sourdough cultures worldwide.

PANETTONE

This dramatic Italian sweet bread, which rises high with a light, fluffy texture, is studded with fruit. Careful monitoring of the fermentation temperature and dough pH is required to ensure its unique flavour and texture. It is incredibly difficult to replicate at home, so is usually bought.

WINE

Wine is a remarkable natural product, loaded with cultural significance. In traditional wine-growing countries it is enjoyed with food, but it is now consumed worldwide on any occasion.

The legal definition of wine is a fermented drink made from fresh grapes. Very little else, if anything, needs to be added, although it is common to use sulfur dioxide at various stages of the production process to prevent unwanted microbial growth and to counter the negative effects of oxidation. In addition, in warmer climates some tartaric acid might be used to correct the must (pressed grapes) before fermentation starts. In many cases selected yeasts and bacteria are used as inoculants for alcoholic and malolactic (converting malic acid to milder lactic acid) fermentation respectively, although these are not essential because wild yeasts and bacteria can carry out the same roles adequately. Since ancient times grapevines have travelled to wherever they will grow well, and today vines occupy 7.3 million hectares, making grapes the most valuable fruit crop worldwide.

KEY STAGES OF PRODUCTION

Grapes are grown on vines, with buds bursting in late spring, followed by flowering in early summer and then berry development, culminating in ripe berries ready for harvest in early autumn. After harvest, winemakers have choices to make. For white wines, grapes are pressed to separate the

HARVEST AND CRUSH GRAPES

PRESS AND REMOVE SKINS

FERMENT IN VATS OR TANKS

AGE IN BARRELS OR TANKS

BOTTLE AND LABEL FOR SALE

WHITE WINES ARE FERMENTED FROM GRAPE JUICE ALONE AFTER PRESSING, SO TEND TO BE PALE IN COLOUR.

WHITE BURGUNDY

WHITE GRAPES

White wine

Whites are usually made from white grapes, but sometimes from red grapes pressed with no contact between the skins and juice.

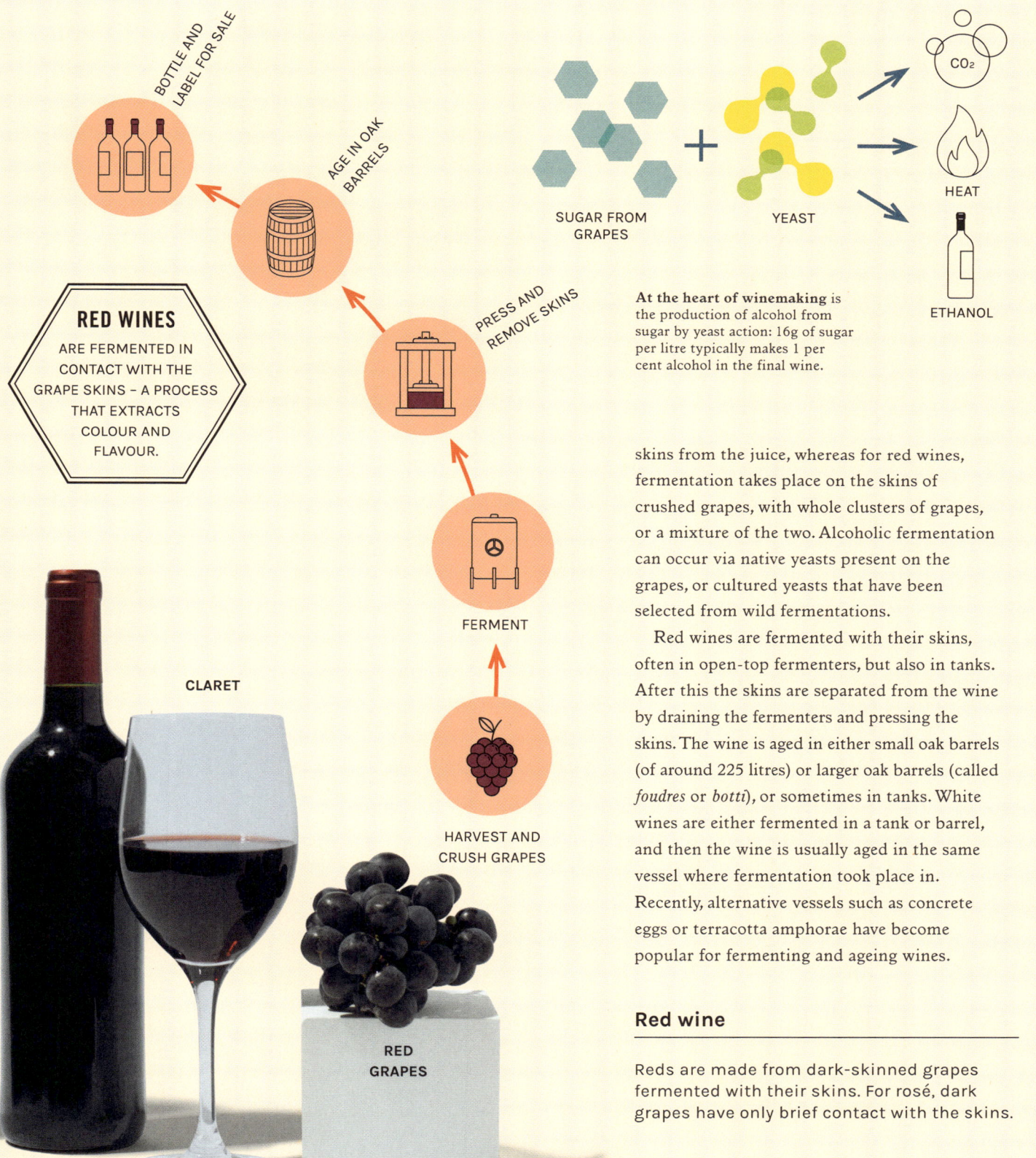

At the heart of winemaking is the production of alcohol from sugar by yeast action: 16g of sugar per litre typically makes 1 per cent alcohol in the final wine.

RED WINES ARE FERMENTED IN CONTACT WITH THE GRAPE SKINS – A PROCESS THAT EXTRACTS COLOUR AND FLAVOUR.

skins from the juice, whereas for red wines, fermentation takes place on the skins of crushed grapes, with whole clusters of grapes, or a mixture of the two. Alcoholic fermentation can occur via native yeasts present on the grapes, or cultured yeasts that have been selected from wild fermentations.

Red wines are fermented with their skins, often in open-top fermenters, but also in tanks. After this the skins are separated from the wine by draining the fermenters and pressing the skins. The wine is aged in either small oak barrels (of around 225 litres) or larger oak barrels (called *foudres* or *botti*), or sometimes in tanks. White wines are either fermented in a tank or barrel, and then the wine is usually aged in the same vessel where fermentation took place in. Recently, alternative vessels such as concrete eggs or terracotta amphorae have become popular for fermenting and ageing wines.

Red wine

Reds are made from dark-skinned grapes fermented with their skins. For rosé, dark grapes have only brief contact with the skins.

MAKE YOUR OWN
RED WINE

If you're making wine the traditional way using grapes, the most important step is sourcing the right ones. Dedicated wine grapes offer the right mix of flavour ripeness; table grapes lack the required sugar levels and acidity. Use healthy, rot-free wine grapes that have a combination of aroma, flavour, and phenolic compounds (such as tannins).

You can also make wine using a kit that contains concentrate, but if you can get fresh wine grapes, the results are likely to be better. Make sure the grapes you use have the correct sugar and acidity levels for either white or red wine – this will be tested by the grape grower. With some simple equipment, this is a rewarding process. When it comes to bottling your wine, cleanliness is vital: sanitize everything before use (see p59). Allow time for each stage of the process – particularly for the wine to settle naturally, then no filtration is needed.

EQUIPMENT
- plastic bucket with lid
- siphon tubing (optional)
- siphon bucket clip (optional)
- 2 × glass or plastic demijohns
- airlocks
- bungs for the demijohns, some with holes for airlocks
- muslin cloth or press bag
- large bowl
- bottles and corks
- hand-corking device

INGREDIENTS (makes approx. 30 litres of wine)
- 50kg wine grapes
- 6 × Campden tablets (or follow pack instructions)
- 5g sachet of cultured wine yeast
- 20g yeast nutrients (optional; if using, follow pack instructions)

Yeasts
S. cerevisiae, H. uvarum, B. bruxellensis

LAB
O. oeni, L. plantarum, Pediococcus spp.

6 MONTHS

1 **Crush the grapes** in a bucket to release the juice. Crush 3 of the Campden tablets and dissolve in a little water or wine. Add to the bucket, cover, and leave at room temperature overnight.

2 **Add the yeast** and yeast nutrients (if using to ensure a steady fermentation) to the juice, transfer to a demijohn (a siphon tube and clip are useful here), cover, and leave in a warm place at 18–24°C (65–75°F) for 5–10 days. Initially an airlock is needed, but when there are no more bubbles coming up through the airlock and fermentation is finished, seal the demijohn with a bung.

DIRECTORY OF FERMENTS • Yeasts 165

3. **Press the liquid through a muslin cloth** into a clean bowl to remove the skins.

5. **Once bubbling has stopped**, add the remaining Campden tablets, crushed and dissolved first in water or wine. Decant the wine into bottles, seal with corks, and leave to settle for a few months. Then drink or store in a cool, dark place for 1–2 years.

Troubleshooting

• To avoid the eggy smells made by hydrogen sulfide during fermentation, ensure the yeasts have the right nutrients and avoid rapid temperature changes.

• After fermentation, keep the wine airtight or it will oxidize, the fruity flavours will be lost, or volatile acidity might develop. Keep vessels sealed and topped up to avoid this.

• When the yeast stops converting sugar into alcohol mid-process your wine can become stuck, leaving you with half-fermented wine. This can happen if the temperature is too low or sugar or alcohol levels are too high, or if the yeast is out of date.

Natural wine

If you want to make wine naturally, then no additions are needed, given the right grapes. If you want to play it a bit safe, check the analysis of the grapes and must, and correct if necessary, using sulfites at appropriate times to protect the wine.

4. **Transfer to a clean demijohn**, leaving the sediment behind, and leave at room temperature for secondary fermentation. This can take 1–6 months and will produce CO_2, so affix an airlock.

WINE IN FOCUS

Wine is unusual among alcoholic beverages in that nothing else needs to be added to the raw ingredient to make it: the grapes contain sugars, acids, and flavour compounds, and the yeasts for fermentation are present on their skins. Stylistically, wine is now hugely diverse and more accessible than ever.

The majority of wines are red, rosé, or white; orange or amber wines are made by fermenting white grapes on their skins.

More than 1,000 different grape varieties are grown commercially, but most wines are made from perhaps 50, which may be blended. Grapes are remarkably sensitive to climate. There are very few places where the red grape used for Pinot Noir can be planted for it to make good wine, for example. Others, like Chardonnay, Shiraz, and Cabernet Sauvignon produce interesting wines across a wide range of climatic bands.

FLAVOUR

Wine's flavour comes from a number of sources. The first is from the grape varieties, and these can vary in taste quite dramatically. The second is from the place: most grape varieties excel only within narrow climatic bands. Even within these bands, the same grape will make wines that taste quite different, according to terroir. The third source of flavour comes from the winemaking process.

Many steps in the winery affect how the wine tastes. Think of the grapes as providing a fermentation medium for yeasts. The crushed grapes contain high levels of sugar, which the yeasts then convert to alcohol and carbon dioxide. Importantly, many of the flavour compounds in wine are made directly by yeasts, and the exact composition of the must influences their production, as does the species and strains of yeasts that carry out the fermentation.

THE ROLE OF BACTERIA

Bacteria also affect how wine tastes. Given too much space in the fermentation, and too much oxygen, acetic acid bacteria produce acetic acid. This leads to the wine fault known as volatile acidity, which also involves another compound called ethyl acetate. The second fermentation (malolactic fermentation) is carried out by lactic acid bacteria and transforms malic acid, which is sharp-tasting, into lactic acid, which has a softer character, resulting in a corresponding drop in acidity.

MALOLACTIC FERMENTATION IS STOPPED IN WHITES SUCH AS RIESLING TO RETAIN FRESHNESS.

UNOAKED REDS ARE BECOMING MORE COMMON AS PEOPLE LOOK FOR FRESH, FRUIT-DRIVEN RED WINES.

MALBEC

Argentina's Mendoza region is a high-altitude desert, but Andes snowmelt means it can make exciting examples of Malbec, which is a floral, fresh, but rich style of red.

RIESLING

The Mosel Valley in Germany is the home of Riesling, a grape that makes crisp, tart wines that taste of lemons, and which can be dry, off-dry, or fully sweet.

BLANC DE BLANCS

France's Champagne region makes the world's most famous sparkling wines. Blanc de Blancs is made from Chardonnay only; it is bright, precise, enthralling.

SAUVIGNON BLANC

An unknown New Zealand wine region 50 years ago, Marlborough Sauvignon, with its grassy, elderflower, passionfruit flavours, has now redefined the variety.

CABERNET SAUVIGNON

Popular worldwide, but California's Napa Valley makes some of the most sought-after examples, with rich, lush blackcurrant fruit and often a kiss of oak.

TERROIR

THIS FRENCH TERM MEANS THE UNIQUE MIX OF CLIMATE, SOIL, AND PLACE THAT GIVES A GRAPE ITS LOCAL FLAVOUR.

SULFUR DIOXIDE

PROTECTS AGAINST OXIDATION AND STOPS GROWTH OF UNWANTED MICROBES.

WINERIES

OFTEN USE SELECTED DRIED YEAST STRAINS TO START FERMENTATION FOR SAFETY AND FLAVOUR PROFILE.

MALBEC • RIESLING • BLANC DE BLANCS CHAMPAGNE • SAUVIGNON BLANC • CABERNET SAUVIGNON

Wild yeasts

Some winemakers use wild yeasts for uninoculated fermentation. They start with non-Saccharomyces yeasts, then after four days or so, wild strains of S. cerevisiae take over. This can create complexity in the wine, although it can be unpredictable.

BEER

The most popular alcoholic drink in the world, beer originated with the earliest farming civilizations around the Fertile Crescent in the Middle East. Its development forms a liquid thread that has weaved through human social history for 10,000 years.

Beer shares an origin with bread, in that water and ground grain are mixed, and a yeast culture starts a fermentation. That process preserved water and grain and transformed them into a hydrating and healthful drink that has been shared communally for millennia. Beer is now arguably the most diverse drink in the world, with over 100 distinct styles, and centuries-old brewing traditions now joined by a modern, creative approach to craft beer.

GRAIN AND HOPS

Beer is brewed with water, grain, hops, and yeast. Wheat, oats, rye, rice, and maize can all be used, but barley is the most common grain owing to its natural enzymes, which can convert its own unfermentable starches into fermentable sugars.

Stages of brewing

Beer is brewed with just four core ingredients – water, grain, hops, and yeast – but it involves numerous different stages to get the best out of them.

YEASTS SUCH AS S. CEREVISIAE AND S. PASTORIANUS CONVERT THE SUGARS IN BEER INTO ALCOHOL.

HOPS ADDED EARLY IN THE PROCESS GIVE BITTERNESS; ADDED LATER, THEY GIVE MORE FLAVOUR AND AROMA.

GRAIN (USUALLY MALTED BARLEY) CONTAINS ENZYMES THAT UNLOCK THE SUGARS FOR FERMENTATION.

H_2O — WARM WATER ACTIVATES ENZYMES

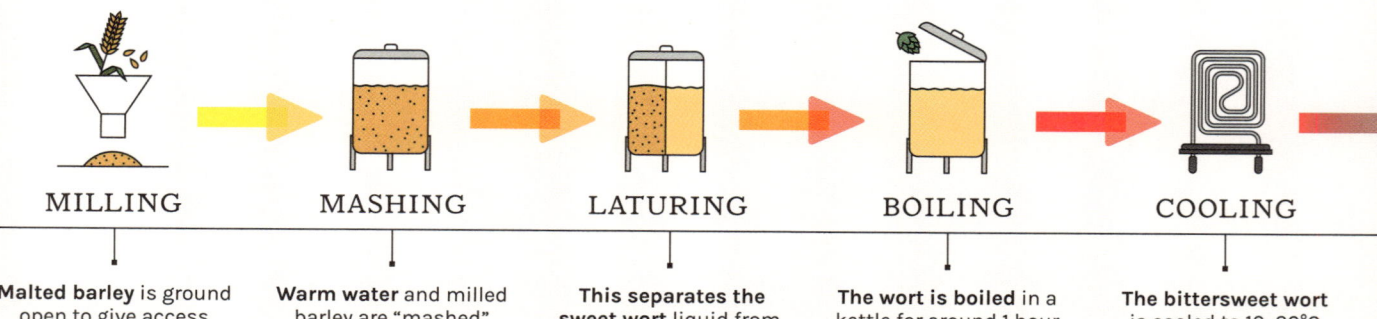

MILLING — Malted barley is ground open to give access to the starches and sugars inside.

MASHING — Warm water and milled barley are "mashed" together for around 1 hour, producing "wort".

LATURING — This separates the sweet wort liquid from the leftover grain.

BOILING — The wort is boiled in a kettle for around 1 hour and hops are added.

COOLING — The bittersweet wort is cooled to 10–20°C (50–68°F).

Barley is malted before brewing; it is soaked in water to encourage germination, which allows enzymes to start breaking down complex starches into simpler sugars, which yeast will later ferment into alcohol. The kernels are then dried in a kiln, where temperature and time determine how pale or dark the malt is.

The grain gives beer its colour, body, and base flavours (toast, biscuits, caramel, coffee), while hops are perennial varietal plants that add bitterness, aroma, and flavour. Their flowers have been the primary "spice" of beer for some 500 years. Other herbs, berries, and spices were once used, but the antibacterial, preservative qualities of hops ensured they became the main flavouring, lending notes of fruits, herbs, spices, grasses, wood, and flowers.

BEER YEASTS

There are three families of beer yeast: *Saccharomyces cerevisiae* (in ales), *S. pastorianus* (in lagers), and *Brettanomyces* (in wild fermentations).

As well as fermentation, yeast is also responsible for a surprisingly wide variety of aromas and flavours in beer, the primary compounds being light, fruity esters, spicy, smoky phenols, and zingy thiols. Alcohol can also give warming, vinous character, especially in stronger beers.

LAGER — YEAST FERMENTS MORE SLOWLY AT LOWER TEMPERATURES THAN ALE, PRODUCING FEWER YEAST FLAVOURS.

Types of beer

There are more than 100 different styles of beer, each with its own identity, story, and drinking character.

LAGER
Around 90 per cent of beer is lager. It's actually a family of beer (ale is another family) and not a specific style. Classic lager styles include pilsner, helles, dunkel, and bock.

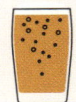
PALE ALE AND IPA
A pale beer with a prominent flavour, bitterness, and aroma from hops. IPAs tend to be stronger and more hoppy than pale ales.

STOUT AND PORTER
A dark ale with a rich, robust flavour of dark malt. Stout and porter are very similar, with stout perhaps having a more roasted flavour profile.

LAMBIC
A spontaneously fermented "wild ale" that naturally develops a tart, dry, complex flavour as it matures for up to 4 years. Different ages of lambic are blended to produce "gueuze".

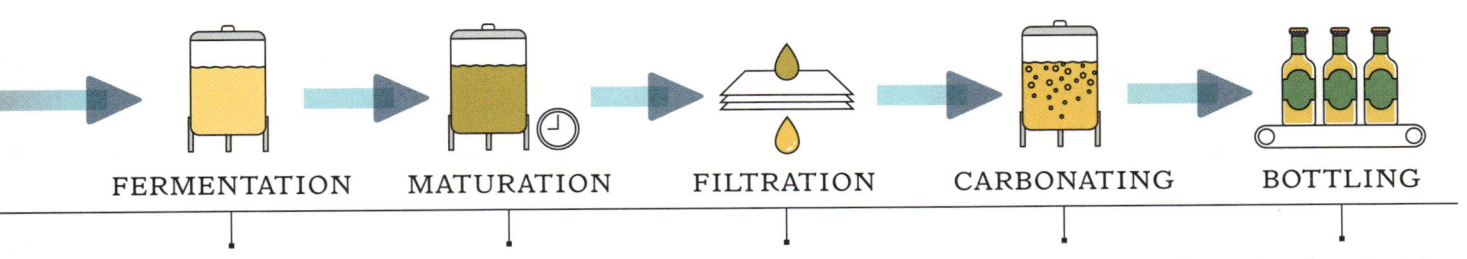

FERMENTATION — **Yeast is added.** Sugars convert to alcohol, CO_2, and flavour compounds. Usually takes 3–9 days.

MATURATION — **Beer matures** for 1–4 weeks or more to develop its flavour profile. More hops can be added here.

FILTRATION — **Any residual yeast** is removed. Not all beer is filtered: if a beer is hazy or cloudy, it is unfiltered.

CARBONATING — **Draft beer is carbonated** in-tank, either naturally with residual yeast in the tank, or by adding CO_2.

BOTTLING — **Beer is packaged.** "Bottle-conditioned" beer develops carbonation inside the bottle.

MAKE YOUR OWN
BEER

This is a recipe for an aromatic modern pale ale – a single-malt, single-hop ale brewed with Citra hops, that will be around 5% ABV. This recipe makes 5 litres and uses a "brew in a bag" method. It will require some specialist equipment, which must all be sanitized before you begin (see p59).

EQUIPMENT
- brewing kettle or large, deep saucepan (approx. 12 litres) with lid
- grain bag
- clamps or other means to secure grain bag
- large plastic spoon
- thermometer
- large pan or bowl
- 2 × hop bags
- large bag of ice
- hydrometer (optional)
- sealable fermenter with tap, airlock, and grommet
- 10 × 500ml bottles

INGREDIENTS
- 1kg crushed pale ale malt
- 30g Citra hop pellets
- 11g sachet pale ale yeast
- 15g sugar (1.5g per bottle)

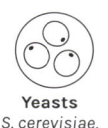
Yeasts
S. cerevisiae,
S. pastorianus,
B. bruxellensis

AAB
A. lambici

4–5 WEEKS

① **Secure a grain bag** to your kettle (or large pan) using clamps, then add 9 litres of water and heat to 75°C (167°F).

② **Put the crushed malt** into the grain bag and stir with a large plastic spoon so that the hot water fully mixes with the grain. This is called "mashing in". The water temperature will drop, but try to get it back to around 67°C (153°F).

③ **Place a lid on the kettle or pan** and remove from the heat. Leave for 1 hour but regularly check the temperature – if it drops below 65°C (149°F), return to a gentle heat (just watch that the grain bag doesn't get scorched inside the kettle).

④ **After 1 hour**, carefully remove the grain sack (ensuring no grain escapes) and allow all the liquid ("wort") to strain into the kettle. Place the grain sack into a separate large pan or bowl (any more liquid that comes out can be added back into the brewing pan or kettle).

DIRECTORY OF FERMENTS • Yeasts 171

⑤ **Bring the wort to a rolling boil**, then put 5g of hops into a hop bag (like a tea bag) and gently stir with the sanitized spoon into the wort. Do not put the lid on the kettle or pan. Set a timer for 1 hour.

⑥ **After 1 hour, remove the kettle from the heat** and add the remaining hops (inside a hop bag), stirring all together. Allow to sit for 10 minutes.

⑦ **Now cool the hopped wort.** Fill a sink with cold water and place the kettle in it. Stir and when it drops below 50°C (122°F), put ice in the sink. Once the wort reaches 20°C (68°F), set the kettle aside for 15 minutes to let the liquid settle.

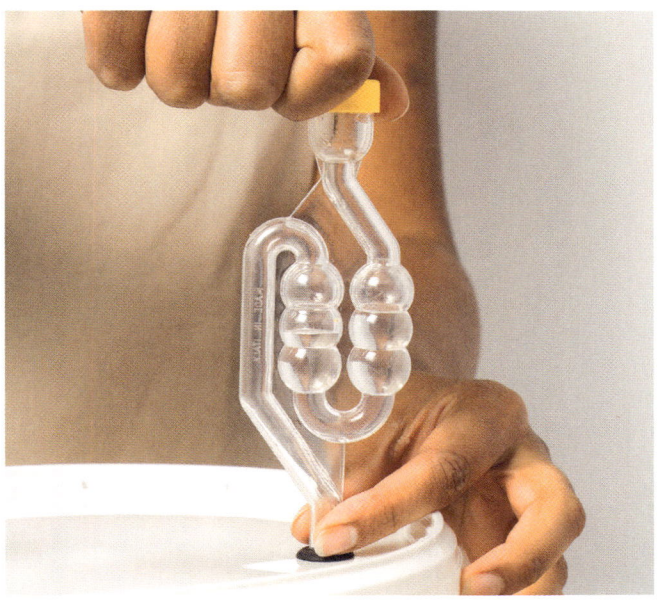

⑧ **If you have a hydrometer**, take a gravity reading of the wort; it should read around 1.050. Carefully transfer the cooled wort to the fermenter, avoiding too much hop residue going in. Add the yeast and seal the fermenter, installing and filling the airlock. Leave in a cool, dark place at 16–19°C (61–66°F). You should see bubbles forming within 12–48 hours.

⑨ **After 7–10 days** the bubbles should slow down and the final gravity should be around 1.010. You can now mature the beer for another week (ideally somewhere colder). When ready, add 1.5g sugar into each bottle, then top up with beer. Seal and leave to ferment/carbonate at around 20°C (68°F); after 2–3 weeks the beer is ready to drink. Store in a fridge or cellar for several months.

Troubleshooting

- If the beer is not fermenting, check the lid is secured and the airlock is working. Gently agitate the liquid to swirl the yeast around, or move it to a warmer area.

- If it's fermenting too quickly, find a slightly cooler place to store your beer.

- If the beer smells like sulphur, give it another week and try it again.

- If your bottled beer is flat, give it another week or two to condition, or move it to a warmer area for a couple of days.

- If it smells and tastes sour, this means you've picked up a bacterial infection and the beer isn't going to be salvageable. Discard it and start afresh.

CIDER

Cider has been consumed for at least 5,000 years, with the earliest evidence coming from the Celts in Britain. Today, it's an alcoholic drink with delicious depth and complexity – all starting from just humble apple juice.

CIDER APPLES ARE CLASSED AS **BITTERSHARP, BITTERSWEET, SHARP,** AND **SWEET.**

As soon as you press the juices out of a fresh apple, time starts ticking before natural fermentation begins. Wild yeast cells will seek out the fruit sugars, which they convert into alcohol and carbon dioxide, plus numerous flavour compounds. The character of the cider will depend on the apple variety, as well as the fermentation and maturation process, which can lend the cider more depth and complexity over time.

CIDER VARIETY AND FLAVOUR

Cider can be champagne-like or perfectly still; be fruity or funky; lightly refreshing or complex and strong; tooth-achingly sweet or puckeringly astringent and dry. It can be made from any apples; in fact, most ciders are made from *many* apples, a mix of different varieties to create a balance of sweetness, sharpness, and tannin.

There are generally two classifications of apple: culinary (dessert or eating, and cooking) and cider. All can be used for cider; the difference is their taste profile, with cider apples typically being more tannic, sharp, and bittersweet than eating apples.

Ciders can also have qualities of citrus, tropical fruit, pear, melon, floral aromas, honey, dried fruit, vanilla, or the "funky" notes of wild fermentation. Like any fermented product, the yeast (or bacteria) involved also add their own distinct esters and phenol compounds.

CLOUDY UNFILTERED CIDER TENDS TO HAVE MORE BODY AND A LITTLE MORE FLAVOUR.

MAKE YOUR OWN

Cider is theoretically easy to make, using either freshly pressed (unpasteurized) apple juice or an apple concentrate mixed with water. This recipe uses fresh-pressed juice for the tastiest results. Natural wild yeast from the apples will likely start fermentation, or you can introduce a "clean" cider, beer, or champagne yeast to get a more controlled, reliable fermentation and flavour profile. Sanitize all equipment before you start (see p59).

EQUIPMENT 2 × 4.5-litre demijohn or plastic fermenter, with airlock • hydrometer (optional) • 8–10 × 500ml bottles

INGREDIENTS 4.5 litres freshly pressed apple juice (plus extra if backsweetening) • 1 Campden tablet (optional but recommended) • 5g dried yeast (a neutral ale yeast is ideal) • ¾ tsp potassium sorbate (optional; if backsweetening) • 30g granulated sugar (3g per bottle)

Yeasts
S. cerevisiae, H. uvarum

LAB
L. brevis

4–7 WEEKS

1. **Add the apple juice** to your sterilized demijohn or fermenter. If you have a hydrometer, measure the original gravity of the juice, as it will help you to know the alcohol content later.

2. **Crush in the Campden tablet** (this is optional, but it releases sulphur dioxide, which will help to stabilize the cider by removing wild yeast and bacteria). Leave for 24 hours.

3. **After the 24 hours,** add the yeast and seal the airlock. Leave in a cool place, at 15–22°C (59–72°F), and fermentation will begin within 12–24 hours. You should see bubbles form on top of the cider, which will increase over a few days.

4. **Fermentation will take 7–14 days.** It is over when the bubbles stop forming and the yeast drops to the bottom of the fermenter (known as "lees"). If you have a hydrometer, take a final gravity reading – ideally it should read 1.000 or very close to it.

5. **Transfer the cider** to another sterilized demijohn or similar vessel, and store in a cool place for 2–3 weeks to allow it to mature and improve in flavour.

6. **Taste the cider.** If you're happy with it, it's ready to be bottled and drunk. If you prefer a sweeter cider, you can "backsweeten" it to taste with fresh apple juice or apple juice concentrate. If so, add the potassium sorbate before you add the juice to stop its sugars fermenting.

7. **Add 3g of sugar to each bottle** (or 6g per 1 litre) to trigger a second fermentation that carbonates the cider, then siphon in the cider and seal the bottle tightly.

8. **Leave at room temperature for 7–14 days** to allow the carbonation to develop, then refrigerate until ready to drink.

Troubleshooting

• The juice must be fresh and without any preservatives. If your cider is not fermenting, check the temperature, as it may not ferment if it's too cold. Gently swirl the fermenter to move the yeast around. If there are no signs of fermentation after 48 hours, move to a warmer place (20–25°C/68–77°F) and add another 5g of yeast. You could also add 50g of granulated sugar.

• There will likely be some cloudiness in the cider, so don't worry. It's more important that the majority of the yeast sediment settles in the bottom of the fermenter.

• If the cider tastes too dry, you can backsweeten it with apple juice after fermentation. You can either do this before bottling, or just mix in fresh apple juice when you pour out the cider.

• If it tastes like cider vinegar, you've got bacteria in the batch. You probably can't save this to drink, and you'll need to be more cautious with sanitizing next time. It's also not drinkable if it develops mould on top.

CLEAR
CIDER IS FILTERED, REMOVING ANY RESIDUAL YEAST AND APPLE SOLIDS, LEAVING YOU WITH A CRISP DRINK.

MEAD

One of the oldest ferments, mead dates back tens of thousands of years to the earliest societies in Africa. It remains a popular ferment for its simplicity, with just two ingredients needed – honey and water.

This alcoholic beverage is the result of yeast fermentation, which converts the sugars present in honey into alcohol. Fruits, spices, and hops can also be added. Historically (and in many home brews) the honey and water mixture was inoculated by wild yeasts, with a blend of many different strains leading to variable results. Modern and commercial production methods use a specific strain or strains of yeasts for consistent fermentation and flavour.

After the initial fermentation the mead can be aged to add complexity, or transferred to barrels to absorb the cask flavours. Secondary fermentation can add another layer of interest; live mead is allowed to ferment and carbonate inside sealed bottles, creating a fizzy mead. The flavour of the final drink is influenced most strongly by the kind of honey used, with the honey flora, species of bee, time of year, weather, and processing methods all affecting the mead's taste.

NECTAR → SUGARS → ETHANOL

Bees produce honey from plant nectar

Yeasts ferment sugars into ethanol

MADHU IS THE SANSKRIT WORD FOR HONEY AND GIVES MEAD ITS NAME.

ROBUST WHOLE SPICES ADD COMPLEXITY AND WARMTH TO CREATE AN EXPRESSIVE BREW.

SEASONAL FRUIT BRINGS FERMENTABLE SUGARS, ACIDITY, AND WINE-LIKE FLAVOURS.

HONEY

CINNAMON AND STAR ANISE

FIGS AND BERRIES

Different types of mead

There are numerous styles of mead, which all vary in flavour and in colour – ranging from pale gold to deep, dark red – and from sweet to astringent. Here is a handful of key styles and their ingredients.

SHOW (BASIC MEAD) is traditionally made with honey, water, and yeast

BOCHET (BLACK MEAD) includes caramelized honey

METHEGLIN is made with added spices

BRAGGOT is made with malted grain such as wheat or barley

MELOMEL is fermented with fruit

MAKE YOUR OWN

Basic mead is simple to make – combine water and honey, then wait for bubbles – but the technique will depend on whether the honey is raw or pasteurized: raw honey already contains yeast; pasteurized does not. To adjust this recipe, use a honey and water mass ratio of 1:4, and 5g of yeast for every 3 litres of mead. Once you've perfected this recipe, you can experiment by adding fruits or spices, fermenting anaerobically, altering the dilution ratio, monitoring alcohol levels, trying specialist yeast strains, or bottle conditioning to carbonate your mead.

EQUIPMENT 5-litre container • muslin cloth • rubber band • bottles (airlocks optional)
INGREDIENTS 750g wild or pasteurized honey • 5g brewer's yeast (optional; see above)

Yeasts S. cerevisiae, H. uvarum, Z. rouxii

2 WEEKS–6 MONTHS

1. **First, measure out 2.25 litres of water**, boil, and then leave to cool to room temperature in your container. When the water is cooled, add the honey and mix until fully dissolved.

2. **If using pasteurized honey**, add the yeast, cover with a clean muslin cloth, and secure with a rubber band. Leave at room temperature, ideally 20°C (68°F), to ferment for around 2 weeks.

3. **Once bubbling slows or stops** and the mead clears, you can bottle and drink it, but most improve with ageing, so ideally seal in airlocked bottles for at least 1–6 months. It should taste dry-to-sweet depending on sugar content, with a clean, alcoholic warmth. It will keep for months to years in sealed bottles, but once opened, refrigerate and consume in 1–2 weeks.

Troubleshooting

• If there is no bubbling after a few days, yeasts are either not present or dead. Add fresh live yeast and mix once a day for a few days.

• If your mead is too yeasty it can be rounded out by filtering, bottling, and ageing.

• Stressed yeast can produce "funky" notes in varying or extreme temperatures. Try to maintain a stable 20°C (68°F). Good hygiene also helps prevent other microbes causing off flavours.

BASIC MEAD   **BLACK MEAD**

SAKÉ

This traditional Japanese alcoholic beverage is the result of a special fermentation process thanks to koji (*Aspergillus oryzae*) and yeast (*Saccharomyces cerevisiae*), which imparts unique flavours, aromas, and textures to the humble rice grain.

UNPOLISHED RICE

POLISHED RICE

Japanese cuisine as we know it would not exist without koji. The word refers to cooked grains or substrate that have been inoculated with koji spores, known as *koji-kin*. Rice, barley, and soya beans are the substrates for traditional saké, shochu, and soy sauce respectively. As with all moulds, koji loves a warm, humid environment. Typical rice koji production for saké brewing takes 48 to 72 hours (see p110).

The main goal of koji production in food is to unlock flavours, while in drinks it's to unlock sugars as well as flavours. Koji is truly an enzyme-producing powerhouse, including over 100 different enzymes, such as lipase, which breaks down fats (lipids). The headline flavour driver, however, is the enzyme protease, which breaks down proteins into smaller amino acids, creating umami. Protease is produced at the lower end of incubation temperature, at around 35°C (95°F). Sugars, meanwhile, are released by the enzyme amylase, which is produced at around 40°C (104°F) and chops up long-chain carbohydrates (like starch in rice) into their simple sugar components. For saké, this process is key to unlocking the sugars within rice.

YEAST STRAINS

Koji and yeast are integral to saké fermentation. They turn the humble rice grain into a delicious, complex, and unimaginably varied beverage. Over the past 100 years, saké yeast strains have been cultivated for their ability to create specific flavour and aroma compounds. Most of these "modern" strains originated as wild yeasts collected from individual breweries across Japan. Historically, these ambient yeasts were synonymous with a particular brewery's saké style. Wild yeast still has a part to play in modern saké production, but most modern breweries use isolated yeast strains to create consistent and relatively predictable saké.

How saké is made

The type of yeast is integral to the style of saké. At least half the flavours and aromas in a saké come from the yeast itself, while a lot of the texture, savouriness, and underlying backbone of a saké can be linked to its koji.

POLISHING

Rice is milled to remove outer layers rich in fats and proteins, exposing the starchy core.

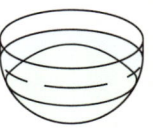

WASHING/SOAKING

Polished rice is washed to remove starch, then soaked to control water absorption, for even steaming.

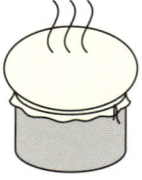

STEAMING

Rice is steamed to gelatinize starches while keeping the grain firm to prepare for koji-making.

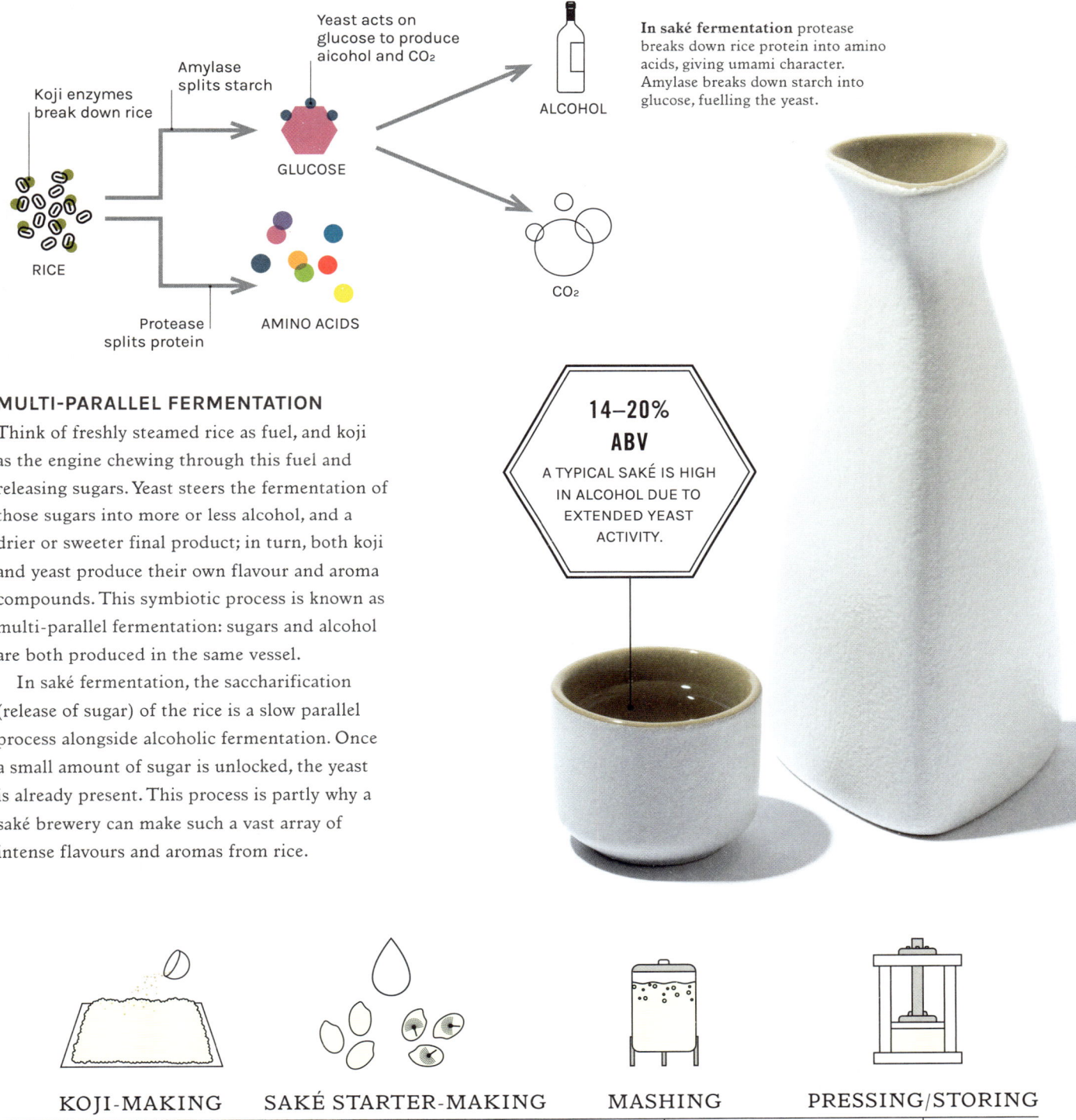

MULTI-PARALLEL FERMENTATION

Think of freshly steamed rice as fuel, and koji as the engine chewing through this fuel and releasing sugars. Yeast steers the fermentation of those sugars into more or less alcohol, and a drier or sweeter final product; in turn, both koji and yeast produce their own flavour and aroma compounds. This symbiotic process is known as multi-parallel fermentation: sugars and alcohol are both produced in the same vessel.

In saké fermentation, the saccharification (release of sugar) of the rice is a slow parallel process alongside alcoholic fermentation. Once a small amount of sugar is unlocked, the yeast is already present. This process is partly why a saké brewery can make such a vast array of intense flavours and aromas from rice.

14–20% ABV
A TYPICAL SAKÉ IS HIGH IN ALCOHOL DUE TO EXTENDED YEAST ACTIVITY.

KOJI-MAKING
Steamed rice is inoculated with *Aspergillus* and grows into koji. Enzymes that convert starches into fermentable sugars are created.

SAKÉ STARTER-MAKING
The koji, steamed rice, water, and yeast are mixed to create the saké starter – the *moto* mash.

MASHING
The main fermentation *moto* mash is built gradually by adding more steamed rice, koji, and water.

PRESSING/STORING
The mash is pressed to separate liquid from solids. The saké is then pasteurized, rested, and aged before dilution and bottling.

MAKE YOUR OWN
DOBUROKU

Doburoku is a traditional, basic form of Japanese saké, which is unfiltered, rustic, and usually sweet. It's an approachable and delicious first leap into the world of saké-style ferments.

Premium saké is typically brewed using a three-stage method known as *san dan shikomi*, where the core ingredients of steamed rice, koji rice, and water are divided into three increasingly larger stages of addition over multiple days. *Doburoku* adds all the ingredients at the start of the fermentation process. This keeps things simple, will yield some funky results, and opens the door for a huge amount of individual experimentation, particularly as the turnaround time is a fraction of its premium cousin. It is intended to be consumed cloudy and milky like a sweet, alcoholic rice pudding drink, which is typically not filtered or strained.

This recipe can easily be scaled up or down using a ratio of 1:1.5 – so for every 1kg of dried rice, add 1.5 litres of water. Make sure you sanitize all equipment before you start (see p59).

EQUIPMENT
- sieve
- 5-litre fermentation jar, or bucket with a vented lid
- steamer or bamboo steamer baskets
- baking parchment or non-stick cloth
- non-rinse brewing sanitizer
- airlock
- blender

INGREDIENTS
- 1kg white sushi rice
- 5g dried ale/wine/champagne/saké yeast
- 250g koji rice

Yeasts
S. cerevisiae

LAB
*L. sakei,
L. mesenteroides,
O. oeni*

Moulds
A. oryzae

Enzymes
Protease, amylase

1–2 WEEKS

① **Wash the sushi rice** in a sieve under running water until the water runs clear. Half fill the fermentation jar with fresh water, add the washed rice, and leave to soak for at least 2 hours.

② **Leave the rice to drain** in a sieve for at least 1 hour, then steam the rice on full power for 30–45 minutes, making sure it does not run dry. It is important that the rice is steamed, not boiled in contact with water.

③ **Cool the rice** by spreading it out on baking parchment or a clean cloth. Sanitize your fermentation jar.

④ **Add the dried yeast** to a cup of 75ml warm water – 40°C (104°F) – to rehydrate it, and set aside.

DIRECTORY OF FERMENTS • Yeasts 179

5 **Once your rice has cooled** to room temperature, transfer to your fermentation vessel, then add 1.8 litres of chilled water (ideally chlorine-free filtered or spring water), followed by the koji rice, and gently stir.

6 **Add the rehydrated yeast and stir.** Seal your vessel and affix the airlock to ensure carbon dioxide can vent out. Place your fermentation vessel in a cool spot, away from direct sunlight. A temperature between 10°C (50°F) and 17°C (63°F) is recommended. Anything below 10°C (50°F) will dramatically slow down your fermentation.

7 **Stir daily to mix up solids** that drop to the bottom. Start tasting after a couple of days. It will be ready in 7–12 days. For a sweeter style pull it sooner; for more funk and alcohol leave it longer. When ready, blitz in a blender, then bottle and seal. Store in the fridge for 5–7 days.

AFTERCARE

Store *doburoku* in a cold fridge. If you want to store it for longer than a week, or potentially outside the fridge, it is possible to pasteurize your brew to halt the fermentation process. This is best done using the water-bath method. Heat water to 80°C (176°F), carefully place your *doburoku* in an open glass vessel into the hot water, raise the temperature of your brew to 65–70°C (149–158°F), and hold it there for 5–15 minutes. Carefully remove and allow to cool. Once cool, add a vented lid. This optional method is particularly recommended to help stabilize your *doburoku* if you choose to add fruit to your fermentation.

Add sweetness
When your *doburoku* is ready, it's possible to add pureéd fruit or conserves.

Make it smooth
For a smoother consistency, you can strain off the larger solids before blitzing with a hand blender.

Troubleshooting

• Remember that your *doburoku* is still alive and fermenting after bottling, meaning it is likely producing carbon dioxide. Avoid airtight containers, which can create very messy explosions.

• You should never smell anything unpleasant from your *doburoku* except a certain amount of funk and high acidity at the start. If you detect any overwhelming sulfur or unpleasant aromas during first fermentation, something has gone awry.

• If you see coloured mould on the surface of your *doburoku*, discard it and start again. Making sure your equipment is well sanitized beforehand is the best protection against this.

SAKÉ IN FOCUS

In Japan, saké production in some form dates to around 600 BCE. Around 1,300 years ago, Buddhist monks incorporated koji (most likely naturally occurring on old rice stores) into brewing saké and it continued to evolve.

The oldest surviving saké breweries date back nearly 900 years, while *koji-kin* production in Japan was commercialized at least 500 years ago for use in both food and drinks.

Today, 90 per cent of saké in Japan is produced using the modern sokujo method of creating a *moto*, or starter, for a saké ferment. This method was developed in the late 1800s and became increasingly popular throughout the twentieth century. Lactic acid is added to reach the desired pH of the starter. Earlier methods had similar objectives of reaching a desired acidic level in the starter ferment. They were slower and harder work, but also tended to produce more complexity, individuality, and a sense of place within the final drink. The three most notable early methods (see right) are all still used today, but they make up less than 10 per cent of all saké produced in Japan.

RICE POLISHING

One of the major developments in saké-making that emerged in the 1900s was the invention of the vertical rice polishing machine. Rice polishing has been part of saké-brewing for centuries, originally performed with a stone by hand and via water or cattle mills. The aim was to remove the brown outside of the grain (which we now know contains elevated levels of protein) to reveal the white starchy grain beneath. Typically brown rice ferments, or rice high in protein, can result in certain off flavours, and may be considered less refined. A certain amount of protein can be desirable, especially when brewing umami-driven styles. But over time, more delicate styles of saké became popular, and the introduction of the vertical polishing machine and its refinement over the past 100 years have allowed breweries to explore this part of modern saké brewing in detail.

Traditional styles

SAKÉ BREWING BEGAN WITH LABOUR AND MICROBES. THESE ANCIENT, SLOW METHODS OF BUILDING STARTER CULTURES HARNESS WILD LAB TO STABILIZE THE MASH AND PRODUCE DEEP, COMPLEX SAKÉS.

BODAIMOTO

Dating to around the 1100s, this approach adds uncooked rice to water, which over time encourages wild lactic acid bacteria (LAB) to thrive, in turn producing lactic acid. That acidic water and sometimes the rice is used to create the starter with the addition of steamed rice and koji.

KIMOTO

This method emerged in the 1600s. A starter of koji, steamed rice, and water is pounded for weeks to encourage LAB from the air to settle and propagate the mash.

YAMAHAI

A less exhausting approach than kimoto, where the principles remain the same but with little to no pounding of the mash. Yamahai emerged at the start of the twentieth century.

YUZU SAKÉ
BLENDS CITRUSY BRIGHTNESS WITH GENTLE SWEETNESS FOR A REFRESHING, AROMATIC TWIST.

TOKUBETSU JUNMAI SAKÉ
IS A STYLE OF PURE RICE SAKÉ MADE BY A "SPECIAL" TECHNIQUE FOR INDIVIDUAL CHARACTER.

CLOUDY NIGORI SAKÉ
IS OPAQUE DUE TO RICE PARTICLES THAT REMAIN IN THE FINAL BREW.

AGED JUNMAI SAKÉ
DEVELOPS EARTHY, NUTTY, UMAMI NOTES WITH DEEP COLOUR OVER 3+ YEARS.

HOW RICE POLISHING AFFECTS SAKÉ

Less polished rice retains more protein, producing richer, umami-forward saké suited to food pairing. Highly polished rice yields cleaner, more elegant styles. Polishing doesn't indicate quality, just style. More polished rice costs more to produce, and is typically served chilled, whereas fuller-bodied styles suit a range of temperatures.

GINGER BUG AND GINGER BEER

A ginger bug is a naturally fermenting starter culture that is used to speed up the process of making fermented beverages, such as ginger beer and root beer. It also gives a slightly tangy flavour to ginger beer and other probiotic fruit drinks.

A ginger bug, like a sourdough starter, is a wild cultured starter that you can make at home and establish, then regularly feed to keep it active. If you use it to make ginger beer that ferments, it gives it a boost by inoculating it with an existing, healthy community of microbes that kick-start the fermentation process. Fresh ginger root can be used to make a starter culture because its skin is teeming with beneficial yeasts and bacteria.

GINGER BEER

BOTTLING
GINGER BEER IN A SEALED CONTAINER FORCES CARBONATION, AS CO_2 CANNOT ESCAPE.

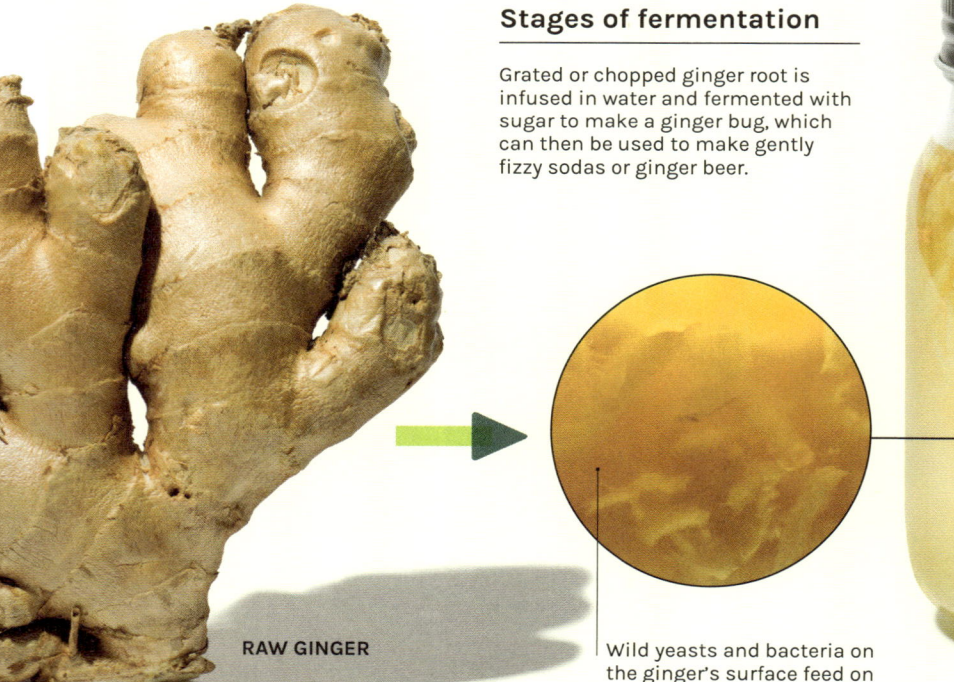

Stages of fermentation

Grated or chopped ginger root is infused in water and fermented with sugar to make a ginger bug, which can then be used to make gently fizzy sodas or ginger beer.

RAW GINGER

Wild yeasts and bacteria on the ginger's surface feed on the sugar and produce CO_2.

GINGER BUG

DIRECTORY OF FERMENTS • Yeasts

MAKE YOUR OWN GINGER BUG

If you want to make your own ginger bug you'll need to find organic ginger, because conventional ginger is sometimes irradiated, which damages existing microbial colonies on the skin and so reduces its ability to ferment quickly.

EQUIPMENT grater • 500ml jar • muslin cloth • swing-top bottle
INGREDIENTS 150g fresh organic ginger • 150g sugar

Yeasts
S. cerevisiae, S. florentinus

LAB
L. hilgardii, L. plantarum, L. mesenteroides

4–7 DAYS

1. **Rinse and scrub** the ginger to remove any dirt, leaving the peel on, then grate.
2. **Add 500ml of water to the jar**, then add 1–2 tablespoons of the grated ginger and 1–2 tablespoons of the sugar. Keep the rest of the grated ginger in a sealed container in the fridge.
3. **Cover the jar with a muslin cloth** or other breathable covering (like a tea towel) and leave at room temperature for 3–5 days. Add 1 tablespoon of ginger and 1 tablespoon of sugar each day and stir.
4. **After 4–7 days**, it will be bubbly and ready to use in homemade sodas. Add 40–60ml to a soda mixture (such as ginger beer; see right), and allow it to ferment in a swing-top bottle for a further 2–3 days.
5. **Store your ginger bug** in the fridge and continue to feed it once a week until it is used up. To feed the ginger bug, take it out of the fridge for a couple of hours to come to room temperature, then add 1 tablespoon each of ginger and sugar. You can then either use it to make more drinks or put it back in the fridge.

Troubleshooting

- Hot liquids kill the microbes in ginger bugs, so if you heat your mixture, wait until it cools to room temperature to add your ginger bug.

MAKE YOUR OWN GINGER BEER

Ginger beer can be made with or without a ginger bug, but adding the ginger bug will help your beer ferment more quickly.

EQUIPMENT grater • mixing bowl • muslin cloth • sieve • 4 × 1-litre bottles
INGREDIENTS 500g fresh organic ginger • 60ml ginger bug (optional) • 3–6 tbsp fresh lime juice • 200g raw sugar

Yeasts
S. cerevisiae, S. florentinus

LAB
L. hilgardii, L. plantarum, L. mesenteroides

1–3 DAYS

1. **Rinse and scrub** the ginger to remove any dirt, leaving the peel on.
2. **Grate the ginger** and add it, together with 3.5 litres of water and the ginger bug (if using), to a large bowl and stir to combine. Cover with a muslin cloth (or tea towel), and leave at room temperature overnight, or for up to 48 hours.
3. **Strain the mixture** using muslin or a fine-mesh sieve, then squeeze the solids to get as much gingery flavour out as possible.
4. **Whisk the lime juice** and sugar into the strained liquid until the sugar has dissolved.
5. **You can now bottle it** and store in the fridge for a lightly fermented, non-carbonated drink. For a carbonated version, ferment in a narrow-necked bottle for 2–3 days before refrigerating.

GO ORGANIC

USE ORGANIC RATHER THAN CONVENTIONAL IRRADIATED GINGER, TO ENSURE THE NATURAL YEASTS ARE INTACT.

KVAS

Kvas – a Proto-Slavic word meaning "sour" – refers not to one single beverage, but a whole category of lightly fermented drinks made across Eastern Europe. These are refreshing, gently tangy, and low in alcohol, with flavour profiles shaped by local ingredients and seasonality.

In much of Ukraine, where kvas remains an enduring part of domestic food culture, the first association will often be beetroot kvas – particularly in regions where it is used to add acidity to borscht, the national broth. It is made simply, with water, a little salt, and raw beetroot, though contemporary versions sometimes include ginger or warming spices.

There are multiple other drinks that are called kvas – from fermented rhubarb kvas, to west Ukrainian lemon kvas and many other lightly fermented berry and fruit beverages. In western Ukraine, raspberries, wild strawberries, blackberries, bilberries, lingonberries, gooseberries, cornelian cherries, and windfall fruit would be used. For berry kvases, the bottom of the barrel would often be covered with oat or rye straw.

The most ubiquitous kvas is bread kvas, which is traditionally made from fermenting stale rye bread crusts, sourdough starter, dried fruits, and spring water. In the past, a tablespoonful of rye flour, *solod* (a special twice-fermented rye malt powder), or buckwheat flour could have been used to introduce the desired yeasts and lactic acid bacteria (LAB) to the starter. Early-twentieth-century recipes describe complex processes where flour would be covered in hot water, then left to cool, then strained and covered in hot water again, sometimes repeated for three to four cycles. Bread kvas is traditionally enjoyed as a cold, fizzy summer drink but is delicious year-round, and the bread kvas starter can be used as the base for lemon, rhubarb, or berry kvases.

SOURDOUGH STARTER, FRESH YEAST, OR A TBSP OF ORGANIC FLOUR AND MALT CAN BE USED TO INITIATE FERMENTATION.

Stages of fermentation

Bread kvas begins with a microbially rich starter culture of stale rye bread, sugar or honey, water, and dried fruits. This starter is used to inoculate a larger batch of liquid, which is bottled to yield a crisp, lightly sparkling drink.

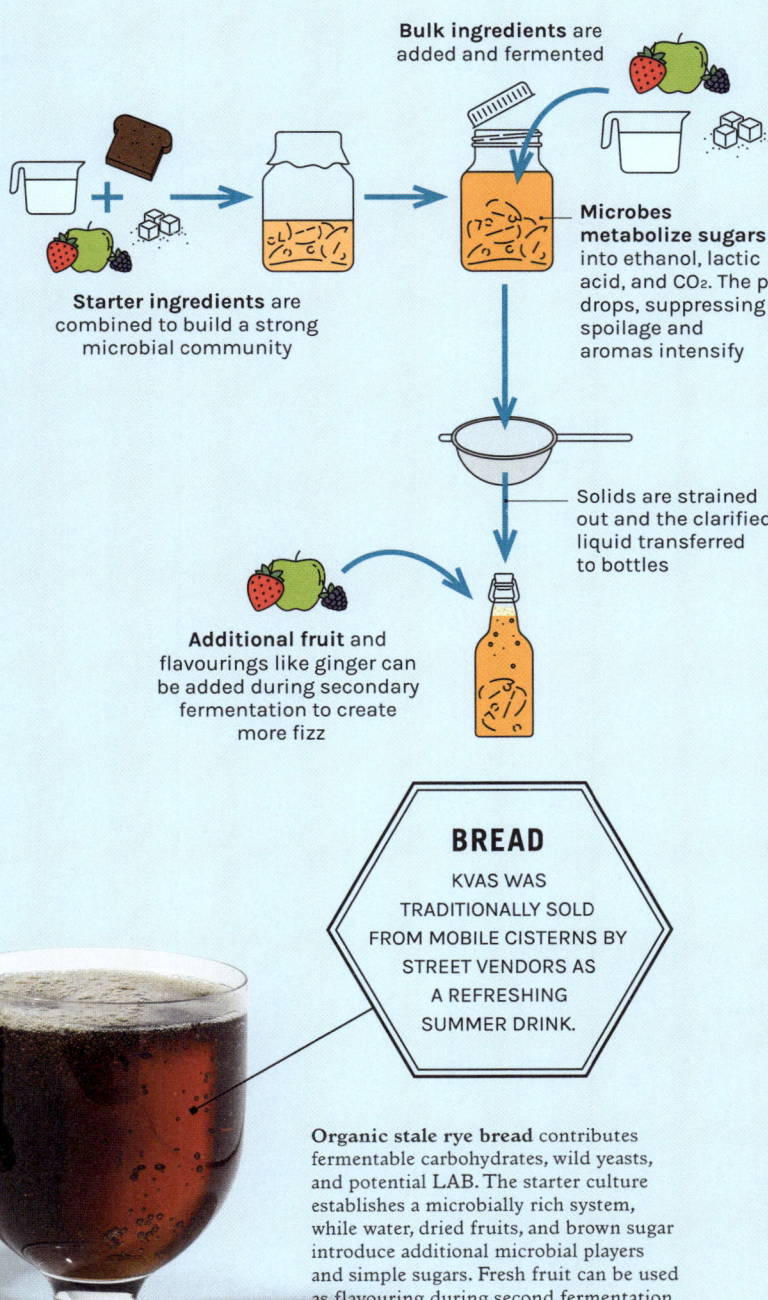

Starter ingredients are combined to build a strong microbial community

Bulk ingredients are added and fermented

Microbes metabolize sugars into ethanol, lactic acid, and CO_2. The pH drops, suppressing spoilage and aromas intensify

Solids are strained out and the clarified liquid transferred to bottles

Additional fruit and flavourings like ginger can be added during secondary fermentation to create more fizz

BREAD KVAS WAS TRADITIONALLY SOLD FROM MOBILE CISTERNS BY STREET VENDORS AS A REFRESHING SUMMER DRINK.

Organic stale rye bread contributes fermentable carbohydrates, wild yeasts, and potential LAB. The starter culture establishes a microbially rich system, while water, dried fruits, and brown sugar introduce additional microbial players and simple sugars. Fresh fruit can be used as flavouring during second fermentation.

MAKE YOUR OWN

This recipe follows a traditional home method for bread kvas. It can be adapted to create lemon, rhubarb, or berry variants using the same starter.

EQUIPMENT 500ml jar or container • muslin cloths • rubber bands • 3-litre jar or container • 2-litre bottle

INGREDIENTS
For the starter 15g sourdough starter (or 3g dry/10g fresh yeast) • 100g dry sourdough rye bread (or good sourdough or yeast-leavened bread), torn or cubed • 15–20g organic raisins (or dried apples, sulfite-free apricots, or pears) • 15g brown sugar or raw honey
For the kvas 100g raw brown sugar (or any sugar/honey/syrup) • 20–30g dried fruit

 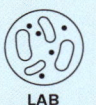 

Yeasts S. cerevisiae, C. krusei | **LAB** L. plantarum, L. mesenteroides | **AAB** A. aceti | 5–7 DAYS

① **Mix the starter ingredients** with 200ml of filtered tap water in a small jar or container, then cover with a muslin cloth secured with a rubber band. Within 1–2 days the starter will start to fizz.

② **When the starter is fizzing vigorously**, pour into a larger jar. Add 3 litres of filtered tap water, the sugar, and fruit for the kvas, then cover with muslin and secure with a rubber band. Leave out of direct sunlight for 3 days or until it tastes a little sweet, sour, and yeasty.

③ **Strain the kvas** through a muslin cloth and squeeze the remaining liquid out of the solids. You can add extra flavourings here, such as 50g of berries or ginger slices (max. 10g per litre), if you wish.

④ **Transfer to a bottle and seal**, ferment for a further 1–2 days, then transfer to the fridge (see p201 for more on carbonation). Drink within 2 weeks.

Troubleshooting

• If the kvas has no fizz, add a little more dried fruit and move it to a warmer spot to get things moving.

• If your kvas turns overly sour or boozy, it's likely fermented for too long or is too warm. Taste as you go and, when happy, transfer to the fridge to slow it down.

• Off, funky, or bitter notes suggest unwanted microbes or over-toasted bread. Ensure your equipment is clean and use dry bread, not toasted.

TEPACHE

Tepache is a traditional fermented soft drink from Mexico. Usually made using only leftover pineapple peel and sugar, it is sweet, tangy, and slightly carbonated. Tepache is incredibly easy to ferment, and makes use of the skin and core of the fruit, reducing food waste.

The origins of tepache in Mexico are not completely clear, although it traces back at least to the Pre-Columbian era (before 1492). It can be fermented from many different fruits, and was probably first made with corn, but the most popular modern version is made using pineapple.

What makes tepache so simple to produce is that it's a wild ferment, which means no starter culture is involved. Pineapple skins are covered with microbes, among them those that excel at fermenting the flesh beneath the peel.

A SELECTIVE ENVIRONMENT

It's the fermenter's job to encourage desirable strains and weed out the bad by creating the perfect conditions for these yeast and bacteria to thrive. In the case of tepache, by submerging the rind and core of the pineapple in liquid we separate them from oxygen at the surface, so the undesirable microbes that need air as well as sweet fruit flesh are starved of it. So, be careful to keep everything under water when making your own tepache.

Stages of fermentation

Once submerged in sugar water, the microbes will get to work converting the sugar into lactic acid, making it taste sour, and carbon dioxide, making it fizzy. As a wild ferment, the exact microbiome of each batch will vary, but yeasts and lactic acid bacteria (LAB) will quickly dominate.

MAIZE, BANANA PEEL, GUAVA, AND THE INDIGENOUS MEXICAN PIÑUELA FRUIT CAN ALL BE USED TO MAKE TEPACHE.

AT 0–3% ABV ON AVERAGE, TEPACHE IS CONSIDERED NO-TO-LOW ALCOHOL.

Pineapple skin hosts wild yeasts that have evolved to nestle into the crevices

PINEAPPLE

A Mexican tradition

Tepache was traditionally made and consumed at drinking establishments called *tepacherías*, which were popular in Mexico City, especially in the early twentieth century. Now it is more commonly sold by street vendors alongside the fermented corn drink *tejuino*. The name tepache comes from the central Mexican language Nahuatl, in which the word *tepiātl* means "corn drink", indicating that the drink was first made with maize.

Floating yeast makes tepache look cloudy

STRAINED TEPACHE

The flavour of tepache should be akin to a sweet and sour spiced scrumpy cider, which will become more acidic over time. It can be cut with lager to make a lovely shandy.

MAKE YOUR OWN

As tepache is made by wild or spontaneous fermentation, timings can be erratic, and depend on temperature, so you may need to experiment.

EQUIPMENT large glass jar (minimum 1.5 litre)
INGREDIENTS 1 pineapple • 100g dark brown sugar (or piloncillo) • cinnamon stick and cloves (optional)

Yeasts
S. cerevisiae,
C. boidinii,
P. membranifaciens

LAB
L. hilgardii,
L. plantarum,
L. mesenteroides

5–10 DAYS

1. **Chop the leaves** and base off the pineapple and discard. Next, peel it, keeping the skin in long, 3–4cm-wide strips. Next, cut out and retain the core. The rest of the pineapple can be eaten or kept for another purpose.

2. **Boil 200ml of water** in a pan, then add the dark brown sugar or piloncillo. Stir to dissolve, then add 1 litre of cold water to bring the mixture down to room temperature.

3. **Arrange the pineapple skin** in the jar securely so it won't float (bending it into horizontal bands with the inner side braced against the walls of the jar works well), then wedge the pineapple core in, too. Pour in the sugar water to fill the jar, making sure the peel is covered and leaving 3–5cm headroom. Add a cinnamon stick and/or a few cloves to enhance the flavour, as desired, then seal the jar.

4. **Leave to ferment** at room temperature for 2–6 days, checking daily until you see evidence of fizzing and/or cloudiness. Once it gets going, let it ferment until it tastes as sour as you'd like (another 1–3 days, depending on temperature).

5. **Strain out the pineapple skin** and core, and keep the tepache refrigerated in a glass swing-top or plastic bottle. It will continue to ferment slowly.

Troubleshooting

• Foam may form at the top, which is the result of top-fermenting yeast – this is not of concern.

• If mould appears at the top, it is due to the peel/core not being fully submerged. Make sure it's all below the water line.

ACETIC ACID BACTERIA

Acetic acid bacteria fermentation	**190**
Acetic acid bacteria, biofilms, and SCOBYs	**192**
Harnessing the power of acetic acid bacteria	**194**
Kombucha	**196**
Kombucha vs vinegar	**202**
Vinegar	**204**
Shrubs	**208**

ACETIC ACID BACTERIA FERMENTATION

A group of about 1,500 microbes collectively known as acetic acid bacteria specialize in converting alcohol into acetic acid – the chemical that gives vinegar, and to a lesser extent kombucha, that characteristic sour tang and acrid smell – via oxidative fermentation.

The large family of microbes comprising acetic acid bacteria (AAB), with genera including *Acetobacter*, *Gluconobacter*, and *Komagataeibacter*, have some interesting features that make them quite distinct from the lactic acid bacteria that are responsible for lactic acid fermentation (see p68). First, they are obligate aerobes, which means they require oxygen for their metabolism. Second, many species are responsible for the production of copious quantities of cellulose. Third, they are uniquely able to oxidize alcohol to acetic acid.

Since the production of alcohol began during the Neolithic era, the alcohol-to-vinegar conversion pathway has caused wine spoilage, but by 3000 BCE the Babylonians had recognized the preservative qualities of soured wine or date beer, and it was extensively used for food preservation in areas where salt was scarce. AAB often have flagella – structures like tadpole tails – that help them swim through liquids, enabling them to access oxygen, and they are ubiquitous, existing on almost all surfaces throughout our homes and in nature. This is why a weak solution of alcohol (7 per cent or less) will readily turn to vinegar without any human intervention if left exposed to the air.

EVOLUTIONARY ORIGINS

AAB have existed on Earth for about 3 billion years and seem to have developed in response to the presence of cyanobacteria, which were able to photosynthesize and produce oxygen. The development of their ability to metabolize alcohol to

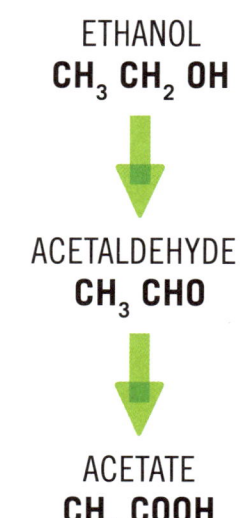

ETHANOL
$CH_3 CH_2 OH$

ACETALDEHYDE
$CH_3 CHO$

ACETATE
$CH_3 COOH$

1. In the first stage, alcohol is oxidized to acetaldehyde in a reaction catalysed by alcohol dehydrogenase.

2. With more oxygen, the second-stage oxidation produces acetic acid, catalysed by aldehyde dehydrogenase.

3. Some acetic acid will react with any remaining alcohol to produce ethyl acetate, which has a strong, solvency odour. This is reversible and indicates fermentation is underway but not complete.

"VINEGAR" DERIVES FROM THE FRENCH VIN AIGRE, MEANING "SOUR WINE" – IN TURN, FROM THE LATIN VINUM ACER.

THE PATHWAY TO ACETIC ACID

The conversion of ethanol into acetic acid is a two-step reaction that requires oxygen. Two specific dehydrogenase enzymes, found in AAB, are needed to catalyse the process. As the name suggests, they remove hydrogen atoms from their substrates, thus oxidizing them.

Acid-producing bacteria

Gluconobacter and *Komagataeibacter* species are capable of oxidative fermentation pathways, producing a range of acids including acetic, gluconic, and glucuronic, depending on substrate and temperature.

produce acetic acid, and in the process ATP (the primary source of energy for our cells), seems to have become aligned with yeast metabolism of fruit sugars to produce alcohol (ethanol) at some point over the last 100 million years. AAB hold a selective advantage because they can tolerate high levels of both alcohol and the acetic acid they produce – compounds that are toxic to many other microbes.

ALCOHOL AND ACID RESISTANCE

Some of the acetic acid generated from this process is used as an energy source for the microbe. The rest is exported via transporter mechanisms in the cell membrane into the surrounding medium. These mechanisms reduce the cellular concentration of acetic acid, which would otherwise become toxic for the microbe. In fact, most AAB are not tolerant of extremely high concentrations of acetic acid, although certain strains such as *Komagataeibacter europaeus* can generate up to 15 per cent acetic acid, if oxygen levels are kept high.

A complete explanation for acid resistance in AAB has not yet been found; many proteins, co-factors, metabolic pathways, and even changes to the shape of the cell are involved. These same factors allow AAB to survive relatively high concentrations of alcohol, through its conversion into acetic acid, which they can metabolize or expel – in some strains, through the formation of protective cellulose cultures or biofilms (see p192).

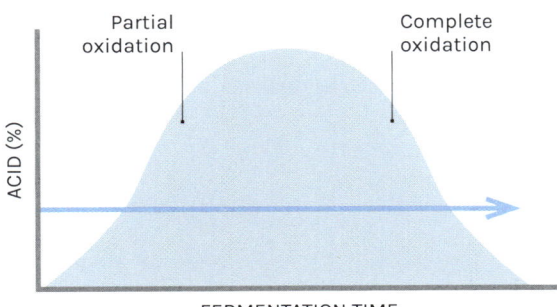

OXIDATION IN VINEGAR-MAKING

Vinegar is the result of partial oxidation. As long as there is alcohol present, and/or no air, the AAB cannot complete the process. However, when all the alcohol has been turned into vinegar, in the presence of oxygen, AAB can use the vinegar as a source of energy, and break it down to CO_2 and water. This is complete oxidation, and it destroys vinegar.

ACETIC ACID BACTERIA, BIOFILMS, AND SCOBYS

Acetic acid bacteria have a long history of symbiotic association with other microbial species, including yeasts and lactic acid bacteria. These prehistoric relationships are remarkable, not least because they can produce physical cultures that help the fermentation process along.

Symbiosis can be an excellent survival strategy for microbes, providing access to food sources, protection from harsh environments, and the chance to occupy otherwise inhospitable niches. Although the microbes are microscopic, they can produce cellulose that binds to form very visible biofilms – the mother of vinegar or a SCOBY (symbiotic culture of bacteria and yeast) – which play a key role in the acetic acid fermentation process.

WHAT ARE BIOFILMS?

Biofilms are symbiotic communities of microbes encased in a self-generated matrix, usually made from polysaccharides (carbohydrates consisting of ten or more simple sugars). They form some of the earliest relationships on Earth, with examples within fossils dating back billions of years, and occupy diverse environments from natural habitats to our oral cavities, and even concrete structures.

From a microbial perspective they are a great way to live; if we consider a kombucha SCOBY, the yeasts and acetic acid bacteria (AAB) are bound together in close association, ensuring that the AAB have ready access to the ethanol produced by the yeast. They also provide other nutrients, including amino acids, fatty acids, enzymes, and vitamins, to promote the growth of AAB. The cellulose provides a protective haven from the harsh acidic and ethanol-rich environment surrounding the microbes, which protects the SCOBY from contamination.

The benefits of living in a SCOBY

The yeasts and AAB are bound together in close association in a SCOBY, and in general, this co-existence enhances fermentation in numerous ways.

- **The biofilm provides a ready supply of nutrients**, including amino acids, fatty acids, enzymes, and vitamins, to promote the growth of AAB and LAB (if present). It may also contain spent yeasts that then go on to provide nutrition for the brew following autolysis (cell or tissue self-digestion).

- **The cellulose provides a protective haven** from the harsh acidic and ethanol-rich environment surrounding the microbes, which in turn protects the SCOBY from contamination.

- **Proximity provides ideal conditions** for horizontal gene transfer between microbe species (this can be useful for microbial survival, but can also potentially cause problems if antibiotic resistance genes are transferred).

- **Protection against attack by bacteriophages** (viruses that can infect bacterial cells).

- **Microbes can collaborate** to share resources via chemical messengers called autoinducers, which can bind to specific receptors on neighbouring microbes and influence gene expression.

SCOBY formation

The physical structure of a SCOBY or vinegar mother is made of bacterial cellulose: biocellulose. At the same time that alcohol, acetic acid, and CO_2 are being produced, specific bacteria, namely *Komagataeibacter xylinus*, convert some of the glucose into cellulose, forming the pellicle.

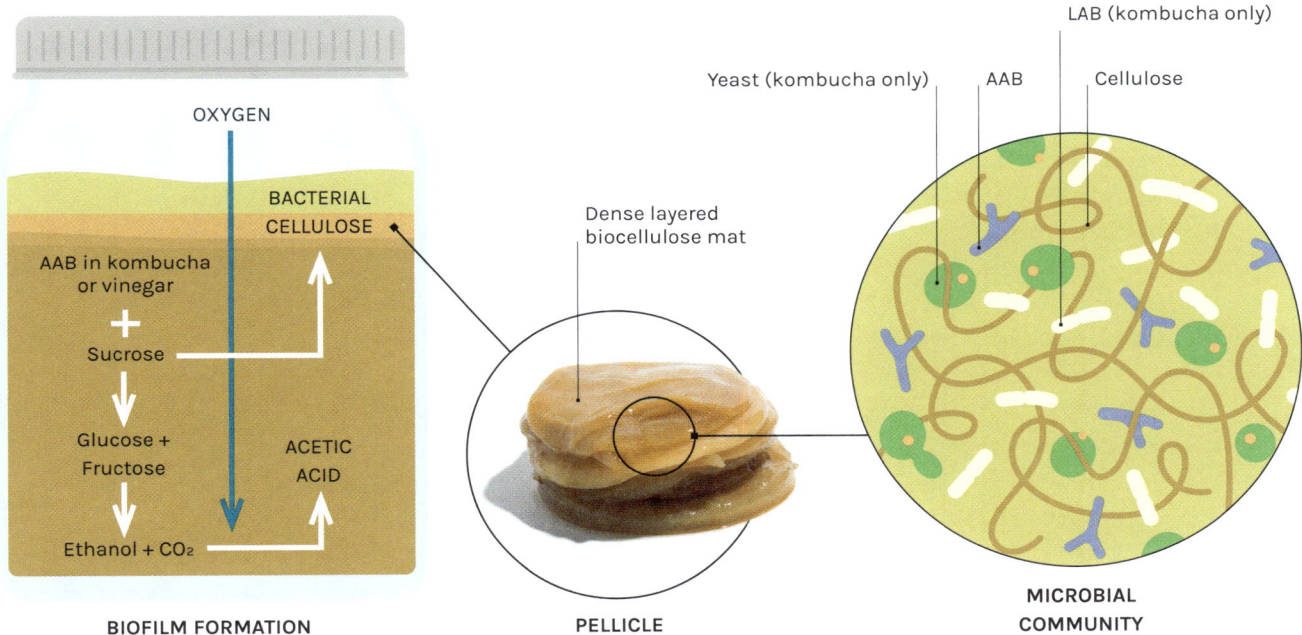

SCOBYS AND VINEGAR MOTHERS

AAB species such as *Komagataeibacter* and *Gluconacetobacter* are particularly voracious producers of cellulose, which help to form kombucha SCOBYs and vinegar mothers. This is controlled by how many copies of the cellulose synthase gene they have, or how efficiently the gene's activity is regulated.

The growth of these biofilms always occurs at the liquid/air interface and is quite incredible to watch; in a couple of weeks, from an almost imperceptible sheen on the surface of a sweet tea or alcoholic solution, a structure several inches thick can develop.

Microbial relationships

Microbes can also have important symbiotic relationships with more complex organisms. In their relationship with our gut microbiota, we provide nourishment for them, while they provide us with the end products of metabolism to support our metabolic health. Then there is the relationship between nitrogen-fixing microbes in the soil and the roots of plants. The microbes in the root nodules convert nitrogen into a form usable by the plant, and in return the plant provides sugars and oxygen for microbial growth.

HARNESSING THE POWER OF ACETIC ACID BACTERIA

Without even realizing it, most of us are in regular contact with the remarkable byproducts of acetic acid bacteria. These microbes can metabolize ethanol from any origin into acetic acid, but that is not their only metabolic pathway of use.

For microbes that were once the scourge of the wine industry (see p166), acetic acid bacteria (AAB) have certainly redeemed themselves and proven to be invaluable in biotechnological processes. In fact, we have been exploiting them for centuries.

VINEGAR

Industrial production of vinegar (see p204) took off in the late 1600s, with makers siphoning off substandard wine and beer specifically for the purpose. Although acetic acid can also be made via a chemical reaction without a microbe in sight, and diluted to make something akin to vinegar, for a product to carry the word vinegar on the label, it must have undergone microbial fermentation.

Making vinegar through the natural development of a mother on a still surface has been replaced with huge, temperature-controlled, aerated tanks of circulating alcohol containing a support structure to increase the surface area upon which AAB can grow, speeding up the conversion rate of alcohol to vinegar.

KOMBUCHA

The kombucha (see p196) industry continues to grow apace, spurred on by consumer demand for low-alcohol drinks. While many artisan producers continue to use the traditional SCOBY, on a commercial scale it's becoming commonplace to engineer the process for consistency and low-alcohol content, often using isolated, specific strains of AAB, such as *Komagataeibacter saccharivorans*, with selected yeasts, or kombucha concentrates as a base, which can be diluted and flavoured.

GLUCONIC ACID

Another useful product of AAB partial oxidation: *Gluconobacter oxydans* can oxidize glucose to gluonic acid via the enzyme glucose dehydrogenase. The acid is excreted into the surrounding medium from the cell via porins (protein channels) in the outer membrane. Gluconic acid has wide-ranging uses in just about every sector: as a concrete additive to control setting time; as an acidulant, flavour enhancer, preservative, and antioxidant in the food industry; it's also found in cleaning products and used as a stabilizer in pharmaceutical preparations.

Acetic acid bacteria are a key part of the process of many different products, from the everyday, like chocolate and table vinegar, to extraordinary biocellulose.

KOMBUCHA AND CHOCOLATE

BIOCELLULOSE

Komagataeibacter xylinus species are particularly proficient at producing cellulose, through a multi-stage pathway that involves several enzymes, including cellulose synthase. The resulting biocellulose is exceptional due to its ultra-pure structure, free from lignin, hemicellulose, and other components found in plant-derived cellulose. It has extremely high tensile strength and excellent water-holding capacity, retaining up to 200 times its dry weight. It can also be produced from various waste streams, so is environmentally efficient. It's come into its own in medical practice, where it is used to dress wounds, treat burns, and create artificial skin. It is gaining traction as a sustainable alternative to plastics for packaging, too, as it is biodegradable, compostable, and even edible, and can also be used as a food thickener and in plant-based meat alternatives.

NATA DE COCO

One of the most interesting uses for AAB is the production of this sweet, chewy, coconut-flavoured jelly from the Philippines. Nata de coco is not ancient in origin, having been invented in 1949 by Teódula Kalaw África, a chemist at the Philippine Coconut Authority, who was looking for an alternative to the pineapple-derived nata de piña, which had been made from piña-fibre industry waste since the 1700s.

The process requires coconut water, which is inoculated with the cellulose producer *K. xylinus*. Just as in kombucha and vinegar, a cellulose mat develops; however, in the case of nata de coco, it's the mat that is kept rather than the coconut water! The cellulose is then washed and cut into pieces before being boiled to improve the texture. The pieces are then soaked in sugar syrup and sometimes flavoured.

CHOCOLATE

Another relatively unknown role for AAB is their importance in the early stages of chocolate production. In cocoa bean fermentation, they convert yeast-produced ethanol to acetic acid and contribute to the development of flavours and the inhibition of unwanted microbes. *Acetobacter pasteurianus* is the species most associated with this spontaneous process.

VINEGARS

The discovery of AAB and pasteurization

Acetic acid bacteria were first isolated by Louis Pasteur in 1857 when he was called upon by the French government to investigate spoilage in the French wine industry. He realized that in spoiled wine, two types of microbe were present: large, oval yeast cells and smaller, longer cells, which he ascribed to newly identified spoilage microbes, *Acetobacter aceti*. He showed that the microbes were obligate aerobes (requiring oxygen), and that controlling oxygen exposure during winemaking could therefore prevent spoilage. His discovery also led to a better understanding of the bacterial production of acetic acid, revolutionizing the vinegar industry.

KOMBUCHA

Kombucha is a fermented drink made from sweetened tea (traditionally *Camellia sinensis*), which can be still or sparkling, sweet, dry, or tart. It is thought to date back over 2,000 years and has recently become one of the most popular soft drinks on the planet, especially by those seeking an alternative to fizzy drinks.

The history of kombucha is murky at best, but it is believed to have been enjoyed during China's Qin Dynasty (221–206 BCE), when it was known as the "Tea of Immortality". From China, kombucha spread to Japan, Russia, Eastern Europe, and then the rest of Europe and around the world, where it is widely enjoyed today as flavours evolve and develop through the enthusiasm and creativity of its makers.

Kombucha is made by brewing black or green tea, sugar, and a mixed culture of bacteria and yeast, via backslopping with unpasteurized kombucha and a SCOBY if you have one. Kombucha needs this microbial community and will not spontaneously ferment without it. The resulting fermentation turns the sugar into alcohol and acids, creating a tangy, sometimes mildly alcoholic drink.

Kombucha can vary in taste from sweet-tart to downright vinegary, depending on the length of the fermentation. Early on, it can also taste slightly yeasty or boozy as a result of the yeast converting sugar into alcohol, while the bacteria bring in the acid flavours as they consume both the sugar and alcohol, leaving only trace amounts of alcohol behind. Simple kombucha can be further flavoured with botanicals, fresh fruit, or fruit juices.

Why and how does a SCOBY form?

A SCOBY (see p192) – the jelly-like cellulose mat (or pellicle) that floats at the top of the kombucha – is not only home to the community of bacteria and yeast that work in tandem to ferment the brew. It also protects the tea from dust, evaporation, and other wild microbes that may be spoilers. As a topper, it even helps keep the light carbonation in place. You can buy a SCOBY ready-made or make your own during your first batch of kombucha (see overleaf). The key is using unpasteurized kombucha as the starter. A transparent film will begin to form in as little as three days. As it grows it will form an initial white layer, then, with each brew you will see a new layer form on top, eventually making the SCOBY quite thick.

The cellulose SCOBY is formed in layers by a community of yeasts, AAB, and LAB

KOMBUCHA STARTER

SCOBY

TEA LEAVES

SUGAR

HEALTH BENEFITS

Many of kombucha's health benefits stem from the bioactive compounds derived from the tea, juices, or herbal extracts used to make it. For example, its strong antioxidant properties come in part from the polyphenols in the green or black tea. It also contains the metabolites of the yeasts, acetic acid bacteria (AAB), and lactic acid bacteria (LAB) that carry out the fermentation. These are most often postbiotics, enzymes, various phenolic compounds, acids, and vitamins.

These benefits are hard to quantify as they depend on the quality of the tea, extraction methods, and all the factors regarding the ingredients and microbes present in the fermentation. Probiotics are even harder to measure and are often spent by the time a batch is finished. Therefore, many commercial brands add probiotics to their kombucha to claim that the drink is probiotic.

Stages of fermentation

Kombucha's fermentation time is influenced mostly by temperature. The AAB, in particular, need warmth to thrive. Fermentation at 24–29°C (75–84°F) will follow this timeline, although in typical home temperatures it may take longer.

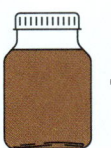

DAY 1
The ferment begins with the bacteria and yeast consuming the sugar and multiplying, with no visible signs. The liquid remains dark, the colour of brewed tea.

DAYS 3–5
CO_2 bubbles are forming, indicating an active ferment. A new SCOBY layer begins to form as a thin film on the liquid's surface – either on the mother SCOBY or on its own if the mother hasn't floated to the top. Acidic flavours are replacing sweetness, and the colour is lightening.

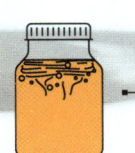

DAY 7 AND BEYOND
CO_2 bubbles continue to be active, slowing down as sugar decreases. The new SCOBY continues to thicken. You may see yeast strands forming below the SCOBY and see spent yeast sediment at the bottom. The flavour becomes sourer as more of the sugar is converted to acid, and the colour becomes lighter.

POLYPHENOLS OFFER PREBIOTIC BENEFITS AND CAN HELP PROTECT AGAINST CELL DAMAGE.

LAB ARE NOT ALWAYS PRESENT AS PROBIOTICS, BUT AS POSTBIOTICS THAT CAN STIMULATE GUT MICROBES.

KOMBUCHA FERMENTATION PRODUCES B VITAMINS LIKE B1, B6, B12, AND TRACE AMOUNTS OF VITAMIN C.

ANTIOXIDANTS COMBINED WITH ENZYMES AND ACIDS SUGGEST GENERAL (BUT UNPROVEN) HEALTH BENEFITS.

START SLOWLY IF YOU HAVE NEVER HAD KOMBUCHA BEFORE, IT MAY UPSET YOUR DIGESTIVE SYSTEM.

MAKE YOUR OWN
KOMBUCHA

Kombucha is quite simple to make at home as you don't need any specialist equipment. Once you've made a batch, you will have a starter and can continue to experiment and develop flavours that you like. To scale the recipe up, add 50g sugar per litre of water. The ratio of brewed tea to kombucha starter is 9:1 (or 90% tea to 10% starter). Before fermenting, remember to wash your hands and any non-reactive utensils and vessels with unscented soap and water, then allow to air-dry. Antibacterial soap can harm your SCOBY.

EQUIPMENT
- 2 × 1.5–2-litre glass jars
- muslin cloth
- rubber band
- bottles

INGREDIENTS
- 1 litre filtered or spring water
- 2 tea bags, or 2g loose tea per litre of water
- 50g sugar
- 100ml kombucha starter, either from a previous batch or unpasteurized, store-bought
- SCOBY (optional; if you don't have one, you will need an extra 50ml kombucha starter)

Yeasts
S. cerevisiae,
Z. bailii,
B. bruxellensis

AAB
A. aceti,
K. xylinus

LAB
L. nagelii

7–21 DAYS if at 24–29°C (75–84°F)

1 **Bring the water** to a temperature appropriate for the tea. Brew the tea in one of the jars, allowing it to steep to the desired strength, then remove the tea bags or strain the tea into the second jar.

2 **Add the sugar** to the brewed tea, stir until fully dissolved, and then allow to cool.

3 **Add the starter** and stir to combine. If you have a SCOBY, add half the starter to the sweet tea; if not, add the full amount of starter plus an extra 50ml (150ml in total). If using a SCOBY, with clean hands place it on top of the tea and gently pour the remaining starter liquid onto the SCOBY. Ideally, the SCOBY will float, but it's fine if it becomes submerged.

4 **Place the muslin cloth** over the top of the jar and secure it with a rubber band. Leave the jar out of direct sunlight in a warm place to ferment for 7–14 days; the microbes work best at 24–29°C (75–84°F). You may see a new SCOBY forming on top or as a thin film in as little as 3 days.

DIRECTORY OF FERMENTS • Acetic acid bacteria 199

⑤ **Begin tasting after day five** by removing the muslin and sliding a clean straw down the side of the jar, under the SCOBY. After tasting, replace the muslin. It is ready when it no longer tastes like sweet tea and the tangy, tart flavour balances out the residual sweetness.

⑥ **Remove the SCOBY** and 200ml starter liquid for the next batch (enough to make a 2-litre brew). Use immediately to start a new batch, or store the SCOBY submerged in its liquid in an airtight jar.

⑦ **Strain the rest of the kombucha.** You can now add flavourings (see overleaf) or funnel directly into clean bottles for storage or consumption. Sealed and refrigerated, kombucha can technically be stored indefinitely, but it's best to consume within a year. Fermentation will be ongoing, yet slower, so over time the flavours will continue to change.

Continuous brewing

If you make your kombucha in a vessel with a non-reactive spigot, you can create a continuous brew once your kombucha is mature. Decant into bottles to flavour it (see overleaf) or drink on tap and replenish with the same amount of sweet tea. For best results, remove no more than one-third at one time, and trim your SCOBY to 1cm thick every few batches.

FERMENTATION TIME:

- **7–14 DAYS**
  (for up to 4 litres)
- **10–24 DAYS**
  (for 8 litres)
- **14–31 DAYS**
  (for 16 litres)
- **31+ DAYS**
  (for kombucha vinegar)

New SCOBY growth
Oldest SCOBY and yeast strands
Spent yeast sediment

Troubleshooting

- Cheesy, rotten, or musty smells signify something is wrong. If there's no mould on the SCOBY, throw away the liquid and try again. If there is mould on the SCOBY, discard both.

- If after 10 days you still have sweet tea with no new SCOBY forming, your culture is probably dead. Try adding fresh starter kombucha or start again with a new SCOBY and starter liquid.

- Discard the SCOBY if it becomes very dark, black, or grows mould, as it's not viable.

- Keep the SCOBY if it develops bumps, dry patches, holes, darker or jelly-like patches – these are normal changes. Problem cultures will show themselves in weaker brews.

- High levels of alcohol are caused by too much sugar and too much yeast. Start a new batch using less sugar and take the starter liquid from the top, with no yeast residue.

- Batches larger than 16 litres are more likely to experience variations or issues due to lack of oxygen deeper in the vessel, causing uneven or weak fermentation.

- When the new SCOBY grows beyond 1cm thick, peel or cut off the bottom layers – anything that is not white or tan.

ACIDITY

CHECK THE PH OF YOUR KOMBUCHA – 2.5–3.5 INDICATES A SAFE DRINK WITH GOOD SHELF LIFE.

FLAVOURING, BOTTLING, AND CARBONATING KOMBUCHA

Once you've made a batch of kombucha you can ferment it for a second time, adding different flavours and carbonation. This is where the creativity happens, as the possibilities are endless and you can create a drink to suit your own taste.

With the SCOBY and starter liquid removed, you are free to experiment with your kombucha. You have two options for the secondary fermentation:

- **Add flavours before bottling.** Add juices, syrups, herbs, or fruit pieces to the whole master brew, ferment at room temperature for 1–4 more days, then strain the kombucha of yeast and flavourings using a muslin cloth or fine sieve. Funnel into a bottle, leaving 2cm of airspace at the top, seal, and store in the fridge, where it will still ferment. If sweet, check after a couple of days and open to release pressure. If it seems extremely active, do this a few more times.

- **Add flavours after bottling, fermenting in smaller batches.** This means you can experiment more, as bottling also reawakens the yeast, leading to carbonation. Strain and bottle the kombucha first, leaving room to add any juice, fruit, herbs, or syrup directly. Leave 2cm of airspace at the top, seal, then allow to ferment at room temperature for 1–4 days. Check and open daily to release pressure. When ready to consume, strain out the flavouring agents if you want to. Store in the fridge. (This option is best if consuming soon after making.)

ADDING FLAVOUR

For inspiration, look in your kitchen cupboards at your favourite herbal tea blends and start with single ingredients to learn how they react. For a 500ml bottle you will use about half a teaspoon of most dried herbs or sweeteners. For fruit juices, start with around 60ml per bottle. If you're using fresh, frozen, chopped, or mashed fruit, use 50–60g per bottle and keep notes of what you've done. After you have tried a few things, you will know what you like and if you want to dial flavours up or down. Remember that added fruit sugars feed the microbes and won't necessarily make your kombucha sweeter; it usually makes it more boozy or sour. For noticeable sweetness you will need to either drink kombucha early in the fermentation, add unfermentable sugars like sorbitol or stevia, or pasteurize and then sweeten. Pasteurization halts fermentation, lengthening shelf life and stabilizing flavour, but it eliminates natural carbonation and kills the live microbes.

Controlling ethanol

Yeast creates ethanol, which is a natural part of the fermentation. Acetic acid bacteria (AAB) convert the ethanol into tart acetic acid during anaerobic fermentation. Straining out yeast when bottling can help reduce levels. Also, if you add sugar or sugary fruit during the secondary fermentation in an anaerobic bottle, the ethanol content can increase. Finally, allowing the oxidative fermentation to work longer will yield a more tart drink with less alcohol.

TO FLAVOUR BEFORE BOTTLING, ADD FRUIT, HERBS, SPICES, OR JUICE TO THE TEA.

DIRECTORY OF FERMENTS • Acetic acid bacteria 201

Strain the master brew before bottling in a sealed container to carbonate

Pour the strained kombucha into the bottle

Open the bottle top every day to release gas and reduce the risk of the bottle exploding

Fill almost to the top, leaving 2cm of airspace, which keeps the CO_2 suspended and the bottle less likely to explode

Moving the kombucha to a bottle enlivens the yeast. Leave the bottle at room temperature for 1–4 days to build carbonation and check daily

Kombucha keeps fermenting once bottled and stored in the fridge, so you may want to bottle it when it is sweeter than you want so that it isn't too sour when you open it. It's a case of experimenting until you find the flavour that is right for you.

CARBONATING KOMBUCHA

BOTTLES
IF GLASS MAKES YOU NERVOUS, FOOD-GRADE PLASTIC IS SAFE FROM EXPLOSIONS AND IS A GOOD OPTION.

FRUIT
ADDITIONS MAY CAUSE STRONGER BATCHES THAT MAY SOUR MORE QUICKLY, AS THEY CONTAIN SUGAR.

Dos and Don'ts

DO USE SWING-TOP BEER OR KOMBUCHA BOTTLES, AS THEY'RE DESIGNED TO WITHSTAND THE PRESSURE OF CARBONATION.

DO KEEP AN EYE ON YOUR BOTTLES IF YOU ADD FRUIT, SYRUPS, OR SUGAR BECAUSE THIS GIVES THE YEAST MORE FOOD AND CREATES MORE BUBBLES, WITH A GREATER RISK OF EXPLOSION.

DO CHILL IN THE FRIDGE FOR AT LEAST 30 MINUTES BEFORE OPENING.

DO USE A TOWEL ON TOP OF THE BOTTLE AND OPEN IN A SINK IF THE PRESSURE IS HIGH.

DON'T USE SQUARE-SIDED OR NOVELTY BOTTLES AS THEY ARE WEAKER IN SHAPE AND MAY NOT HAVE PROPER SEALS.

RASPBERRY AND PASSION FRUIT KOMBUCHA

KOMBUCHA VS VINEGAR

Kombucha and vinegar have many similarities. At their core, they are both products of yeast, acetic acid bacteria (AAB), and sometimes lactic acid bacteria (LAB), which transform sugars into acidic liquid, but they have key differences, too.

The difference between kombucha and vinegar is less about microbial cultures than about the type of substrate used. This and the sugar content determine the growth rate of the microbial families, genera, and species to create the final product. Just the tea alone, depending on where it was grown, affects the taste of kombucha, just as the varieties of fruits and carbohydrates used to make vinegars can deliver endless flavours. Other influences are pH level, temperature, oxygen, and the chemical changes throughout the process.

YEAST AND SUGAR

Both vinegar and kombucha involve two-step oxidative fermentation, but kombucha is done simultaneously with a reliance on yeast in the culture. For example, without the SCOBY you are not likely to get kombucha by leaving sweet tea exposed to oxygen. This is in part because sweet tea does not have a high enough pH to sit on the

Sugar fuels kombucha and vinegar fermentation. The process creates various acids, but it is acetic acid that dominates the final product.

Kombucha vs vinegar microbes

The two-step fermentation of kombucha or vinegar takes place by microbial cooperation, where a few species dominate.

KOMBUCHA SCOBY

DIRECTORY OF FERMENTS • Acetic acid bacteria

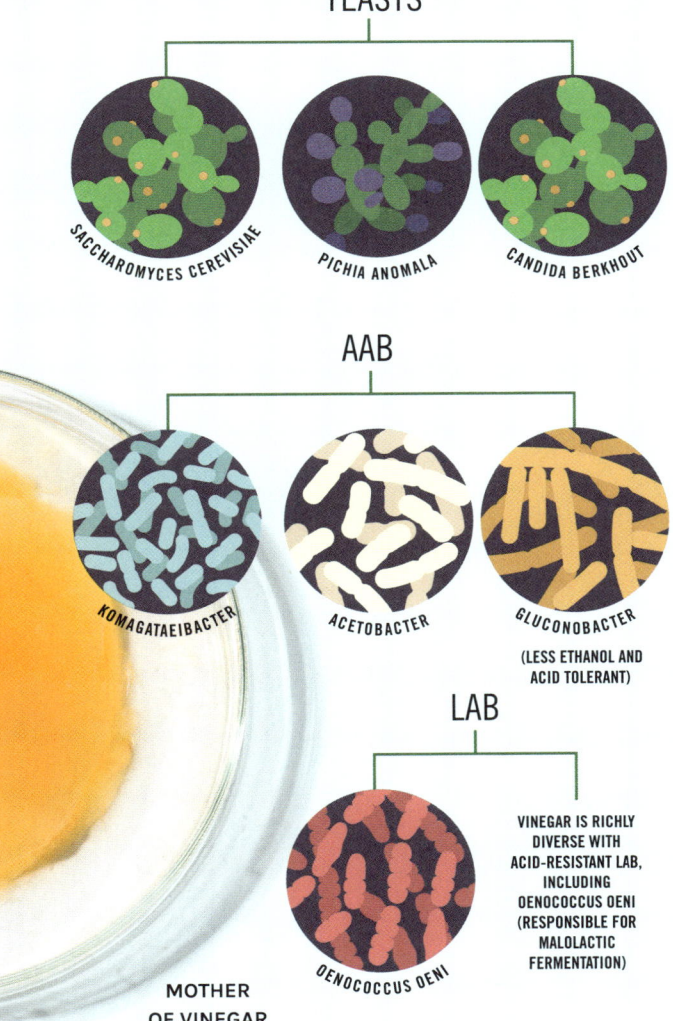

counter safely and does not already contain alcohol for the AAB to feed on. While vinegar cultures also have yeast present, it is not as important as the AAB in the culture, as the fermentation generally begins after the alcohol has been established.

There is a direct relationship between sugars and acetic acid in both kombucha and vinegar; sugar content increases or decreases the amount of ethanol the yeast will produce, which then determines the amount of acetic acid in the final product. Kombucha uses less sugar, and therefore produces less ethanol, so will never be as acidic as vinegar. When kombucha becomes too sour it is because most or all of the sugar has been consumed by the microbes. This sour liquid is often called kombucha vinegar.

PROBIOTICS AND POSTBIOTICS

Vinegar shows more LAB activity than kombucha early in fermentation; however, they are significantly reduced during fermentation, so no vinegar contains enough to be labelled probiotic. With kombucha there is also no evidence that the microbes are probiotic, so probiotic strains are often added to commercial brands. Kombucha's healthful properties shouldn't be generalized, as so many variables affect it.

However, kombucha and vinegar do both have high postbiotic content, as the early growth of LAB kills off many microbes. It has been well established that even these dead microorganisms have prebiotic-like properties and can stimulate the gut microbiome.

No culture?

You can make kombucha without the SCOBY, and vinegar without a mother, if you need or want to, as the active microbes are in the starter liquid. These physical cultures are simply tangible evidence that we are adding a proven community of microbes, providing extra insurance that the fermentation process is working properly. That said, with kombucha in particular, an established SCOBY can make the process faster.

VINEGAR

The first condiment, used to brighten and balance food with acidity, vinegar was also one of the earliest medicines, and has been used around the world for thousands of years in various different forms.

Where there is alcohol, there will be vinegar, and they have both been occurring in nature long before humans figured out how to control their natural fermentation progression. Indeed, we have to work hard to keep our wines, ciders, and beers alcoholic. As soon as fruit is ripe, yeast begins to break down the sugars into alcohol, and acetic acid bacteria (AAB) is just waiting for a little bit of oxygen to quickly turn that ethanol into vinegar. It was only a matter of time before man harnessed this product.

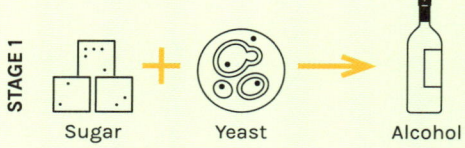

STAGE 1: Sugar + Yeast → Alcohol

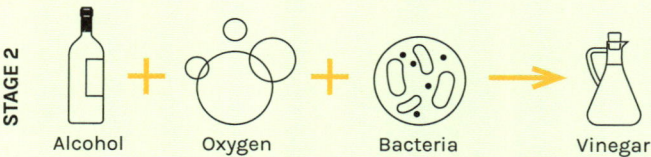

STAGE 2: Alcohol + Oxygen + Bacteria → Vinegar

There are two stages to the fermentation process when making vinegar. In the first stage, sugars are converted to alcohol by yeast. In the second, AAB convert the alcohol to acetic acid via oxidation. Through this process, the essence of the base ingredients is maintained.

WHITE WINE VINEGAR

APPLE CIDER VINEGAR

BALSAMIC VINEGAR

*c.*5000 BCE — IRAN
The first known wine vessel was discovered in Iran, in the Zagros Mountains, providing evidence, in turn, of vinegar.

*c.*3000 BCE — ANCIENT EGYPT
In Ancient Egypt, vinegar was used as payment for labour, as recorded on a pottery-shard receipt. Barley wine vinegar was the most common variety, and most documentation shows it was used for medicinal purposes.

*c.*2000 BCE — ANCIENT BABYLON
In Ancient Babylon, vinegar was made of beer, date palm sap, date wine, and raisin wine. The concentrated sugars from wines made of sun-dried fruits were probably rich, like a balsamic vinegar.

*c.*2000 BCE — CHINA
Xia dynasty legends (2070–1600 BCE) tell that rice vinegar was discovered by Heita, the Chinese god of wine. The first professional vinegar production, however, was during the Zhou dynasty (1046–256 BCE).

*c.*1000 BCE — INDIA
In India, vinegar is made from sugar cane, coconut, honey, and tamarind. Ayurvedic manuals from the first millennium BCE mention vinegar in traditional medicine.

Traditional is best

In modern production, alcohol is circulated in generators to aerate the AAB, thereby producing vinegar quickly. Some also add synthetic acids to speed things up further. These methods don't feature lactic acid and don't allow for flavours to develop. Vinegars made using traditional methods, however, have a mix of lactic acid and AAB. They also contain more vitamin B, flavonoids, amino acids, and organic acids, and have higher antioxidant capacity and more volatile compounds, enhancing flavours.

Vinegar varieties

All vinegar is mostly water with a percentage of acetic acid and some trace acids and compounds from the base ingredients. These produce distinct varieties, with a unique molecular make-up.

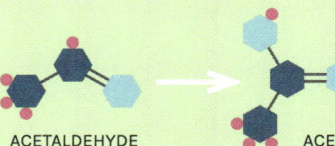

KEY
- Carbon
- Oxygen
- Nitrogen
- Hydrogen

ETHANOL → ACETALDEHYDE → ACETIC ACID

While AAB are converting ethanol to acetic acid, acetaldehyde is produced, so when vinegar smells like nail polish remover it is half done.

Distilled vinegar
A colourless diluted form of acetic acid with very few trace compounds, made from distilled ethanol.

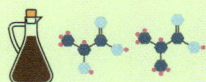

Balsamic vinegar
Commercial-grade balsamic of Modena is widely available but this only imitates the traditional product.

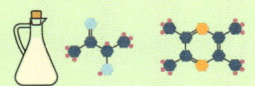

Wine vinegar
Varies by grape and wine type. Grapes bring tartaric acid and other phenolic compounds and esters.

Apple cider vinegar
Rich in phenolics and volatile compounds from the malic acid in the apples fermented to make cider.

Malt vinegar
Made from oxidized ales, malt vinegar contains some lactic acid and traces of isobutyric acid.

Rice vinegar
A vast family. The process, which begins with koji grown on rice, is as varied as the regions that make it.

ABV
PREDICTS THE PERCENTAGE OF ACETIC ACID IN VINEGAR. IN PERFECT CONDITIONS THERE IS A 1:1 CORRELATION.

BALSAMIC
STARTS AS A 25% SUGAR MUST. THIS SLOWS FERMENTATION, AND EVAPORATION CREATES A SYRUPY VINEGAR.

---

c. 500 CE — JAPAN

Japan's modern vinegar production began about 1,500 years ago, with methods from China. Two types of rice vinegar are made: *komesu*, an amber rice vinegar, and *kurozu*, a black rice vinegar.

1050 CE — ITALY

Traditional balsamic vinegar is made from cooked Trebbiano grape must and syrup, not wine. As it ages it is moved through several barrels, each wood imparting its own aromas and flavours.

1346 CE — BRITAIN

During the medieval plague, vinegar was used for sterilizing. A legendary formula combined with herbs, known as "four thieves" vinegar, hails from this time.

1492 CE — THE AMERICAS

The Pre-Columbian Americas don't have a written history of vinegar, but they do have a rich history of fermented drinks, so are likely to have used vinegar in multiple ways.

c. 1800 CE — FRANCE

Orléans was the port before Paris where soured wine was unloaded to avoid tax. Here, a new industry emerged to take advantage of this, and by 1800 the city produced 80% of the vinegar in France.

MAKE YOUR OWN VINEGAR

You can either start this two-stage fermentation method at the beginning with a fruit juice and some yeast, or at Step 4 using pre-made alcohol such as wine, beer, or cider. Before you start, make sure all containers are sanitized to avoid contamination (see p59). To scale the amount up or down, maintain a ratio of 20% raw vinegar to juice (1:5).

EQUIPMENT
- thermometer
- beaker or cup
- 2-litre jar
- muslin cloth
- rubber bands
- pH test strips
- bottles with air-tight, non-reactive lids

INGREDIENTS
- 1g active dry wine yeast
- 1.6 litres apple juice, organic if possible
- 320ml raw, unpasteurized vinegar
- mother of vinegar (MOV) pellicle (optional)

AAB
A. aceti, A. cerevisiae, A. malorum, G. oxydans, K. europaeus

2–4 MONTHS

2 **Pour the room-temperature apple juice into the jar.** Stir the yeast to mix it with the warm water, then pour into the juice and stir.

1 **Heat 60ml of water** in a pan to 40°C (104°F), testing the temperature with the thermometer. Put the water in a beaker and add the yeast, allowing it to sit on the surface for 20 minutes.

3 **Cover the jar with a muslin cloth**, securing it with a rubber band. Leave for 7–14 days out of direct sunlight at room temperature to ferment. You may notice some bubbling (though with a breathable covering, pressure will not build up) and a yeasty, boozy smell as the ethanol develops.

⑥ **Check every few weeks**, trying not to jostle the jar. If you had no MOV, or it sank, you should see a new MOV forming. It is done when it tastes like vinegar, with no residual sweet, boozy, or yeasty flavours: this may take 2–4 months.

⑦ **When the vinegar is ready, remove the MOV** and reserve some of the vinegar as a starter liquid, then fill each bottle to the top, leaving very little airspace. You can use the vinegar immediately, or seal and age it further – for a few months or several years – to continue to develop nuanced and mellow flavours.

④ **Pour the raw vinegar** into the fermented alcoholic juice. If you have an MOV, add it now, taking care to place it on top to float (although it's fine if it doesn't). Using a pH strip, test the acidity level. It should be 4.0 or lower.

⑤ **Cover the jar with a muslin cloth** and fasten with a rubber band, then place out of direct sunlight at room temperature, or preferably somewhere a little warmer, as the microbes work best at 25–30°C (77–86°F).

Troubleshooting

• If a white film that breaks apart when touched develops, you have kahm yeast rather than an MOV. This is harmless but not good for vinegar, so scoop it off, stir, and spritz the surface daily with "magic spray" (see p59) until no more yeast appears.

• Sometimes vinegar in production will smell like acetone. The smell will go away. If it doesn't, fermentation may have slowed or stalled. Stir regularly to increase oxygen. If this doesn't help, the alcohol may be too strong, so dilute with a small amount of raw vinegar.

• If your vinegar starts becoming less sour, it has fermented for too long. Add a little alcohol back into the mix and allow to ferment for a week or two more; this will create more acid.

• If your vinegar tastes weak, the per cent acid (the number of grams of acetic acid per 100ml of vinegar) was low. Most vinegar is 5 per cent (i.e. 5ml acetic acid and 95ml water). Store this vinegar in the fridge.

SHRUBS

These sweetened drinking vinegars are usually made from fruit, vinegar, and sugar, and were originally developed as a way of preserving fruit. They can be enjoyed in cocktails and other drinks to add fruity, refreshing flavour.

Shrubs are simply vinegar infusions: aromatic ingredients are steeped in vinegar over the course of days or weeks, then the vinegar is strained and sweetened to taste. When most people think of shrubs, they think of fruit flavours, but they can be made with a wide variety of other ingredients, too: herbs from the garden, or flowers, including lavender, and even carrots or beetroot.

As well as the aromatics you add to the vinegar, the flavour profile of shrubs is influenced by the vinegar itself. Apple cider vinegar is a good, all-purpose choice, as it marries well with most flavours, as are red or white wine vinegars. Consider how the vinegar will pair with the flavourings you're using. You can also experiment with other vinegars you enjoy, although if you've never used them in a shrub before, start with a small batch first to see if you like the flavour before making a large amount.

The process of making shrubs is largely intuitive and based on your own flavour preferences – however, there are standard steps you can follow.

APPLE CIDER VINEGAR

ACETIC ACID IN VINEGAR INHIBITS MICROBIAL GROWTH, HELPING TO KEEP FRUIT FROM SPOILING.

STRAWBERRY **POMEGRANATE** **BLUEBERRY**

DIRECTORY OF FERMENTS • Acetic acid bacteria 209

The perfect mix

Shrubs can be made with varying amounts of vinegar, sugar, and fruit depending on taste. Start with equal parts, then adjust from there.

33% VINEGAR — Experiment with different kinds of vinegar. Apple cider vinegar works well with most kinds of fruit, and balsamic vinegar goes with darker-skinned fruits such as cherries.

33% SUGAR — The variety of sugar you use is flexible, from regular caster sugar to brown sugar or raw.

33% FRUIT  — You can use almost any kind of fruit, which means shrubs are a good way to cut down on food waste, by using up berries that are too soft to eat fresh.

INFUSION
THE FRUIT'S CELL WALLS SOFTEN AS THEY INFUSE; JUICE AND AROMATICS FLAVOUR THE VINEGAR.

ORANGE AND CINNAMON

SHRUB MIXED WITH SODA

MAKE YOUR OWN

Start with equal amounts of vinegar, sugar, and fruit. Then, when you are more confident, you can begin to experiment, adding as little or as much of each ingredient as you wish.

EQUIPMENT glass jar with lid • sieve • storage jar
INGREDIENTS fruit, fresh herbs, or flavourings of your choice • apple cider vinegar • sugar

AAB
A. aceti,
G. oxydans,
G. liquefaciens

Yeasts
S. cerevisia,
Candida spp.

LAB
L. plantarum

1–2 WEEKS

① **Fill the jar about halfway** with your desired flavourings (if using dried spices and herbs, use less as the flavours are more intense).

② **Pour over a good-quality** vinegar to cover the flavourings completely.

③ **Seal the jar with the lid** and leave at room temperature, out of direct sunlight, either on the counter or in the fridge, for 1–2 weeks (or longer), until it has a flavour you enjoy. If your aromatics float to the top of the jar, give it a shake once or twice a day.

④ **Once the shrub** has reached a flavour that you're happy with, strain through a sieve into a clean storage jar and either discard or repurpose the pickled fruit (they make a great garnish in cocktails or a topping for ice cream).

⑤ **Sweeten the vinegar** to taste: start by whisking in 12g sugar until dissolved, then taste, and add more as needed.

⑥ **Store the finished shrub** in the fridge, where it will last at least a month.

Troubleshooting

• If you use lots of aromatics, place the shrub in the fridge rather than leaving it to steep on the counter at room temperature to prevent spoilage.

• If you use lots of watery fruit, it can cause the acidity of the solution to drop, leading to mould – you can increase the sugar and/or vinegar to help with this, or reduce the amount of watery fruit. Or simply let it develop in the fridge.

INDEX

A

acetaldehyde 190
acetate 45, 190
acetic acid 190, 191
acetic acid bacteria (AAB)
   biofilms 192–93
   evolution 35, 190
   fermentation stages 190
   history 190, 195
   kefir 95
   microbiology 191
   microbiome 44
   byproducts 194–95
   SCOBYs (symbiotic cultures of bacteria and yeast) 192–93
   shrubs 208–9
   sourdough 156–57
   types 190
   see also kombucha; vinegar
Acetobacter pasteurianus 195
acetone aroma, troubleshooting 63, 129
acid coagulation 98
acid hydrolysis 119
Actinomucor elegans 145
adaptation 34
aerobes 31
África, Teódula Kalaw 195
ageing, cheese 100
airlocks 55
aka miso 130–31
alcohol
   cider 172–73
   Crabtree effect 151
   fermentation stages 71
   ginger bug and ginger beer 20, 182–83
   history 35
   mead 174–75
   saké 25, 110, 111, 153, 176–81
   tepache 186–87
   troubleshooting 63
   vinegar 190, 191
   yeast evolution 35
   see also beer; wine
aldehydes 125
ale 169
alliinase 125
alpha-amylase 38–39, 116
amasi 91
amazake 111, 116–17
amazuzuke 132
amino acids 22, 25, 37, 95, 125
amino pastes 126
amylases 36–37, 38–39, 176
anaerobic fermentation 80–81
anchovy sauce 147
antibiotics resistance 34
apples
   apple cider vinegar 205, 206–7
   cauliflower leaf kimchi 88–89
   cider 172–73
archaea 30
asazuke 132
Aspergillus flavus 106
Aspergillus niger 108
Aspergillus oryzae 23, 34, 37, 40, 104, 106–7, 110, 116, 118
Aspergillus sojae 116, 118
Aspergillus spp. 108, 111
ATP (adenosine triphosphate) 30, 32, 191
autolysis 147
autotrophs 31
avocado 25
awamori 111
awase miso 130–31

B

Bacillaceae (*Firmicutes*) 137
Bacillus cereus 115
Bacillus subtilis 44, 115, 118, 142–43
backslopping 60, 126, 196
bacteria
   evolution 30
   gochujang 137
   gut health *see* microbiome
   microbiology 32
   nattō 142–43
   probiotics 44
   SCOBYs (symbiotic cultures of bacteria and yeast) 152–53
   spores 32
   see also acetic acid bacteria; lactic acid bacteria
bacteriophages 31, 192
baechu kimchi 84, 87
baek kimchi 84, 87
baker's yeast 156
balsamic vinegar 205
barley
   gochujang 136–38
   koji 116
   malting 169
   miso 116, 126–31
   saké 25, 110, 111, 153, 176–81
   whisky 36, 37
   see also beer
Basidiomycota 150, 153

beans 25
beer
   brewing stages 168–69
   flavour 25
   history 12, 168
   low and no alcohol 41
   method overview 170–71
   types 169
   yeast selection 152
beetroot kvas 184
beta-amylase 39
Bifidobacterium animalis 42
Bifidobacterium spp. 44
binary fission 32
bioavailability 8, 36, 44
biocellulose 195
bioethanol 27
biofilms 31, 94, 142–43, 191, 192–93
biogas 27
biomass fermentation 18
bioplastics 152
bioreactors 19, 27
bitterness 25
black garlic 124–25
bloom 35
bochet 175
bodaimoto 180
bottles 52
botulism 56, 57
braggot 175
bread
   history 156
   injera 15
   kvas 15, 184
   sourdough 25, 45, 151, 152, 156–59, 161
   soy sauce alternative 26–27

   types 160–61
Brettanomyces spp. 40, 151, 153, 169
Brevibacterium linens 101
brewer's spent grain 25
brewer's yeast 40, 150, 156
brine, dill pickles 76–77
broad beans, doubanjiang 134–35
budding 150
burping 70
butyrate 45
butyric acid 37

C

cabbage
   kimchi 84–89
   sauerkraut 74–75
calcium-sensing receptors 24–25
Camembert 17, 101, 106
Candida spp. 137
canning 57
capsaicin 80, 81, 137
carbonation 201
carbonic maceration 80–81
carboys 55
carotenoids 41
carrots, cauliflower leaf kimchi 88–89
casein 19, 90–91
catalysts, enzymes 38
cauliflower leaf kimchi 88–89
cells
   mould spores 105
   types and structure 30–31
   yeasts 33
cellulases 39
cellulose 190, 191, 192, 193, 195

cEVG (glutamyl-valyl-glycine) 25
Cheddar 101
cheese
   enzymes 36
   history 13, 17, 27, 68, 98, 105, 106, 107
   kokumi 25
   lipase 37
   method 98–99
   moulds 99, 100, 104, 105, 109
   precision fermentation substitutes 19
   spores 109
   types 100–101
chemosynthesis 31
cheonggukjang 143
chicha, history 14
chillies
   doubanjiang 134–35
   gochugaru 84, 88
   gochujang 136–38
   hot sauce 80–83
chitin 105
chocolate 195
chonggak kimchi 87
chou 121
chou doufu 144
cider 172–73
citric acid 108, 111
clarification 21
Clostridium botulinum 56, 57
cloudiness 62
cocoa beans 25, 40, 195
coconut, nata de coco 195
coffee 40
colatura di alici 147
colonocytes 45
colonies 31

competitive exclusion (CE) 56, 58
conidia 105
corn, chicha de jora 14
Crabtree effect 151
crocks 53
crunch, tannins 76
cryopreservation 107
Cryptococcus curvatus 41
cucumber
   dill pickles 76–77
   kimchi 87
   tsukemono 133
cyanobacteria 35, 190
cytoplasm 30

D

dahi 91
dairy foods
   plant-based alternatives 19, 20, 153
   see also cheese; kefir; yogurt
Darwin, Charles 34
dashi 22
dawadawa 143
Debaryomyces hansenii 12–17, 153
demijohns 55
dextran 95
dextrins 39
diet, increasing functional foods
   consumption 48–49
digestion
   enzymes 36
   umami 23
dill pickles 76–77
disease, inflammation 48
DNA

   bacteria 32
   horizontal gene transfer 32, 192
   moulds 33
   single nucleotide polymorphisms
     (SNPs) 34
   yeasts 33
doburoku 178–79
doenjang 121
doko beds 133
domestication 12, 106–7
dosa 154–55
doubanjiang 121, 134–35
douchi, history 14
doufuru 144
durian 25
dysbiosis 42–43

E

EF (glutamyl-phenylalanine) 25
EL (glutamyl-leucine) 25
Emmental 100
endoplasmic reticulum 30, 31
energy production
   biogas 27
   microbiology 31
Enterobacter spp. 70
enzymes 31, 36–39, 108, 125
epithelial cells 43, 45
equipment 52–55
Escherichia coli (STEC) 56, 57
ethanol 35, 151
eukaryotes 30, 34
EV (glutamyl-valine) 25
evolution
   acetic acid bacteria (AAB) 35, 190–91

   lactic acid bacteria (LAB) 34, 68
   microbes 30, 34
   moulds 34–35
   phylogenetic tree 35
   yeasts 35
extremophiles 30

F

fats, lipase 37
fatty acids 37, 45
fat washing 21
fenugreek seeds, idli and dosa 154–55
fermentation
   biomass fermentation 18
   compared to pickles 48
   definition 8
   gastronomic techniques 21
   glossary 60
   history 6, 12–17, 68, 107, 137
   industrialized 107, 108, 119
   key principles 60–61
   multi-parallel 177
   precision fermentation 17, 19, 27, 41, 153
   sustainability 26–27
   wild fermentation 60, 118, 143, 144, 167
fermentation boxes 53
fermenters' percentages 61
fibre 45, 47
fill levels 60
filmjölk 91
fish
   protease 37
   umami 23
fish sauce
   fermentation stages 146–47

history 12, 14, 26, 146
   kimchi 86
   kokumi 25
   protease 38
   shottsuru 130
   types 146
   umami 23
five Ks 46
flagella 190
flatbreads 160
flavour
   kokumi 24–25
   umami 22–23
   wine 166–67
food security 14
food waste reduction 26
France, cheese 17
freeze clarification 21
fruit
   kvas 184
   lacto-fermentation 72–73
fuel production 27
functional foods 46–49
fungi
   biomass fermentation 18
   see also moulds
furans 125
furu 144
Fusarium venenatum 18

G

gamma-glutamylation 25
ganjang 120, 121
garlic
   accidental fermentation 57
   black garlic 124–25
   kimchi 84–89
   kokumi 24, 25
garum 14, 26, 146–47
gastroenteritis 56–57
gastronomic techniques 21
genetic modification, precision fermentation 19
gene transfer, horizontal 32, 192
genome editing 107
Geotrichum candidum 100
ginger
   ginger beer 20, 182–83
   ginger bug 182–83
   kimchi 84–89
Global Hansik Campaign 15
glossary 60
glucans 105
Gluconacetobacter spp. 193
gluconeogenesis 45
gluconic acid 191, 194
Gluconobacter oxydans 194
Gluconobacter spp. 191
glutamate 22–23
glutamic acid 119
glutathione 24–25
glycerol 37, 41
glycolysis 151
GMP (guanosine monophosphate) 22–23
gochugaru 84, 88
gochujang 136–39
Golgi apparatus 30, 31
Gorgonzola 37
Gouda 100
grapes
   varieties 166–67
   see also wine

Grigorov, Stamen 17
gueuze 169
gut–brain connection 43
gut function 43, 44–45
gut microbiome *see* microbiome

H

Hanseniaspora uvarum 41
hatcho miso 116, 127, 130–31
heat
   enzymes 38
   moulds 105
heat mats 55
heterotrophs 31
Hibiscus tiliaceus 140
history of fermentation 6, 68, 107, 137
   see also specific ferments
honey, mead 174–75
hops, beer 168–69
hot sauce 80–83
humidity 125
hydrogen sulfide 165
hydrometers 55
hygiene 57
hyphae 33, 104, 140

I

Ideonella sakaiensis 34
idli 154–55
Ikeda, Kikunae 22
immersion circulator 55
IMP (inosine monophosphate) 22–23
incubators 55, 125
industrialized food 26, 108

inflammation 48
injera 15, 160
inoculation 60
insulin 17
invertase 125
IPAs 169

J

Japan
  koji 107, 110
  soy sauce 16
jars 52
jelly pellicles 152
Jerusalem artichokes 48
jiang 120, 121, 130
jiangyou 120, 121
juicing 21
junmai saké 180–81

K

kahm yeast 60, 62, 75, 83, 89, 123, 153, 207
kecap 121
kefir
  bacteria strains 94–95
  history 17, 94
  method 96–97
  microbiology 95
  SCOBY 152
kefiran 94, 95, 152
Kern, Edward 17
kimchi
  flavour profile 86
  history 16, 27, 84
  Korean identity 15, 84–85, 86

types 87
yeasts 153
kimjang season 84
kimoto 180
kinema 15, 143
kioke 16, 120, 126, 130
Kioke Craftsmen Revival Project 16
kiselo mlyako 91
kkakdugi 87
Klebsiella spp. 70
Kluyveromyces marxianus 40, 152
Kluyveromyces spp. 95
koikuchi 120, 121
koji
  amazake 116–17
  enzymes 110, 176
  fermentation stages 110–11
  fermented tofu 144–45
  gastronomic techniques 20–21
  history 106, 110
  method overview 112–15
  mirin 116–17
  miso 126
  sakadane 160
  saké 176
  shio koji 116–17
  soy sauce 16
  spores 109
  substrates 116
  tamari 122–23
  troubleshooting 115
kokumi 24–25
Komagataeibacter europaeus 191
Komagataeibacter saccharivorans 194
Komagataeibacter spp. 191, 193
Komagataeibacter xylinus 44, 193, 195

kombucha
  bottling 201
  carbonation 201
  compared to vinegar 202–3
  fermentation stages 197
  flavouring 200–201
  history 196
  industrialized 194
  method overview 198–99
  nutrition 48, 197
  SCOBY 152–53, 192, 193, 196
  yeasts 33, 41
kombu dashi 22
Korea
  gochujang 136
  kimchi and identity 15, 84–85, 86
Ks, the five 46
kvas 15, 184–85
kyurizuke 133

L

labneh 91
lactic acid 69
lactic acid bacteria (LAB)
  evolution 34
  fermentation stages 70–71
  idli and dosa 154
  kefir 152
  kombucha 197
  microbiology 68
  microbiome 44, 71
  sourdough 156–57
  types 70–71
  see also lacto-fermentation

Lactobacillus acidophilus 90
Lactobacillus brevis 70, 75
Lactobacillus bulgaricus 40, 44, 90, 91, 95
Lactobacillus hilgardii 95
Lactobacillus kefiranofaciens 44, 95
Lactobacillus kefiri 44, 95
Lactobacillus plantarum 69, 70, 71, 75, 90
Lactobacillus rhamnosus 90
Lactobacillus sanfrancisensis 161
Lactobacillus spp. 58, 98, 126
Lactococcus spp. 98
lacto-fermentation
    cheese 98–101
    dill pickles 76–77
    fermentation stages 70
    history 16, 68
    hot sauce 80–83
    kefir 94–97
    kimchi 84–89
    method overview 72–73
    microbiology 68–69
    pathogen prevention 56
    sauerkraut 74–75
    umeboshi 78–79
    vacuum-sealed 21
    yogurt 90–93
lager 169
lambic ales 169
lead contamination 57
lemon kvas 184
lentils
    idli and dosa 154–55
    miso 126
Leuconostoc mesenteroides 70, 74, 95
Leuconostoc spp. 71, 99
lipases 37

lipids 41
Listeria monocytogenes 56
locust bean seeds 143
longevity 45

M

"magic spray" 59, 75, 83
Maillard reaction 119, 124–25, 126
maize, tepache 186–87
malolactic fermentation 71, 166
malting 169
maltose 37, 39
malt vinegar 205
mannoproteins 105
mao doufu 144, 145
mash-fermentation
    basic guide 73
    hot sauce 82–83
matsoni 91
mead 174–75
meat
    protease 37
    soy sauce alternative 26–27
    umami 23
meat alternatives, biomass fermentation 18
medicine
    biocellulose 195
    precision fermentation 19
meju 110, 137, 138
melanoidins 125
melomel 175
Metchnikoff, Élie 17, 44
metheglin 175
methi 154
Mexico, tepache 186–87

microbes
    colonies 31
    competitive exclusion (CE) 58
    energy sources 31
    enzymes 39
    function 30
    serial passaging 106, 107
    specialists 40–41
    structure 30–31
    types 30–31
microbiome
    custom nutrients 19
    fermented foods 44–45
    function 42–43
    functional foods 47
    lactic acid bacteria (LAB) 71
    parabiotics 69
    probiotics 69
    symbiosis 193
microbiota 42
milk
    cheese 98–101
    kefir 94–97
    yogurt 90–93
mirin 116–17
mishti doi 91
miso
    enzymes 39
    fermentation stages 126
    history 121, 130
    koji 111, 116
    kokumi 25
    method overview 128–29
    types 130–31
    umami 23
    varieties 127

miso-dama 130
misozuke 132, 133
mitochondria 30, 31
monosodium glutamate (MSG) 22
mothers (vinegar) 193, 207
moulds
   cheese 99, 100, 104, 105, 109
   culinary types overview 108–9
   domestication 106–7
   doubanjiang 136–39
   evolution 34–35
   fermented tofu 144–45
   microbiology 31, 33, 104–5
   protease 37
   troubleshooting 62
   tsukemono 132–33
   see also koji; tempeh
mouthfeel 24–25
mozzarella 100
mucilage 154
Mucor spp. 118, 144, 145
mugi miso 116, 127, 130–31
multi-parallel fermentation 177
mushrooms
   kokumi 25
   umami 23
mycelium 33, 104, 140
mycoprotein 18

N

nail polish aroma, troubleshooting 63, 129
nam pla 146
naru 144
nata de coco 195
nattō 15, 38, 142–43

nattokinase 143
natural wine 165
nigori saké 180–81
Nishio 121
nitrogen fixation 193
nuka-doko beds 133
nukazuke 132
nunu 91
nuoc-mam 146
nutrition
   bioavailability 8
   functional foods 46–49
   umami 23
   see also specific ferments

O

Oenococcus oeni 71
Oenococcus spp. 71
oil production 41
oi sobagi 87
oleaginous yeasts 41
onggi 84, 120
onions
   kimchi 84–89
   kokumi 25
organelles 30
osmosis 77
oxidation 191

P

pain de campagne 160
pale ale 169
panettone 160–61
parabiotics 69

pasteurization 16, 60, 195
Pasteur, Louis 16, 195
pathogens
   myths and misconceptions 57
   removal 44, 69
   safety 57
   sources 56–57
patis 146
pears, cauliflower leaf kimchi 88–89
peas, miso 126
pecorino 36, 37
pectinase 39, 74, 76–77
Pediococcus spp. 70, 71, 75
pellicle 193
Penicillium biforme 107
Penicillium fuscoglaucum 107
penicillin 105, 109
Penicillium camemberti 104, 106, 107, 109
Penicillium candidum 101
Penicillium chrysogenum 105, 109
Penicillium roquefortii 100, 104, 109
Penicillium spp. 109
peptides 24–25, 37
photosynthesis 31, 35, 68, 69
pH strips 54
phytases 108, 157
phytates 44
Pichia kudriavzevii 40
pickle packers 54
pickles
   compared to ferments 48
   tsukemono 132
pineapple
   nata de piña 195
   tepache 186–87
plasmids 32

plastics
    biodegradable 27, 153, 195
    Ideonella sakaiensis 34
plums, umeboshi 78–79
poha 154
polyphenols 197
porter 169
postbiotics 47, 48, 197, 202
prebiotics 46–47, 48
precision fermentation 17, 19, 27, 41, 153
preservation beds 133
Prevotella copri 42
probiotics
    fermented sources 44, 48, 69
    health benefits 46–47
    history 17
    kombucha 197, 202
    vinegar 202
prokaryotes 30, 34
propionate 45
Propionibacterium freudenreichii 100
protease 37, 38, 110, 176
proteins 37
Prunus mume 78–79
pyridines 125

Q

qū balls 110
Quorn 18

R

radishes
    kimchi 84–89
    tsukemono 132

raib 91
rancidity 37
ratios 61
refractometers 55
rehydration 113
rennet
    cheese 98–99
    skyr 91
resistant starch 45
Rhizopus oligosporus 104, 140
Rhizopus oryzae 31, 33, 34, 37
Rhizopus spp. 108, 118
Rhodosporidium toruloides 41
ribonucleotides 22
rice
    amazake 116–17
    cauliflower leaf kimchi 88–89
    dosa 154–55
    gochujang 136–38
    idli 154–55
    koji 110–15
    mirin 116–17
    miso 126–31
    polishing 180–81
    sakadane 160
    saké 25, 110, 111, 153, 176–81
    vinegar 205
ripeness 37
RNA (ribonucleic acid) 22
Roquefort 100
Ruminococcus gnavus 42
rye breads 160–61, 184–85

S

Saccharomyces brettanomyces 33
Saccharomyces kluyveromyces 33
Saccharomyces boulardii 44, 47
Saccharomyces cerevisiae 40, 150, 151, 156, 169
Saccharomyces pastorianus 153, 168, 169, 170
Saccharomyces spp. 95
Saccharomycodes fragilis 152
Saccharomycodes ludwigii 41, 152
saishikomi 121
sakadane 160
saké 25, 110, 111, 153, 176–81
sakurazake 132
salivation 23
Salmonella 56
salt
    cheese 100
    lacto-fermentation 69
    "magic spray" 59
    pathogen prevention 56
    percentage calculations 61
    troubleshooting 62
    umeboshi 78–79
San Francisco sourdough 161
sanitization 59, 60
satiety 45
sauerkraut
    fermentation stages 70
    history 16, 74
    method 74–75
    soil remediation 69
scales 53, 55
SCFAs (short-chain fatty acids) 45, 47
SCOBYs (symbiotic cultures of bacteria and yeast) 152–53, 192–93, 196

seafood, shiokara 130
seaweed, umami 23
serial passaging 106, 107
serine proteases 38
shinshu miso 130–31
shiokara 130
shio koji 116–17
shiro miso 127, 130–31
shiro shoyu 119, 121
shiso leaves 78–79
shochu 111
shokupan 160
short-chain fatty acids (SCFAs) 45, 47
shottsuru 130
show (mead) 175
shoyu 16, 111, 116, 119, 121
shrimp, fermented
    kimchi 86
    kokumi 25
shrubs 208–9
Sichuan doubanjiang 134–35
skyr 91
sliminess
    nattō 142
    sauerkraut 75
    troubleshooting 63, 129
softness, troubleshooting 62, 63
soil
    nitrogen fixation 193
    remediation 69
    source of pathogens 56
sourdough 25, 45, 151, 152, 156–59, 161
sourness, troubleshooting 63
soya beans
    cheonggukjang 143

douchi 14
gochujang 136–38
kinema 143
koji 116
nattō 15, 38, 142–43
tofu 144–45
types 119
umami 23
see also miso; soy sauce; tempeh
soya milk, kefir 95
soy sauce
    alternative ferments 26–27
    Aspergillus strains 111
    history 16, 120
    koji 111
    kokumi 25
    production methods 16, 118–19
    types 120–21 *see also* tamari
    umami 23
sporangiospores 33
spore banks 107
spores 32, 104, 105
spring onions, cauliflower leaf
    kimchi 88–89
starch 36
starters
    bread 158
    cheese 98, 100
    definition 60
    saké 180
    yogurt 93
stout 169
Streptococcus thermophilus 44, 90, 95
sugar
    amylase 36
    lacto-fermentation 68, 71, 73

mishti doi 91
tepache 186–87
sulfur dioxide 167
sustainability 20, 25, 26–27
symbiosis 31, 192–93
synbiotics 47
systems theory 8–9

T

takana 133
takuan 132
Taleggio 101
tamari 111, 116, 120, 121, 122–23
tannins 76
taste
    bioavailability 8
    kokumi 24–25
    umami 22–23
tea, kombucha 198–203
tempeh
    growth 31, 104, 108, 140
    history 16, 140
    method overview 140–41
    nutrition 48
    spores 109
temperature
    enzymes 38
    moulds 104
    specialist microbes 41
    troubleshooting 63
tepache 186–87
terroir 19, 167
Tetragenococcus halophilus 40
textiles 27
tofu, fermented 144–45

tokubetsu junmai saké 180–81
Torulaspora delbrueckii 41
troubleshooting 62–63
tsukemono 132–33
tyrosine 100

U

umami 22–23
umeboshi 78–79
urad dal 154
usukuchi 120, 121

V

vacuum distillation 21
vacuum-sealed fermentation 21
vacuum sealers 55
vegetables
   lacto-fermentation 72–73
   tsukemono 132–33
viili 91
vinegar
   cider 173
   compared to kombucha 202–3
   fermentation stages 204
   history 13, 204–5
   industrialized 194, 205
   "magic spray" 59, 75
   method overview 206–7
   mothers 193, 207
   oxidation 191
   shrubs 208–9
   word origin 190
vinegar mothers 193
viruses 31, 192

vodka, "magic spray" 59

W

washing powders 37
waste reduction 26
water kefir 95
Weissella spp. 44
wheat bran 25
whisky 36, 37
wild fermentation 60, 118, 143, 144, 167
wine
   fermentation stages 71
   flavour 25, 166
   low and no alcohol 41
   method overview 164–65
   production methods 162–63
   types 166–67
   vinegar 205
   wild fermentation 167

XYZ

yamahai 180
Yamamoto, Yasuo 16, 120
Yarrowia lipolytica 41, 153
yeasts
   aerobic and anaerobic fermentation 150–51
   biodegradable plastics 153
   cheese 99
   cider 172–73
   domestication 12
   dosa 154–55
   evolution 35
   ginger bug and ginger beer 20, 182–83
   gochujang 137
   idli 154–55
   kefir 95
   kimchi 153
   kombucha 200, 202
   kvas 184–85
   low and no alcohol 41, 152
   mead 174–75
   microbiology 31, 33, 150–51
   microbiome 44
   miso 126
   oleaginous 41
   precision fermentation 19
   saké 25, 110, 111, 153, 176–81
   salty ferments 153
   SCOBYs (symbiotic cultures of bacteria and yeast) 152–53, 192–93
   tepache 186–87
   types 150
   see also beer; bread; kahm yeast; wine
yeolmu kimchi 87
yogurt
   bacteria strains 90
   fermentation stages 90–91
   history 12, 17, 68, 90
   method 92–93
   starters 93
yuzu saké 180–81

Zygosaccharomyces 137, 153
zygospores 33

BIBLIOGRAPHY

To access a full list of research citations supporting the information in this book, please visit: **www.dk.com/science-of-fermentation-biblio**

Bamforth, C.W. (2005) *Handbook of Food & Beverage Fermentation Technology*. Boca Raton, FL: CRC Press.

Cooper, S. (2024) *The Fermentation Kitchen: Recipes and Techniques for Kimchi, Kombucha, Koji and More*. London: DK Red

Coucquyt, P., Brunst, B. and De Clippeleer, J. (2020) *The Art & Science of Foodpairing: 10,000 Flavour Matches That Will Transform the Way You Eat*. London: Mitchell Beazley.

Davidson, A. (2014) *The Oxford Companion to Food*. 3rd edn. Oxford: Oxford University Press.

Gilmartin, C. (2021) *Fermented Foods: A Practical Guide*. Bristol: Ferment Books.

Hunter, B.T. (2011) *Fermented Food and Beverages: Creative Recipes for Everything from Kombucha to Sauerkraut*. New York: Square One Publishers.

Hutkins, R. (2006) *Microbiology and Technology of Fermented Foods*. Ames, IA: Blackwell Publishing.

Katz, S. (2003) *Wild Fermentation: The Flavor, Nutrition, and Craft of Live-Culture Foods*. White River Junction, VT: Chelsea Green Publishing.

Katz, S. (2012) *The Art of Fermentation: An In-Depth Exploration of Essential Concepts and Processes from Around the World*. White River Junction, VT: Chelsea Green Publishing.

McGee, H. (2004) *On Food and Cooking: The Science and Lore of the Kitchen*. New York: Scribner.

Mouritsen, O.G. and Styrbæk, K. (2014) *Umami: Unlocking the Secrets of the Fifth Taste*. New York: Columbia University Press.

Nout, M.J.R. and Sarkar, P.K. (2018) *Microbiology of Fermented Foods*. New York: Springer.

Read, J. (2023) *Of Cabbages and Kimchi: A Practical Guide to the World of Fermented Food*. London: Kyle Books.

Ray, B. and Panda, S.H. (2014) *Food Fermentation and Microorganisms*. 2nd edn. Boca Raton, FL: CRC Press.

Read, J. (2024, April 17). "Living Fermented Foods and Drinks". *Oxford Research Encyclopedia of Food Studies*. https://oxfordre.com/foodstudies/view/10.1093/acrefore/9780197762530.001.0001/acrefore-9780197762530-e-15. doi:https://doi.org/10.1093/acrefore/9780197762530.013.15

Segnit, N. (2010) *The Flavour Thesaurus: Pairings, Recipes and Ideas for the Creative Cook*. London: Bloomsbury.

Shockey, K.K., Shockey, C. and Kunkel, E. (2014). *Fermented Vegetables: Creative Recipes for Fermenting 64 Vegetables & Herbs in Krauts, Kimchis, Brined Pickles, Chutneys, Relishes & Pastes*. North Adams, Ma: Storey Publishing.

Smith, D.V. and Firestein, S. (2017) *Tasting and Smelling: The Chemical Senses*. San Diego, CA: Academic Press.

ABOUT THE AUTHORS

ROBIN SHERRIFF is the CEO of the Fermenters Guild (@fermentersguild) and owner of the Koji Kitchen (@thekojikitchen). After studying chemistry and biology, Robin took the scenic route from park ranger to bike mechanic, animal-vaccine researcher and then Victorian confectionery plant site manager before going back to university for an MSc in Gastronomy. Robin researched his thesis on Japanese whisky philosophy in Kyoto, which led him to learn about saké, and, in turn, to koji. In 2020, he started the Koji Kitchen in Edinburgh, Scotland, and in 2025, he co-founded Slow Sauce (@slow.sauce), Scotland's first miso and shoyu brewery. This is his first book.

DR CAROLINE GILMARTIN is an author, microbiologist, vinegar specialist, and fermentation educator at Every Good Thing.

HERO HIRSH is a chef, award-winning cheese maker, educator, and fellow at the Academy of Cheese.

JAMES READ is an author, journalist, and founder of Kim Kong Kimchi.

DR JAMIE GOODE is an award-winning author, wine journalist, and science educator.

DR JOHNNY DRAIN is an author, chef, materials scientist, and co-founder of Win-Win, an ethical, sustainable, cocoa-free chocolate producer.

DR JOSH SMALLEY is a *Great British Bake Off* finalist, chemist, and food-science educator at Leicester University.

DR JULIA SKINNER is an award-winning author, food scientist, and expert in the history of fermentation.

KENJI MORIMOTO is an author, content creator, and fermentation specialist.

KIRSTEN K. SHOCKEY is an author, writer, and fermentation educator at the Fermentation School in Oregon.

MARA JANE KING is an educator, filmmaker, and Director of Fermentation for Id Est restaurant group in Colorado.

MARK DREDGE is an award-winning beer writer, presenter, and author of DK's *Beer: A Tasting Course*.

NABILA RODRÍGUEZ VALERÓN is a food scientist and food development researcher.

OLIA HERCULES is an award-winning author, chef, activist, and food and cookery educator.

PAYAL SHAH is a fermentation specialist and fermentation educator at Kobo Fermentary.

PRATAP CHAHAL is a chef, restaurateur, and fermentation specialist.

REBECCA GHIM is a kimchi specialist, sustainability researcher, and founder of the Ferm, a low-waste kimchi and jangajji producer.

RYAN CHARLES WALKER is head of fermentation at innovative zero-waste restaurant SILO in London.

TOM WILSON is the head brewer and co-owner of Kanpai, the UK's first saké brewery.

ACKNOWLEDGMENTS

AUTHOR'S ACKNOWLEDGMENTS
Fermentation teaches us that all things are interlinked, and as such, everyone I've ever met has contributed to this book in some way, regardless of how small.

First and foremost I would like to thank my incredible partners Hannah, Kai, and Nina. Your support, kindness, and love throughout made this whole thing possible. It's been a wild ride.

Lucy Sienkowska, thank you for approaching me to begin this project, ensuring its integrity, and kindly tolerating a manic fermenter for a year. You are truly amazing.

Holly Kyte, Sarah Snelling, Amy Child, Clare Double, Cara Armstrong, Barbara Zuniga, and everyone at DK. You are some of the kindest, most diligent people I've had the pleasure to meet.

All of the incredible contributing writers that made this book possible – Dr Caroline Gilmartin, Hero Hirsh, James Read, Dr Jamie Goode, Dr Johnny Drain, Dr Josh Smalley, Dr Julia Skinner, Kenji Morimoto, Kirsten K. Shockey, Mara Jane King, Mark Dredge, Nabila Rodríguez Valerón, Olia Hercules, Payal Shah, Pratap Chahal, Rebecca Ghim, Ryan Charles Walker, and Tom Wilson.

Thanks to the marvellous Neil Watson for photography, Sonali Shah for food styling, and Daisy Shayler-Webb for prop-styling wizardry.

Payal Shah, my friend in fermentation since I started and the first person to encourage me to ferment for a living.

My wonderful sister Jill Sherriff, for providing a rational sounding board for my more wild ideas. My parents, Anne and Garry, for offering up their office for me to grow my first ever batch of koji in.

Chikara Shimasaki, Dan Devoy, and Abbi Welch for your unwavering friendship and relief.

Sam Cooper – fellow fermenter, and legend – for keeping me sane.

James Read, Jules Goddard, Jono Hope. Thank you for being my copilots and navigators in all things fermentation.

My lab mate, Liam Kerr, for calm understanding, creative kinship.

Haruko Uchishiba, for giving me my first koji spores and starting me on my mouldy journey.

Torben Hutchings, for the invaluable advice on mead and many delicious drinks over the years.

And to the Fermenters Guild, the most marvellous collection of fermenters, oddballs, inventors, educators, geniuses, and heroes. Thank you all for being who you are and what you do.

PUBLISHER'S ACKNOWLEDGMENTS
DK would like to thank the contributing authors for their essays and recipes:

Dr Caroline Gilmartin 30–31 Microbiology 101; 32–33 Food-fermenting microbes; 34–35 How do microbes evolve?; 42–43 Why is gut health important?; 44–45 How do fermented foods affect our gut health?; 46–47 What are functional foods?; 48–49 How can I include functional foods in my diet?; 56–57 Should I be worried about pathogens?; 94–97 Kefir; 190–191 Acetic acid bacteria fermentation; 192–193 Acetic acid bacteria, biofilms and SCOBYs
Hero Hirsh 98–101 Cheese
James Read 14–18 A timeline of fermentation; 186–187 Tepache
Dr Jamie Goode 162–167 Wine
Dr Johnny Drain 6–7 Foreword; 18–19 What are the latest advances in fermentation technology?; 40–41 How do niche microbes affect fermentation?
Dr Josh Smalley 156–161 Bread
Dr Julia Skinner 182–183 Ginger bug and ginger beer; 208–209 Shrubs

Kenji Morimoto 132–133 Tsukemono
Kirsten K. Shockey 68–69 Lacto-fermentation; 70–71 Lactic acid bacteria; 196–201 Kombucha; 202–203 Kombucha vs vinegar; 204–207 Vinegar
Mara Jane King 134–135 Doubanjiang; 144–145 Fermented tofu
Mark Dredge 168–171 Beer; 172–173 Cider
Nabila Rodríguez Valerón 22–23 Why is fermented food so tasty?; 24–25 How does fermentation enhance flavour?
Olia Hercules 184–185 Kvas
Payal Shah 90–93 Yogurt
Pratap Chahal 136–139 Gochujang; 146–147 Garum
Rebecca Ghim 84–89 Kimchi
Ryan Charles Walker 20–21 What role does fermentation play in modern cooking?; 26–27 Can fermentation bring about a sustainable future?
Tom Wilson 176–181 Saké.

The publisher would like to thank Aditya Kaytal for data clearance, Sonali Shah for food styling, Daisy Shayler-Webb for prop styling, Clare Double and Nicola Hodgson for editorial assistance, John Friend for proofreading, and Ruth Ellis for providing the index. Thanks go to the following producers and fermenters for kindly supplying some of the products photographed for this book: Dr Caroline Gilmartin; Liam Kerr of Heriot Hott; Pratap Chahal; Tom Wilson of Kanpai Saké; and Zak Tozer of Zak's Kombucha.

PICTURE CREDITS

The publisher would like to thank the following for their kind permission to reproduce their photographs:

(Key: a-above; b-below/bottom; c-centre; f-far; l-left; r-right; t-top)

13 Adobe Stock: Atlas (cr); Gresei (cr/Vinegar).
14 Dreamstime.com: Zkruger (crb).
Shutterstock.com: tolobaluger.com (cl). **15 Dreamstime.com:** Pr2is (clb). **16 Adobe Stock:** Ange1011 (cl). **Science Photo Library:** (cr). **17 Dreamstime.com:** Picture Partners (clb). **Science Photo Library:** SCIMAT (c). **27 Adobe Stock:** Ange1011 (bl). **Dreamstime.com:** Oksana Ermak (bl/Paste). **34–35 Dreamstime.com:** MK Studio (bc). **36 Adobe Stock:** Fabiano Goremecaddeo (bc). **Dreamstime.com:** Oksana Ermak (bl/Paste). **48 Adobe Stock:** Bergamont (cb). **Dreamstime.com:** Picture Partners (clb). **53 Dreamstime.com:** Sundraw (br); Valio84sl (tl). **54 Shutterstock.com:** Tiagoz (cra). **75 National Library of Medicine:** Sauerkraut Fermentation reference taken from National Research Council (US) Panel on the Applications of Biotechnology to Traditional Fermented Foods. *Applications of Biotechnology to Fermented Foods: Report of an Ad Hoc Panel of the Board on Science and Technology for International Development.* Washington (DC): National Academies Press (US); 1992. 5, "Lactic Acid Fermentations". Available from: https://www.ncbi.nlm.nih.gov/books/NBK234703/ (crb).
78 Getty Images / iStock: K--K (bl/Plum).
84 Dreamstime.com: Noam Armonn (bc).
94 Dreamstime.com: Picture Partners (bl).
95 Dreamstime.com: Picture Partners (bl).
109 Dreamstime.com: Onlyfabrizio (br).
126 Adobe Stock: Amy Lv (tl, cla); Koosen (clb); Innafoto2017 (bl). **146 Dreamstime.com:** Siarhei Nosyreu (l). **153 Adobe Stock:** Ange1011 (bl); Eric Hood (bc). **155 Dreamstime.com:** Aala Images (br, bc). **160 Dreamstime.com:** Ppy2010ha (tc); Takoyaki3 (tl). **168 Adobe Stock:** Stone36 (cra). **Dreamstime.com:** Hort73 (cr). **168-169 Adobe Stock:** Stone36 (ca). **169 Adobe Stock:** Eric Hood (cl). **172 Getty Images / iStock:** Olena Koliesnik (l)

All other images © Dorling Kindersley

Senior Editor Lucy Sienkowska
Design Manager Barbara Zuniga
Editorial Director Cara Armstrong
Production Editor David Almond
Senior Production Controller Stephanie McConnell
Art Director Maxine Pedliham
Publishing Director Stephanie Jackson

Jacket Design and Art Direction Sarah Snelling
Editorial Holly Kyte
Design Amy Child
Photography Neil Watson
Illustration Andrew Torrens

First published in Great Britain in 2025 by
Dorling Kindersley Limited
DK, One Embassy Gardens, 8 Viaduct Gardens,
London, SW11 7BW

The authorised representative in the EEA is
Dorling Kindersley Verlag GmbH. Arnulfstr. 124,
80636 Munich, Germany

Text on pages 6-7, 14-19, 20-27, 30-35, 40-49, 56-57,
68-71, 84-89, 90-101, 132-139, 144-147, 156-167, 168-173, 176-187,
190-193, and 196-209 copyright © Dorling Kindersley 2025
All other text copyright © Robin Sherriff 2025
Robin Sherriff has asserted his right to be identified as the author of this work
Copyright © 2025 Dorling Kindersley Limited
A Penguin Random House Company
10 9 8 7 6 5 4 3 2 1
001-345514-Oct/2025

All rights reserved.
No part of this publication may be reproduced, stored in or introduced into
a retrieval system, or transmitted, in any form, or by any means (electronic,
mechanical, photocopying, recording, or otherwise), without the prior written
permission of the copyright owner.
DK values and supports copyright. Thank you for respecting intellectual
property laws by not reproducing, scanning or distributing any part of this
publication by any means without permission. By purchasing an authorised edition,
you are supporting writers and artists and enabling DK to continue to publish
books that inform and inspire readers.
No part of this publication may be used or reproduced in any manner for the purpose
of training artificial intelligence technologies or systems. In accordance with Article
4(3) of the DSM Directive 2019/790, DK expressly reserves this work from the text and
data mining exception.

A CIP catalogue record for this book
is available from the British Library.
ISBN: 978-0-2417-2728-7

Printed and bound in Slovakia
www.dk.com

This book was made with Forest Stewardship Council™ certified paper – one small step in DK's commitment to a sustainable future. Learn more at www.dk.com/uk/information/sustainability